Richard Wagner
Der Ring
des Nibelungen

Richard Wagner
Der Ring des Nibelungen

a companion volume
by Rudolph Sabor

For Emmi

Phaidon Press Limited
Regent's Wharf
All Saints Street
London N1 9PA

Phaidon Press Inc
180 Varick Street
New York
NY 10014

www.phaidon.com

First published 1997
Reprinted 2001

ISBN 0 7148 3650 8

A CIP catalogue record for this book is available from the British Library

Printed in Hong Kong

Frontispiece, Richard Wagner; portrait in oils by Franz von Lenbach (1871)

Contents

Foreword

A newcomer to Wagner's *Ring des Nibelungen* is apt to experience difficulties arising from its origins, its idioms and the thought-world it inhabits. Approaching the *Ring* can be a bewildering experience. Wagner's German can be convoluted and sometimes obscure; modern renditions into English tend to transfer these characteristics. Productions freely adapting the *Ring* to the producer's own ideas about society abandon Wagner's relatively simple locales for the action and choose others considered to have more strictly contemporary resonance. So, recently, we have seen the action take place in brothels, tunnels, a space ship, on the wing of an aeroplane, or the entire work set in a world devastated by a nuclear catastrophe.

The would-be initiate remains confused by the seemingly infinite diversity of interpretations, in print or on the stage. But that, however, testifies to the profundity of the work. This present work (and the volumes it accompanies) aims to provide a guide through the labyrinth of Wagner's *Ring* cycle, in order to clarify its literary and musical idiom for a contemporary audience – especially in those areas where our received ideas and expectations depart from those of Wagner.

The first essay, 'Translating Wagner's *Ring*', discusses the vital topic of the German *Idiom* and the individual language assigned by Wagner to each of his characters; it also specifies the objectives of the author in his own translation of Wagner's libretto. This the reader will find in the four volumes to which this book is a companion and guide. 'Wagner's Life and Music' chronicles the composer's progress from gifted child to Meister of Bayreuth and stresses the interaction between the creator and his creations. We then proceed to an investigation into Wagner's treatment of his literary sources, such as the Poetic Edda, the *Volsunga Saga*, the *Nibelungenlied* and many others. The next chapter discusses the *Ring*'s genesis, the twenty-six years of its creation, from 1848 to 1874. It examines the work's essence and its relevance for our time. The reader's attention is drawn to the common aspects and surprisingly close parallels between the *Ring* and one of Wagner's earlier works, *Lohengrin*, and the essay concludes with the case history of the golden ring itself, and the fortunes and adversities of its owners.

The essay discussing the Wagnerian leitmotif reveals the function and usage of the composer's unique system, of which his grandson, Wieland Wagner, remarked: 'To trace the course of the motifs through the whole *Ring* amounts to a journey into the realms of depth psychology.' (At the end of the book the reader will find an alphabetical list of all the leitmotifs of the *Ring* cycle.) There then follow brief biographies of the *Ring*'s dramatis personae and a synopsis of the four music dramas. The essay entitled 'Performance History' features stagings of the *Ring* in Bayreuth, from the opening of the Festspielhaus in 1876 to the present day, and also evaluates major productions elsewhere.

The History of Composition section traces all relevant stages of the work's creation within a tabulated biographical survey. Wagner's instrumental forces are specified in a discussion of the *Ring*'s orchestra. The discography comments on performances of the *Ring*, ranging from pre-war recordings, now on CD, to the present day. The bibliography lists all publications used by the present author, as well as others which may be of interest to the reader.

A number of people have helped me in a number of ways. Hilde Pearton, Dr Maurice Pearton and Stewart Spencer have provided comments in detail and depth. Their generous assistance far exceeds the accepted norm of collegial co-operation, and I hope the present volumes reflect their good counsel. Eric Adler has supplied valuable information about Ring performances in distant climes. The unquenchable thirst for Wagnerian enquiry and intelligence, displayed by the students of my Wagner seminars at Crayford Manor and Higham Hall, has been largely responsible for the growth and scope of these five volumes. Several enlightening conversations with Wolfgang Wagner, wise guardian of the Bayreuther Festspiele, have claimed the author's attention and have contributed to smoothing his path through the complexities of the *Ring*.

Emmi Sabor has double-checked the manuscript, and I am grateful for her labour and for the serenity with which she has tolerated Richard Wagner as lodger for the best part of our lives. Lady Young, with Wagnerian seductiveness, was instrumental in persuading Phaidon Press to publish a series of books whose structural and typographical intricacies were formidable. To my editors, Edmund Forey and Ingalo Thomson, and to Hans Dieter Reichert of hdr design, I owe particular thanks for their masterminding of our joint Wagnerian safari.

Rudolph Sabor, Petts Wood, 1997

Translating Wagner's *Ring*

Mimi hight a manikin grim,
who in nought but greed granted me care,
to count on me, when manful I'd waxed,
in the wood to slay a worm,
which long had hidden there a hoard.

More than a hundred years ago the English-speaking world was treated to a translation of the *Ring* by Frederick and Henrietta Corder, husband and wife; the above is a sample of their craft. The Corders had many successors. The most noteworthy are:

Frederick Jameson 1896
Margaret Armour 1911
Ernest Newman 1912
Stewart Robb 1960
William Mann 1964
Peggie Cochrane 1965
Lionel Salter 1966
Andrew Porter 1976
Stewart Spencer 1993

Their translations have much to offer. I have admired and envied many of their neat solutions to intricate problems, and I am indebted to them all for suggesting a phrase here, a telling word there, and for the comfortable assurance of being a successor rather than a pioneer.

So why attempt a new translation? Because Wagner's *Ring*, in spite of minor flaws, is a literary masterpiece, something that none of the existing translations quite manages to convey. But the *Ring* is not only a literary work of art. Its intricate system of metrical patterns, its use of alliteration, its rare but telling rhymes, its imaginative metaphors, its occasional punning, its astonishing ambiguities, its sheer singability – all these combine to create something unique in the history of the opera libretto: the music is in the text. The present translation aims to provide the reader and singer with a libretto which does not sound like a translation, but rather like the text Wagner might have written had he been born not in Leipzig but in London.

My objectives are:
– Accuracy
– Matching German and English lines, and retaining the position of key words
– Preserving the original metre
– Retaining alliteration and rhyme where possible
– Elucidating where Wagner is obscure
– Emulating the original by allowing each character to speak in his/her particular idiom

Accuracy

Confusion can arise not only from grammatical errors in translation, but also from misunderstood figures of speech; mistranslation can obscure an already complex plot. In the second act of *Siegfried*, Alberich hopes to regain the ring from Siegfried:

Und doch seinem Herrn	To its rightful lord
soll er allein noch gehören	shall it at last be surrendered

Alberich is, of course, referring to himself as the future 'rightful' lord. One translation misleadingly gives:

The boy is its lord,
Siegfried alone is its master.

In the second act of *Die Walküre*, Siegmund searches for the sword which his father, Wotan, had promised him:

Wo ist dein Schwert,	Where is your sword,
das starke Schwert,	that mighty sword
das im Sturm ich schwänge,	I might wield in battle,
bricht mir hervor	when from my bosom
aus der Brust,	shall burst
was wütend das Herz noch hegt?	the fury that fells my foe?

In one version this is translated:

Where is your sword?
The stout sword
that I shall wield in
adversity:
will it burst from my breast,
where my raging heart
hides it?

Burst from his breast? Had he swallowed the sword?

The *Ring* abounds with figures of speech, some archaic even in Wagner's time; these idioms seem to embarrass many translators. In *Das Rheingold*, for just one example, Flosshilde's flirtation with Alberich ends when Alberich accuses her of trifling with him. Flosshilde replies, 'Wie billig am Ende vom Lied.' 'Wie billig' is 'how cheap'. Alas, it can also mean, as it does here, 'as it is fitting'. Furthermore, 'Ende vom Lied' is 'end of the song'. But it is also a common figure of speech meaning 'the end of the matter' or 'that's that'. So when Alberich asks 'Are you trifling with me?', Flosshilde replies 'Yes, and that's the end of this affair.' Among the existing translations are:

Your love song thus merrily ends.
How trite at the end of the song.
How easy at the end of the song.
And laughter's the end of the song.

Matching Lines and Key Words

To assist the reader it is essential that the German text and English translation run in parallel; lines must not be transposed just to satisfy grammatical demands. Equally important is the location of key words. Where the German speaks for example of 'Schwert' (sword) or 'Liebe' (love), the word may have been given a particular melodic or instrumental setting, which would be lost if the word were displaced in translation. In *Götterdämmerung*, Brünnhilde addresses her horse Grane:

Dem Freunde zu folgen, wieherst du freudig?	So join your own master, neighing with pleasure.

Wagner illustrates the neighing with an orchestral equivalent: flutes, piccolo, oboes, violins and violas neigh together, expressing sheer animal joy. The translator will miss this at his peril. One version gives:

Thou neighest with joy
to think thou shalt join him.

Wagner's neighing thus accompanies the word 'think'! And in another version, the word 'just' is made to neigh!

You're joyfully neighing,
just to be with him.

In *Rheingold*, Fafner remonstrates with Donner, the god of thunder:

Ruhig, Donner, rolle wo's taugt.	Quiet, Donner, rumble elsewhere.

Wagner gives Fafner's bass voice a mocking trill on the first syllable of 'rolle'. To render this, as one translator did, 'not so much noise', transposes the trill, incredibly, to the word 'not'.

Metre

It has earlier been asserted that Wagner's music is already discernible in the text. This is achieved, partly, by the astonishing variety of metre: iambs (.–), trochees (–.), anapests (..–) and spondees (––), long lines and short lines. All coexist without ever disturbing the natural flow of the text. One example, from *Walküre*, shall suffice – tap the metre and hear the music in the text!

Ein trauriges Kind	.–. .–	An ill-fated girl
rief mich zum Trutz	–. .–	cried for my aid;
vermählen wollte	.–.–.	in loveless marriage
der Magen Sippe	.–.–.	her kinsfolk threatened
dem Mann ohne Minne die Maid	.–. .–. .–	to market the sorrowful maid

Alliteration and Rhyme

Wagner regarded alliteration as the textual equivalent of the musical leitmotif. In three of his prose works, *Das Kunstwerk der Zukunft*, *Eine Mitteilung an meine Freunde* and *Oper und Drama*, he stresses the importance of that method of versification which is 'another kind of rhyme'. Indeed, the German term *Stabreim* means 'spelling rhyme', as in 'Wasser, wie du gewollt', 'Water, won by your wish' (*Walküre*). The following passage from *Walküre*, Act I, will yield some of its verbal music when read aloud:

Ich weiss ein wildes Geschlecht,	I know a turbulent tribe;
nicht heilig ist ihm,	not sacred to them
was andern hehr:	what we esteem,
verhasst ist es Allen und mir.	and hated by all men and me.

The counterpart of the *Stabreim* is the true rhyme. Wagner uses it most sparingly in the *Ring*, but when he does, it heralds a matter of special importance. It is unhelpful of translators to ignore those instances, but they do.

Stark und schön steht er zur Schau,	Bright and brave stands it up there,
hehrer, herrlicher Bau.	fortress radiant and rare.

Dem Wälsung und Wotan zum Hohn:	See Wälsung and Wotan undone!
Schwörst du mir's, Hagen, mein Sohn?	Swear to me, Hagen, my son!

Another poetic device, often overlooked by translators, is the pun. In *Rheingold* we find a superb example of not just a pun, but a double pun, as Wotan is waiting for Loge's advice:

Reicher wiegt seines Rates Wert, zahlt er zögernd ihn aus.	Apt advice flows from Loge's lips; patient waiting will pay.

The double pun is on 'waiting' and 'pay', as Fafner assigns different, more immediate and personal meanings to these words in his reply:

Nicht gezögert, rasch gezahlt!	No more waiting, promptly pay!

Only Jameson and Spencer have spotted the double pun. All the others ignore it.

Obscurity and Ambiguity

On the few occasions when Wagner's language is convoluted and the meaning becomes opaque, the translator must lend a helping hand. A good example occurs in the final act of *Walküre*, when Brünnhilde justifies her decision to aid Siegmund in spite of Wotan's command. She tells Wotan:

Weil für dich im Auge das Eine ich hielt,
dem, im Zwange des Andren schmerzlich entzweit,
ratlos den Rücken du wandtest!

A literal prose translation reveals Wagner's rare clumsiness:

Because on your behalf I concentrated on the one thing
which you, compelled by the other, sadly at odds
with yourself, helplessly relinquished ...

Wagner means:

Because I took your place in caring for Siegmund
whom you in your confusion forsook, when Fricka forced
you [i.e., when Fricka insisted on the sanctity of marriage]
to be sadly untrue to yourself ...

Turning prose into verse, preserving original metre and alliteration, and elucidating the cryptic passage, we propose:

When I aided Siegmund,
I acted for you,
since you dared not stand up
to Fricka's demand.
Then you cast off your own kindred ...

What is one to make of one existing version:

Because my eyes are yours
I held to the one thing
which the alternative forced you
in a painful dilemma
summarily to turn your back on ...

Another bewildering passage is encountered towards the end of *Rheingold*. Wotan invites Fricka to live with him in Walhall, his newly built stronghold. Fricka asks him to explain the meaning of the word 'Walhall'. He replies:

Was mächtig der Furcht
mein Mut mir erfand,
wenn siegend es lebt,
leg' es den Sinn dir dar.

Literally:

Fear being conquered,
thought out by my fancy,
when it lives victoriously,
you will understand my meaning.

Porter solves this neatly:

When all that I've dreamed
and planned comes to pass,
when victory is mine,
you'll understand that name.

One translation suffers from confusing 'when' and 'if':

The fort I have found
to finish all fear,
if born to success,
soon will explain its name.

And this version would baffle Fricka and audiences alike:

What might 'gainst our fears
my mind may have found,
if proved a success,
soon shall explain the name.

The author suggests:

Audacious and free,
conceived by my will,

victorious life:
that is what Walhall means.

Wagner's libretto can also include deliberate ambiguity, which must be preserved in the translation. In *Götterdämmerung* Siegfried drinks to the memory of his beloved Brünnhilde:

Vergäss' ich alles,	Were all forgot
was du mir gabst,	you granted to me,
von einer Lehre	one sacred lesson
lass ich doch nie:	lives in my heart:
den ersten Trunk	this drink, my love,
zu treuer Minne,	with love undying,
Brünnhilde, bring ich dir!	Brünnhilde, shall be yours!

The drink is a potion of forgetfulness – a symbol of man's capacity for falling in and out of love. When Siegfried proposes to barter Brünnhilde for Gutrune, he assures Gunther, 'Brünnhilde bring ich dir!' ('Brünnhilde shall be yours!'). In this momentous passage the ambiguity of one single line reveals a man's monstrous fickleness. Wagner achieves this by the removal of just one comma. To ignore this in the translation amounts to short-changing the reader.

Characterization

The most important aspect of Wagner's versification is the individual idiom of his characters. Wagner's characterization does not begin on the stage: it is already planned in the language of the text, where each character is given his or her own distinctive mode of expression. It is up to the translator to retrace Wagner's design.

When we first meet Wotan, in *Rheingold*, he is viewing his new fortress, Walhall. His speech is grave and dignified:

Vollendet das ewige Werk!	Achieved is the hallowed abode!
Auf Berges Gipfel	On mountain summit
die Götterburg;	the gods' own gates;
prächtig prahlt	solid, proud
der prangende Bau!	the swaggering pile.

The brass instrumentation is anticipated in the text by the use of such brassy words as 'prächtig prahlt' and 'prangende'. The translation must not lag behind. Hence, 'solid', 'proud' and 'swaggering'.

Alberich's vernacular, on the other hand, lacks dignity. He prefers lecherous impetuosity, precision and short snatches. In *Rheingold* he proves to be a poor climber of rocks, as he complains:

Slippery, slimy, ghastly glimmer!
I slip and slide;
my hands cannot hold
and my feet cannot fetter
those slithery nixies!

When Alberich goes a-wooing, his language, and his eyes, become even more sharply focused:

Your arms so comely coil round me now,
that I may fondle your face with my fingers;
enraptured, enthralled,
let me nuzzle your billowy bosom!

Gloom, menace and a touch of sadness distinguish Hunding's style. In *Walküre*, he bids Siegmund (the son of Wolfe, hence 'Wölfing') beware:

My house holds you,
Wölfing, today;
for this night – nothing to fear.
But with stout weapons
withstand me tomorrow.
That day is marked for your death!
For their blood your blood must flow.

As for Siegmund, his language is tender and lyrical, even in his hour of triumph when, at the end of the first act of *Walküre*, he presents Sieglinde with his bridal gift, the sword Nothung:

Siegmund the Wälsung,
here I stand.
As bride-gift
I bring you this sword.
I woo with it a glorious wife.
This hostile house,
no longer your home.
Far from here
follow me now
forth into springtime's blissful abode.
Your shield is Nothung, the sword,
as Siegmund lies captive to love.

Mime and Alberich, the rascally brothers, are linguistically matched; in the second act of *Siegfried* they are at each other's throats, spitting eloquent venom at top speed:

Alberich
Slinking this way,
nimble and sly?
Slippery knave!

Mime
Accursed brother,
unbidden lot!
What brings you here?

Alberich
Is it your greed
for all my gold
and all my goods?

Mime
Off with you, ruffian!
This region is mine:
no rummaging here!

Alberich
Have I found out
your secret intent,
pilfering sneak?

Both Siegfried and Brünnhilde are endowed with an extraordinarily powerful, ardent idiom, as they seal their union at the end of the last act of *Siegfried.* The tone is positively orgiastic:

Brünnhilde
O hero-like child,
o child-like hero!
Of loftiest feats
the unwitting lord!
Laughing, so will I love you.
Laughing, let me be blinded.
Laughing, so let us perish,
laughing defy our doom.

Siegfried
Laughing, you wake in wonder to me;
Brünnhilde lives,
Brünnhilde laughs.
Blest the day that blazes around us;
blest the sun that gives us this day;
blest the light that has burst from night;
blest the world where Brünnhilde lives.

As the fortunes, moods and circumstances of Wagner's characters wax and wane, so does their language. In the second act of *Götterdämmerung,* Siegfried and Brünnhilde each accuse the other of treachery. Their spear-oath language is ritualistic:

Siegfried
Shining steel,
holiest weapon,
come to the aid of my honour!
On this piercing spear point
swear I this oath.
Spear point, witness my words!

At the end of the *Ring*, in the Immolation scene, Brünnhilde grows, morally and linguistically, beyond herself. We have seen her as the ecstatic lover, then as the betrayed avenger, and now as the wise and sole custodian of the world. Her mode of speech reflects that status:

Eternal gods
who guard solemn pledges,
turn, turn your eyes
on my full flowing shame:
behold your own shame in full flow!
Hear my heart-sick moan,
you mighty god!

———

Grane, my steed,
I greet you here.
Do you know, my friend,
what course we shall follow?
In flame-girt glory
there lies your lord,
Siegfried, the star of my life.
So join your own master,
neighing with pleasure,
lured by the flames,
their light and their laughter.
Now feel my breast, friend,
its fiery blaze;
sacred fever
lays hold of my heart;
him to embrace,
and embraced but by him:
our love is eternal,
our love – it is now!
Heiajoho, Grane,
ride we to greet him.
Siegfried! Siegfried! See,
Brünnhild brings you her life.

'Poetry is what gets lost in translation,' someone once said. It is the author's sincere wish that this may not be so.

Richard Wagner, oil sketch by
Franz Hanfstaengl (c. 1871)

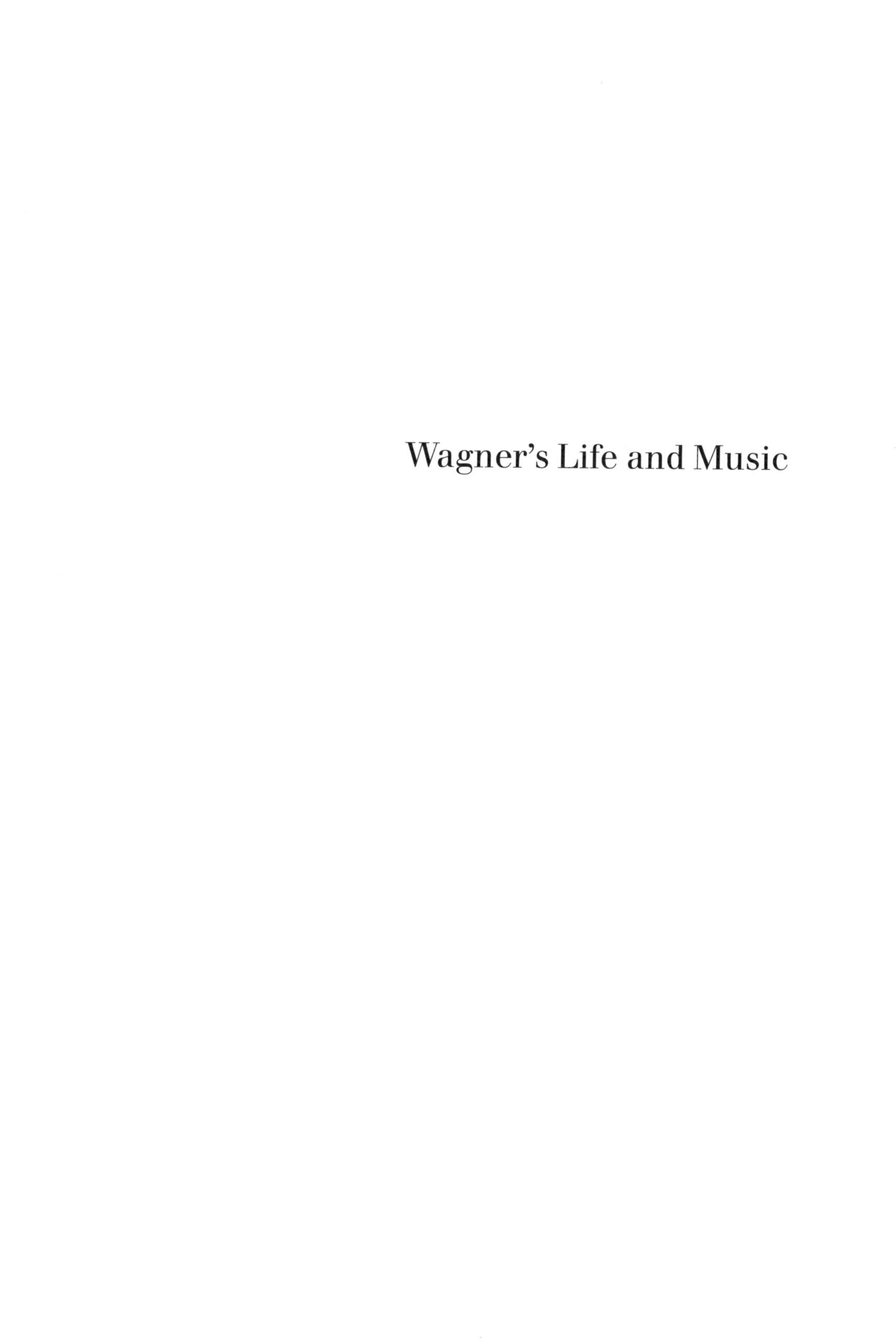

Wagner's Life and Music

Wagner's Life and Music

Early Years

Im wunderschönen Monat Mai
kroch Richard Wagner aus dem Ei.
Ihm wünschen, die zumeist ihn lieben,
er wäre besser drin geblieben.

A maytime chick, we know it well,
was Wagner, when he burst his shell.
Today it cannot be denied,
he might as well have stayed inside.

Johanna Rosine Pätz, Wagner's mother; oil painting by actor-playwright Ludwig Geyer (1813)

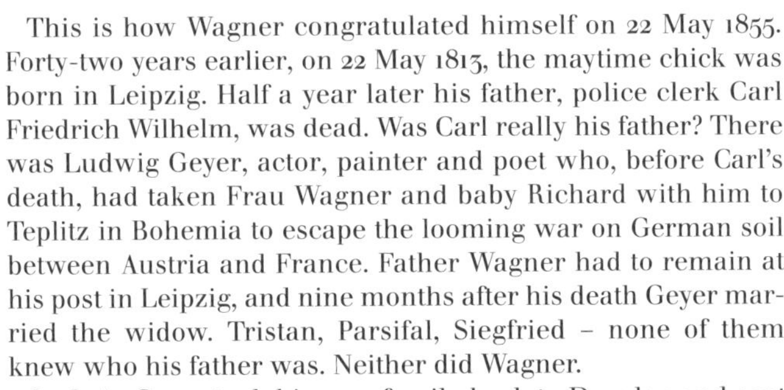

This is how Wagner congratulated himself on 22 May 1855. Forty-two years earlier, on 22 May 1813, the maytime chick was born in Leipzig. Half a year later his father, police clerk Carl Friedrich Wilhelm, was dead. Was Carl really his father? There was Ludwig Geyer, actor, painter and poet who, before Carl's death, had taken Frau Wagner and baby Richard with him to Teplitz in Bohemia to escape the looming war on German soil between Austria and France. Father Wagner had to remain at his post in Leipzig, and nine months after his death Geyer married the widow. Tristan, Parsifal, Siegfried – none of them knew who his father was. Neither did Wagner.

Ludwig Geyer took his new family back to Dresden and sent the four-year-old Richard to school. Around this time the brothers Grimm published their *Deutsche Sagen* (German Sagas) and Arthur Schopenhauer had written his *Die Welt als Wille und Vorstellung* (The World as Will and Idea). Both works were to exert a powerful influence on the *Ring*.

When he was seven, Wagner moved from his infant school to Pastor Wetzel's private boarding establishment. Only one year later, Geyer died, and Richard went to live with Geyer's brother, goldsmith Carl. A year later he entered the Kreuzschule in Dresden, under the name of Wilhelm Richard Geyer. There he received piano lessons, studied and fell in love with ancient Greek mythology, and was allowed to recite passages from Homer's *Iliad* to the class. He also wrote a bombastic poem on the death of a fellow pupil. On hearing this, 'my mother piously folded her hands', as Wagner later wrote in his autobiography, *Mein Leben*. The thirteen-year-old translated a large section of Homer's *Odyssey* into German, and began his first major work, *Leubald*, a tragedy in five acts.

In 1827 he dropped the name Geyer and was confirmed, as Wilhelm Richard Wagner, in Dresden's Kreuzkirche. Twenty-two years later he was to climb the tower of that church, to assist the Dresden uprising as a military observer.

Another change of schools brought him to Leipzig, where he completed his *Leubald*. The plot, he said in *Mein Leben*, was inspired by Hamlet: 'My hero, confronted by his father's ghost who was crying for vengeance, is roused to such violent action that he commits a series of murders and finally becomes insane.' Intended as a libretto for his first opera, *Leubald* proved intractable. Wagner left the task of attempting to rescue a feeble text through less feeble music to his Beckmesser in the *Meistersinger* of 1867. The world had to wait until 1989, when *Leubald* was given its first performance, in a Bayreuth theatre.

Richard was now determined to learn the craft of composing. The loan from a library of the most up-to-date textbook led to the composition of a string quartet and two piano sonatas, while the non-payment of the escalating lending charges established a lifelong pattern. At that time – he had turned seventeen – he found part-time employment as proof-reader for several volumes of a world history, one of which dealt with the Middle Ages. Here he probably encountered Tannhäuser, Lohengrin, Siegfried, Tristan and Parzival.

Having lost all appetite for attending school, Wagner now concentrated exclusively on learning how to become a real composer. To that effect he laboriously copied out, note by note,

Wagner with his half-sister Cäcilie; drawing by Ernst Benedikt Kietz

the complete score of Beethoven's Ninth Symphony. In the process, he absorbed the elements of orchestration, such as the range of the instruments, harmony, counterpoint, orchestral colouring and architectural principles. He then made a piano arrangement of the symphony which he offered, unsuccessfully, for publication. Undeterred, he composed three overtures, one of which achieved a public performance. In *Mein Leben* he recalled that 'the audience was startled'. Audiences have remained startled ever since, on hearing new works from the same pen.

A few months before his eighteenth birthday Wagner became *studiosus musicae* at Leipzig University, at a time when he was about to compose incidental music to Goethe's *Faust*. But his first term as a student smacked more of Mephistopheles than of the learned doctor. He neglected his studies, kept bad company, gambled, engaged in and got out of duels and drank. Deplorable? Or grist to the mill? His descent into the nether regions may well have expedited his writing and composing of those chaotic events in the *Ring*, such as Alberich's curse on love, the enslavement of the Nibelungs, Wotan's connivance in his son's murder, fratricide, Mime's wickedness, the breaking of treaties and the swearing of false oaths. Wagner was to emerge from the Nibelheim of his own making and delivered what he had long promised to deliver, his first worthwhile compositions. Under the inspiring tutelage of Theodor Weinlig, his new teacher, he produced the *Sieben Kompositionen zu Goethes Faust*, two piano sonatas (one of them for four hands), a concert overture in D minor, and his fine Fantasia in F sharp minor for piano which, inspired by Beethoven, contains melodic germs which were to ripen in *Rienzi*, *Tannhäuser*, *Tristan und Isolde* and in the *Ring*.

To encourage his pupil, Weinlig paid for the publication of one of Wagner's piano sonatas. He thus established another precedent, labour of love elicited by Wagner's charm, that was to be a pattern in the future. The young composer was on his way. Soon he was asked to conduct his new Concert Overture in C major. He composed another piano sonata and a Symphony in C major which was performed in Prague. His new overture to *König Enzio* was promptly given in Leipzig. He later wrote, in *Mein Leben*, 'the audience was not particularly worried.' But he also knew when to abandon a profitless enterprise. He had written and partly composed the libretto for a projected opera, *Die Hochzeit* (The Wedding), at the end of which Ada, the luckless heroine, breathes her last over her lover's body. He showed the manuscript to his sister, the actress Rosalie Wagner. 'She disliked it, so I destroyed it' (*Mein Leben*). The macabre denouement was to find a worthier location, twenty-six years later, at the end of *Tristan und Isolde*.

It did not take Wagner long to tackle his next opera, this time complete and performable. *Die Feen* (The Fairies) betrays the influence of Marschner and of Weber, but it also contains elements of Wagner's future works. The heroine of his aborted *Die Hochzeit* was named Ada. So was the present chief character of *Die Feen*, a fairy who loves a mortal (the theme heralds *Lohengrin*) but who is not allowed to ask Ada's name (*Lohengrin* again). There is an oath-scene in Act 1 (as there is in the first act of *Götterdämmerung*). Ada renounces immortality (as does Brünnhilde), but the opera ends happily, with both lovers elevated above other mortals and allowed to live, literally, for ever. Among the dramatis personae are a Gunther (as in *Götterdämmerung*), and a Morald (heralding *Tristan's* Morold). We also meet the intriguing line: 'Then you are not my father?' The vexed paternity question haunts Wagner's life and works.

Wagner completed *Die Feen*, his first opera, in January 1834, but he never saw it performed. Five years after his death it was given in Munich (1888), where it remained in repertory for a whole decade. The BBC broadcast it in 1976, and Munich marked the centenary of Wagner's death with one more performance in 1983.

In 1833 the twenty-year-old had his Symphony in C performed in Leipzig, his home town, in the famous Gewandhaus. *Mein Leben* remarked, 'Reviewed by all newspapers, none of them malicious.' In the same year Wagner was offered his first professional engagement, as chorus director in Würzburg. His duties included preparing the choruses for *Der Freischütz*, *Fidelio* and Meyerbeer's *Robert le Diable*, in which his elder brother, Albert, sang the title role.

At the age of twenty-one Wagner found himself in charge of a long-established operatic company which held a summer season in Bad Lauchstädt. There he met and fell in love with his future wife, the celebrated actress Minna Planer. 'I ran into her outside her front door ... and immediately rented a room in the same house' (*Mein Leben*). Minna was by no means the young music director's first love, neither was he hers. There was Leah David, a Jewish banker's daughter whom he renounced on meeting her fiancé. There was Therese, a grave-digger's daughter to whom he gave singing lessons 'according to a method which still remains a mystery to me'. There was Friederike, a Würzburg chorus member, engaged to the orchestra's oboist. Both she and Therese were to meet Senta's fate in *Der fliegende Holländer* – they had to be renounced. In Pravonin, near Prague, Wagner had flirted with Auguste and Jenny, pretty daughters of Count Pachta. Since he was out of their social class, neither was for him. He did not bother to renounce Auguste, but of Jenny he confided to his friend Theodor Apel that 'she was not worthy of my love.' But Minna

Planer was. Leah, Therese, Friederike, Jenny and Auguste were mere episodes. His life's tragic drama was entitled Minna.

The actress is twenty-five. The 21-year-old director of music does not mind. She has many admirers. Wagner scorns them. She had an illegitimate daughter before she was seventeen. Wagner forgives, and welcomes the opportunity for renouncing plebeian morals. The child, Natalie, is passed off as Minna's baby sister. This appeals to the author of *Leubald* and *Die Hochzeit*. In his operatic enterprises Wagner spent considerable time studying his source material and the historical or legendary background. But in personal affairs he tended to be less meticulous. Being in love, as he saw it, required no further

Minna Planer, Wagner's first wife and his life's 'tragic drama'; painting by Alexander von Otterstedt (1835)

deliberation, lest he fell out of love. They would be married in November 1836.

As Fräulein Planer, Minna had allowed herself to be seduced, but she was determined to hide the disgrace under a mantle of utter respectability. As Frau Wagner, however, she was to deceive her husband, more than once, with a less impecunious man. This was when Wagner's mounting debts would drive her, ironically, to betray him, in order to avoid being branded as the wife of a bankrupt. All through her life Minna regarded respectability as the height of her ambition. When her husband became a celebrated opera composer, her only wish was to perpetuate that period of comparative prosperity. But she was quite unable to tolerate or support his withdrawal from writing further lucrative operas, when he turned to territories inhabited by such dubious fund-raisers as Brünnhilde, Tristan and Hans Sachs. Minna changed little, while Wagner never stopped metamorphosing himself. Minna was surely in his mind when, much later, he composed Fricka's argument with Wotan, in *Rheingold*:

FRICKA
Handsome our palace,
precious our household,
such as to charm you
to cherish our home.

WOTAN
If it befits
my own wife to confine me,
her lord will also endeavour,
chained to his hearth,
to conquer the world from without.
Ranging and changing,
life's own law:
that thrill I cannot relinquish.

The artistic leap from Wagner's first opera, *Die Feen*, to *Das Liebesverbot* (The Ban on Love) was prodigious. Brilliant orchestration, especially in the overture, memorable tunes and fine concerted pieces are its hallmarks. With *Das Liebesverbot* Wagner left the realm of fantasy and the supernatural, a world which he was to revisit only twelve years later, in *Lohengrin*. *Das Liebesverbot*, based on Shakespeare's *Measure for Measure*, celebrates sensual pleasure. It also pokes fun at the puritanical German governor of Sicily, and contrasts his draconian rule with the people's healthy passion for joy and liberty. Echoes from the scores of Beethoven's *Fidelio* and from Mozart's *Figaro* are balanced by premonitions of Wagner's later works. The theme of forgiveness in the third act of

Tannhäuser, for instance, is anticipated in the Nuns' Chorus of *Das Liebesverbot.*

Wagner performed this opera in Magdeburg in 1836. The cast had not studied their parts, leaving such details as text and music to the prompter; the second performance had to be aborted, since the singers engaged in arguments, fisticuffs and open warfare. 'And so my career as conductor and opera composer at Magdeburg came to an end' (*Mein Leben*). Thirty years later, Wagner presented the score to King Ludwig II with these verses:

In boyish ignorance I strayed a little.
What penance for my juvenile caprice?
Permit this work to sue for its acquittal.
May your kind favour grant it lasting peace.

The second owner of the manuscript was Adolf Hitler, who managed to lose it in 1945, while otherwise engaged.

We next meet Wagner in Königsberg, where his fiancée Minna Planer was employed at the local theatre. In November 1836 the wedding took place. *Mein Leben* tells us that the preacher promised the couple imminent help from an unexpected quarter. 'Then he named him – Jesus. I felt let down.'

Financially ruined, with scant prospect for professional advancement, Wagner turned his attention abroad. To interest British audiences and publishers he wrote an overture *Rule Britannia*, which he posted to Sir George Smart, President of the Philharmonic Society in London. This remained unacknowledged, and Wagner considered whether he should seek out Sir George in person. He had also sent a prose sketch for an opera libretto, *Die hohe Braut* (The High-Born Bride) to Eugène Scribe, Meyerbeer's librettist, in Paris. Scribe however was too busy to reply. The more reason for Wagner to start winding up his affairs in Germany and to prepare for a trip, or a protracted journey, or a new domicile in Paris, via London. His tenure as music director in Königsberg was cut short, because the theatre had gone bankrupt. As always, Wagner had raised money in anticipation of future fees, and the number and potency of his creditors was becoming alarming.

It was all too much for Minna: with a wealthy protector, a Herr Dietrich, she left her husband, without a forwarding address. To pay for information and travel expenses, Wagner sold their wedding gifts (Wagnerian justice) and followed her by fast mail coach to where he had been told she was hiding. Halfway there, with no money left for the next stage, he had to sell the remaining silver to pay for the return home. Minna, meanwhile, had lost interest in her protector and had gone back, with Natalie, to her parents in Dresden. A week later she absconded once more, resuming her liaison with Dietrich, while Wagner consoled himself with writing the prose sketch for his next opera, *Rienzi*.

In August 1837 he took a step preliminary to emigration by accepting a post as conductor in Riga, at that time a Russian sea port which might offer an escape route, unblocked by creditors, into exile. The Riga theatre had an auditorium shaped like an amphitheatre, an orchestra below the surface and, in contrast to the custom of the time, the spectators were seated in the dark. Wagner was to adopt these features when, thirty-five years later, he built his own opera house in Bayreuth. By October Minna had had enough of life with a wealthy nobody and returned to her insolvent somebody.

Rienzi was progressing well, and during the next fourteen months Wagner was able to complete the libretto and to compose the entire first act. This opera was to persuade the Parisians that Richard Wagner was the composer of the future, so he imagined. In 1839 matters came to a head. Wagner lost his position in Riga. In April Minna announced her retirement from the stage and gave four farewell performances, and in June her husband took an intensive course of lessons in French.

The Romantic Operas

Applying for passports would have alerted Wagner's creditors. So he, Minna, now pregnant, and Robber, their Newfoundland dog, fled by night over the Russian border. On the way to the sailing vessel their conveyance overturned, causing Minna to have a miscarriage. To add to their ordeals, the ship's captain had to be bribed to ferry them, before dawn, past the harbour authorities to his boat, where they hid below deck to evade passport control. The voyage to London was due to take eight days. Several storms and a near-shipwreck almost trebled that forecast. They had to make an emergency stop on the Norwegian coast, near Sandvigen; the place name, and the rhythmical chanting of the sailors weighing anchor, were to find their way two years later into *Der fliegende Holländer*. Minna, already suffering from wretched health, was so afflicted by seasickness that she asked her husband to tie her to his body, so that they might at least drown together. After twenty-two days, they arrived in London. 'So we reached London Bridge, the unique centre of this immense, densely packed universe' (*Mein Leben*).

Soon Wagner called on Sir George Smart, to present himself as the composer of the overture *Rule Britannia*. Sir George was out of town. Next he tried to contact the author of *Cola Rienzi*, Sir Edward George Bulwer-Lytton MP, on whose work Wagner had based his own libretto for *Rienzi*. Sir Edward was not to be found in the House of Commons, but Wagner was able to witness a debate in the Lords. 'The Bishop of London was the only one whose voice and bearing struck me as artificial and unsympathetic, but this may have been due to my dislike of all clergymen' (*Mein Leben*). The next day Wagner, wife and dog boarded the steamship for Boulogne. But London was to see him twice more: in 1855, when he conducted a series of concerts and was rejected by the press but cordially received by Queen Victoria, and in 1877, when he was awarded laurel wreaths and great public acclaim.

Giacomo Meyerbeer (1791–1864), composer of *Robert le Diable*, *Les Huguenots*, *L'Africaine* and *Le Prophète*, was taking the waters at Boulogne when Wagner called on him. Meyerbeer listened attentively to the young unknown's reading of his *Rienzi* libretto, was impressed by the neat manuscript and provided several letters of introduction to Parisian institutions and notables. At that time Wagner was no more anti-Semitic than most central Europeans, and he admitted that 'Meyerbeer made an altogether favourable impression on me' (*Mein Leben*).

In September 1839 the Wagners moved, with Robber, to Paris. They soon made friends with other German emigrants, all barely able to make even a lean living. There was Ernst Benedikt Kietz, a fine painter and lithographer; Samuel Lehrs, a philologist of Jewish descent, who introduced Wagner to the teachings of Feuerbach and Proudhon, and was featured by Wagner in his novella, *Ein Ende in Paris* (An End in Paris); and Gottfried Engelbert Anders, seventeen years older than Wagner, an archivist and custodian at the Imperial Library in Paris. They all met frequently, making plans for the conquest of Paris, and Minna cooked for them.

Meyerbeer's well-intentioned letters of introduction failed to provide either hope or sustenance, and the Wagners' table began to carry even poorer fare than in their worst days in Germany. The sole glimmer of a possible breakthrough was provided by Habeneck, conductor at the Paris Opera, who consented to peruse Wagner's overture to *Columbus*, which dated from his time in Magdeburg (1835). It had already been performed twice, in Dresden and in Riga, and now Wagner pinned his hopes on the auspicious title – discovery and conquest of new territory. The music is quite specific in that respect: toward the end, success within reach, we hear orchestral chords, rising tone by tone and culminating in a euphoric *presto* rejoicing. No rejoicing at all at *Columbus*'s presentation to a Parisian audience. Nobody was impressed.

Facing page, Richard and Minna Wagner in Paris; illustration by Ernst Benedikt Kietz

Ever resourceful and not easily discouraged, Wagner tried to reach the public with some French songs. When no publisher showed interest, he offered them to a journal which printed them. *Dors mon enfant*, a charming lullaby, reveals Wagner's talent, foreshadowing the Spinning Chorus of the *Der fliegende*

Holländer. The meagre fee was soon exhausted, and Wagner became a frequent customer at his local pawnbroker's, where his and Minna's wedding rings were followed by pieces of furniture.

He also managed, as always, to persuade friends, and friends of friends, to part with loans which invariably turned into gifts. 'Necessity not only teaches us to pray,' he wrote to his brother-in-law, Eduard Avenarius, 'it also forces on us a measure of impertinence. You are once more, and for the last time, my only refuge.' A few weeks later he asked Avenarius, 'Could you advance me 500 francs?' Butchers, tailors, landlords had to be paid, or so they thought, and Wagner's conquest of Paris turned rapidly into a battle for survival. No wonder that Robber escaped and was not seen for a whole year. The only ray of light for Wagner was his visit to a performance of Beethoven's Ninth Symphony. It reminded him of his roots, of his own copying of the score, and it provided a grim contrast to the 26-year-old's present achievements. It was not a good period for the Wagners.

Wagner originally designed the *Faust-Ouvertüre* as a first movement to a 'Faust' Symphony. This fine piece, composed in 1840 but revised in 1855, has found its way into the repertoire of many leading orchestras, although its composer never thought highly of it. It actually achieved a rehearsal, but no more, at the Paris Conservatoire.

The title hero, Faust, ever probing, never at rest, resembled the composer in his quest for spiritual and material uplift. To effect his own uplift Wagner pursued two avenues, literary work and operatic projects. The former ranged from occasional articles to highly original, valuable novellas, written while *Rienzi* and *Der fliegende Holländer* were in their gestation periods. His writings and his compositions were meant to secure his precarious French foothold, but as it turned out, they were instrumental in propelling him homeward.

Maurice Schlesinger edited the *Revue et gazette musicale de Paris*. When he heard of Wagner's musical talents – and of his financial straits – he offered him part-time employment as arranger, or rather as musical hack. Among his duties were to write transcriptions for piano, piano duet, harmonium, violin, cello, flute, clarinet and cornet of popular arias, duets, choruses and overtures from the current operatic repertoire. Schlesinger also asked him to contribute journalistic work. Wagner wrote articles about the operas of the day; he occasionally examined philosophical ideas in essays such as *On German Music*, *The Artist and his Public* and the intriguingly titled *Pariser Fatalitäten für Deutsche* (Parisian Pitfalls for Germans); he also wrote three novellas for the journal. The remuneration for these works and, equally important for Wagner, the evidence of his creativity in his three novellas, combined to make existence slightly less of a burden for his household. Of the three novellas, *Eine Pilgerfahrt zu Beethoven* (Pilgrimage to Beethoven) is an outstanding example of Wagner's stylistic flair and musical insight. The views on opera which Wagner has Beethoven express in this novella are remarkably prophetic of Wagner's own concept of music drama as exemplified in his later *Der Ring des Nibelungen*:

> 'If I were to write an opera after my own heart, people would run away. There would be no arias, no duets, no trios, none of the stuff that makes our operatic patchwork world. No singer would want to sing it, and no audiences would listen. He who would write a true musical drama would be taken for a fool.' 'A musical drama?' I scribbled excitedly. 'How could that be done?' 'As Shakespeare did it, when he wrote his plays,' he replied.

A less rewarding enterprise of that time was Wagner's attempt at writing a method for the cornet. This was commissioned by Schlesinger, who was unabashed when Wagner confessed that he knew nothing about that instrument. Schlesinger lent him five existing methods and asked him to cobble together a sixth from the five. Wagner did so, but Schlesinger found that nobody would be able to learn to play that instrument by using Wagner's method. Schlesinger did not, however, lose faith in his non-cornetist. In fact, he offered him a seat on the editorial board of his *Gazette*. Among his co-editors were Berlioz, Liszt, Rellstab, Georges Sand and Schumann.

The prose draft of *Der fliegende Holländer*, which Wagner had sent via Meyerbeer to Léon Pillet, director of the Paris Opera, resulted in a sale. Pillet bought the work and passed it to a couple of writers who made scant use of it in their own libretto for *Le Vaisseau fantôme* (The Spectre Ship), composed by Pierre-Louis Dietsch. The opera was performed in Paris, a little later, but proved a failure. Wagner and Dietsch were to meet in 1861, when Dietsch conducted the ill-starred Paris version of *Tannhäuser*.

The prose draft of Wagner's *Rienzi* was dated July 1837. Now, in 1840, Wagner completed the composition of the score. He had learnt, by then, that Paris and the Parisians were not to be conquered by any grand heroic opera; that genre was monopolized by Meyerbeer. He therefore sent the work to Wilhelmine Schröder-Devrient, the Maria Callas of her time. He also petitioned the King of Saxony to order the work's performance at Dresden's new opera house. This was granted, and Wagner found that circumstances were pointing to the desirability of an exercise in loss-cutting. Dresden might prove less resistant to his claims and offerings than Paris, and a return home might be indicated. In *Rienzi* Wagner emphasized several themes of his earlier *Das Liebesverbot*, such as the liberty of the individual, equality before the law and condemnation of feudal despotism, the very themes that were to find forceful expression, a few years later, in the Dresden uprising. Wagner, fate seemed to say, was needed in Dresden, both as the composer of *Rienzi* and as a herald, on the barricades, of the work's battle cry.

Der fliegende Holländer, too, seemed to urge its composer homewards. Selling his prose draft did not stop Wagner from writing his own libretto and from composing the score, all in one sustained bout of vitality. In ten days he finished the libretto and in a mere six months the whole score. On its last page we find the entry, 'Finis Richard Wagner, Meudon [his domicile], in anguish and distress.' So deep was his artistic anguish and so unlooked-for his material distress that, in the absence of even the slightest chance of performing his works in France, he now was near to admitting defeat. He made Minna write a begging letter to Theodor Apel, friend of his youth, pretending that he had been taken away to the debtors' prison. What is more, he himself had sent a letter to Meyerbeer, in May 1840, which he must have regretted the moment he posted it:

> The time has come for me to sell myself to someone, in order to exist in the most basic sense of the word. But my head and my heart are no longer my own – they are already your property, my Master; all I have left are my hands. Would you like to make use of them? I realise that I shall have to be your slave in mind and body, if I am to gather food and strength for the work which shall one day express my gratitude to you. I shall be a faithful and honest slave. I feel immensely happy when I can give myself unconditionally, recklessly, and in blind faith ... Therefore buy me, good sir, your purchase shall be worth your while! Unpurchased, I should perish, and my wife with me. Would that not be a pity?

Such self-abasement was unbearable for Richard Wagner. Instead of despising himself for having written so humiliating a letter, he chose to despise the recipient and his whole race to boot. Here we encounter one of the reasons for his later anti-Semitism.

Wagner's scant earnings, perpetually topped up by loans, threatened to cease altogether. His creditors now became a serious threat to his freedom of movement. *Rienzi* had been accepted by Dresden, and Frau Schröder-Devrient had consented to sing the part of Adriano, and she would surely be his first Senta in *Der fliegende Holländer*. Why linger in France?

Return of the Native

From Germany to France to Germany. Once again Wagner was forced to relocate. It was during his fourth decade that he displayed a development of his musical and dramatic powers which produced temporary financial independence and comparative prosperity. At the same time his artistic and political convictions, bolstered by his social conscience, were beginning to undermine this very prosperity by replacing any thoughts of writing further popular operas – such as *Rienzi*, *Holländer*, *Tannhäuser* and *Lohengrin* – with writing essays that covered such subjects as the relation between republican ambitions and the monarchy, man and existing society and revolution. Thus, the Wagners were to encounter, within less than seven years, acclaim and respectability, then decline into defeat, notoriety and banishment.

The grand tragic opera *Rienzi* mirrors its composer's peregrinations. Wagner wrote the prose draft in Germany (Blasewitz, 1837), the libretto in Russia (Riga, 1838), completed the music in France (Paris, 1840) and conducted the première in Germany (Dresden, October 1842). Influenced by Meyerbeer, Bellini, Spohr and Weber, this spectacular work stirred the audience with its choral oath scene at the end of Act I, its famous battle for freedom in Act III, Rienzi's prayer in Act V and the final scene, with Rome's Capitol in flames. Joseph Tichatschek and Wilhelmine Schröder-Devrient, who sang the main parts, were instrumental in launching the work on its brilliant career, and Wagner remained grateful to them throughout their lives – so much so that he permitted the soprano to lend him a vast sum of money.

With his next opera, *Der fliegende Holländer*, Wagner departed from the operatic tradition of musical numbers (separate

The final scene of *Der fliegende Holländer* as depicted in the *Illustrirte Zeitung* of 1843

arias, duets, choruses etc.) without attaining, as yet, the 'through-composed' style which he reserved for the *Ring*, *Tristan*, *Die Meistersinger* and *Parsifal*. The chief themes of this opera – salvation through love, cursed existence and eternal fidelity – were to recur in later operas. The original feature of this work, which was perpetuated in all subsequent operas, was the role of the orchestra as carrier of the drama, and commentator. This was new territory for the Dresdeners, and their reluctance to surrender as unreservedly as they had done to *Rienzi* resulted in only four performances, but the composer became known as a dynamic force. A month later, in February 1843, he was appointed Royal Saxon Court Conductor, and Minna's dreams were fulfilled. A splendid new residence, an extensive library, friends and acolytes for dinner – all combined to bring out the best in the Frau Kapellmeister. Gustav Adolf Kietz, sculptor brother of Ernst Benedikt, Wagner's Parisian fellow sufferer, sketched a pleasing picture of the Wagners at home:

> I arrived one lunchtime to find him and his wife still in a state of helpless mirth at a dubious pleasure they enjoyed almost every lunchtime in these apartments when the local band passed beneath their windows. In order to give me a better impression of the musical pleasures provided by the Riflemen's Battalion as it passed the house, Frau Minna took up her position and imitated the sound of the clarinets, while Wagner, laughing all the time, accompanied her on the piano. She was such an excellent mimic, her performance so virtuosic and the effect so comical that at the end we all collapsed in a heap of laughter. On such occasions they were both as happy as sandboys.

A Wagnerian triumvirate, Schröder-Devrient as Venus, Tichatschek as Tannhäuser and Wagner's niece Johanna as Elisabeth, adorned *Tannhäuser* at its Dresden première in October 1845. Wagner conducted, the critic Eduard Hanslick smiled on it, Liszt performed it at Weimar, and many other opera houses were eager to enjoy its benefits.

The opera's chief theme, salvation through love, is complemented by another, the fate of the outsider, as exemplified by Tannhäuser himself (and previously by the Dutchman, and subsequently by Lohengrin, Siegmund, Walther von Stolzing and Parsifal). *Tannhäuser* reveals the composer's considerable mastery of orchestration, especially in the Venusberg scene, and his deft handling of the complicated choral finale of the second act. The Rome Narration of Act III is a dramatic, musical and psychological forerunner of later narrative set pieces, such as those of Loge (in *Rheingold*), Wotan (in

Walküre), Waltraute (in *Götterdämmerung*) and Gurnemanz (in *Parsifal*).

Even while the Wagners were enjoying the agreeable appurtenances of success, counteracting forces were at work. A disastrous agreement with a music publisher was just one of several causes of his financial ruin. The firm of C. F. Meser was to publish *Rienzi*, *Holländer* and *Tannhäuser*, and Wagner undertook, recklessly, to pay for it. He never recovered even a fraction of the cost. Neither did he ever pay Meser in full. When Frau Schröder-Devrient recalled her considerable loan, through the courts, Wagner was forced to raise capital from a ruthless money-lender. Minna's costly household would soon cease to be.

More was at stake. Wagner's position as court conductor and pillar of the establishment required him to conform, rather than to conspire against king and country. Wagner tested this requirement in his memorandum of March 1846, *Die königliche Kapelle betreffend* (Concerning the Royal Orchestra), in which he points out organizational defects and proposes improvements in the running of the orchestra. After a whole year's delay the opera director rejected his conductor's suggestions. At the same time, Wagner's operas contained elements which tended to irritate his superiors. Tannhäuser is shown to revel in the sensual delights of Venus and to revolt against

The soprano Wilhelmine Schröder-Devrient, Venus in the première of *Tannhäuser*; photograph by Franz Hanfstaengl (1840)

feudal and spiritual authority. Lohengrin, potential redeemer of a society in decline, is defeated by the imperfections of that society. It is even doubtful whether the Dresden authorities could welcome Wagner's triumph when, on 5 April 1846, he performed Beethoven's Ninth Symphony. Was not that expensive, 300-strong choir extolling the brotherhood of man?

Politics and Revolution

A month after the completion of *Lohengrin*, in May 1848, Wagner wrote his pamphlet, *Entwurf zur Organisation eines deutschen Nationaltheaters für das Königreich Sachsen* (On Establishing a German National Theatre in the Kingdom of Saxony). In it he demands that the theatre personnel, not the king, should appoint their director, and that the staff's wages were in need of an overdue rise. He criticizes the mediocre standard of the existing theatre and opera whose repertoire, with a few exceptions, was pandering to the audience's desire for shallow entertainment. He quoted the Emperor Joseph II's dictum, 'The function of the theatre is to refine people's tastes and morals.' The pamphlet was passed over, and Wagner was confirmed in his long-held conviction that a revolution was needed to effect a thorough reformation of the theatrical and operatic scene.

In his next pamphlet Wagner was more outspoken. *Wie verhalten sich republikanische Bestrebungen dem Königtume gegenüber?* (Republican Aspirations and the Monarchy, 1848) demands the abolition of the monarchy, universal suffrage, 'man's emancipation from fiscal clutches' and the establishment of a republic, with the king as the 'foremost republican'. Wagner's prose draft of the same year for a projected opera, *Friedrich I*, discusses the relation between church and state, and the desirability of secular sovereignty based on the will of the people.

Two preliminary *Ring* studies date from the same time, the prose drafts *Die Wibelungen* and *Die Nibelungensage (Mythus)*. Here Wagner proclaims, astonishingly, the close affinity of the Nibelung's hoard with the Holy Grail, and of Jesus with the character of Siegfried.

Jesus von Nazareth (1849) is another prose draft, for a drama in five acts. Here Jesus informs his mother of his desire to redeem mankind. Wagner depicts him as a social revolutionary who proclaims universal love as the destroyer of sin. The project was abandoned, but its theme was bequeathed to the *Ring* and to *Parsifal*. In *Der Mensch und die bestehende Gesellschaft* (Man and Existing Society, 1849) we read, 'Man's struggle against society has begun. Our society is depraved. Once we recognize this, it will perish by itself.' *Die Revolution*

(1849) goes further: 'I shall destroy the rule of one over many, of the dead over the living, of matter over spirit. I shall abolish the rule of the powerful, of law and of property.'

Once more, on Palm Sunday 1849, Wagner conducted Beethoven's Ninth Symphony in Dresden. At the rehearsal Mikhail Bakunin, a Russian anarchist and one of the leaders of the imminent insurrection, sat in the auditorium. 'He came up to me and told me that, though all music might perish in the coming world conflagration, this symphony must be preserved, even at the peril of our own lives' (*Mein Leben*).

The Dresden uprising and Wagner's prominent participation were preceded by a number of significant events.

Revolutions, revolts, uprisings and street barricades in Paris, Vienna, Berlin, Frankfurt and Prague, all in 1848, had encouraged the discontents in Dresden. The appearance, in March of that year, of Karl Marx's *Communist Manifesto* provided additional incentive. King Friedrich August of Saxony had attempted to tranquillize his people by appointing a liberal government and by promising abolition of censorship and tax reforms. Wagner and his friends demanded more, and the police were instructed to regard the former Royal Court Conductor as a dangerous individual who had to be kept under close observation. Another artist/revolutionary, Robert Blum, former secretary of the Leipzig Theatre and editor of a seven-volume *Theaterlexikon*, was captured during the Vienna uprising in November 1848, and was executed. The sword of Damocles hung uneasily over Wagner's head.

On 30 April the King of Saxony dissolved the two Chambers of Deputies, committing a breach of the constitution. On 3 May the government appealed for Prussian troops to reinforce their own small numbers. Saxon soldiers opened fire on protesting Dresdeners and on the newly recruited people's militia. Wagner attended an emergency meeting of the revolutionary Popular Front. The next day the King and his cabinet withdrew from Dresden to the fortress of Königstein. The Popular Front formed a provisional government. Wagner had leaflets printed: 'Are you on our side and against foreign troops?' He distributed them among the King's soldiers. With barricades all over the town, fighting broke out on 5 May between the army and the people's militia. The soprano Schröder-Devrient encouraged the insurgents from her window. Wagner took his post on the 300-foot tower of the Kreuzkirche (Church of the Holy Cross), where he acted as an observer, reporting on troop movements. Roaring canons, bullets flying past, booming bells – the composer of *Rienzi* was in his element. On 6 May Prussian troops joined the battle. The next day, Dresden's opera house was on fire. Bakunin joined Wagner on the tower. The perilous association may have prompted Wagner's departure, with Minna, to Chemnitz, while Bakunin advised the insurgents to withdraw.

Facing page, Wagner's arrest warrant, 1849

August Röckel, Wagner's close friend and fellow revolutionary, was arrested. Wagner then returned to Dresden, where the fighting had stopped, but a day later left again for Chemnitz. Bakunin was arrested. Both he and Röckel would later be tried and given the death penalty, subsequently commuted to life imprisonment. Röckel would be released after thirteen years; Bakunin would be extradited to Russia, eventually escaping from Siberia to London, via Japan and North America.

Wagner then travelled, alone, to Liszt in Weimar, and on 14 May wrote to Minna: 'I herewith break with the revolution.' The following day Wagner, still evading arrest, travelled to Jena and visited the Wartburg, locale of *Tannhäuser*. The title hero's wanderings had led him from Venus to Elisabeth, to the pope and back to Venus. Wagner, on the other hand, had journeyed into exile in Paris, back to Dresden, to the Wartburg and was soon to go into exile again. On 16 May a warrant was issued for Wagner's arrest. It read: 'Wanted, in connection with the recent disturbances in which he has played an active role, Richard Wagner, Court Conductor of this town ... The police are requested to look out for the said Wagner and, in case of his arrest, to report immediately to headquarters ... Aged thirty-six to thirty-seven, medium height, brown hair, wears glasses.'

On 17 May Wagner returned to Weimar, where he found Minna's letters, imploring him to seek immediate asylum abroad. Instead, with Liszt's financial and moral support, Wagner went into hiding in Magdala, a Thuringian village, under the name of 'Professor Werder'. Meanwhile, police searched his Dresden apartment. On 22 May Minna visited him in Magdala. Together they celebrated his thirty-sixth birthday. The next day they travelled to Jena, she by coach, he on foot. Wagner said farewell to Minna and with an out-of-date passport travelled south, this time as 'Professor Widmann'. Successfully slipping through border controls, he arrived in Zurich on 28 May.

Wagner had dodged arrest and the death penalty; he had avoided being sent back on account of his false passport; he had lost position and income; his longed-for revolution had collapsed; he had had to leave Minna behind, penniless. He ought to have been shattered and utterly demoralized. A Richard Wagner could not afford such bourgeois luxuries. Had he not recently completed his libretto of *Siegfrieds Tod* (later to become *Götterdämmerung*)? The day after his arrival in Zurich he asked one of the few people he knew there to round up some friends and, himself taking all the parts, read to them the first finished quarter of his *Der Ring des Nibelungen*. First things first.

Switzerland, Paris and the *Ring* Poems

Four personal leitmotifs ran through Wagner's life: his stage works, his prose writings, great men, and his beloved women.

Politisch gefährliche Individuen.

Richard Wagner

ehemal. Kapellmeister und politischer Flüchtling aus Dresden.

Steckbrief.

Der unten etwas näher bezeichnete Königl. Capellmeister

Richard Wagner von hier

ist wegen wesentlicher Theilnahme an der in hiesiger Stadt stattgefundenen aufrührerischen Bewegung zur Untersuchung zu ziehen, zur Zeit aber nicht zu erlangen gewesen. Es werden daher alle Polizeibehörden auf denselben aufmerksam gemacht und ersucht, Wagnern im Betretungsfalle zu verhaften und davon uns schleunigst Nachricht zu ertheilen.

Dresden, den 16. Mai 1849.

Die Stadt-Polizei-Deputation.

von Oppell.

Wagner ist 37 — 38 Jahre alt, mittler Statur, hat braunes Haar und trägt eine Brille.

In the course of the next six years he was to achieve significant progress in all of them. In spite of, and sometimes because of setbacks, diversions and dead ends, he never relented in the pursuit of his four expectations.

The day after his reading of *Siegfrieds Tod* in Zurich he obtained a Swiss passport. The next day he was on his way to Paris. Why? Both Minna and his new friend Liszt wished it. Both urged him to seek fame and material independence there. A month later he returned to Zurich, without having achieved anything at all. But he had pleased his wife and, more important for him, he had strengthened his bonds with Liszt. Twenty years later he was to write to Liszt, 'You came into my life as the greatest man ...'

Wagner's literary pursuits in 1849 yielded three works – two minor and one major. *Die Kunst und die Revolution* (Art and Revolution) and *Das Künstlertum der Zukunft* (Artistry of the Future) reveal his continued hopes for a revolution, but they hint at his imminent conversion from political to artistic reform. The really effective revolution would not be enacted on the barricades, but on the stage. In *Das Kunstwerk der Zukunft* (The Art-Work of the Future) Wagner indicates the desirability of an amalgamation of music, poetry and dance, as on the ancient Greek stage, to form a new dramatic entity, the *Gesamtkunstwerk* – the totality of the arts. Wagner dedicated his work to Ludwig Feuerbach (1804–72), whose *Das Wesen des Christentums* (Essence of Christianity) was to influence the *Ring* and *Tristan und Isolde*. Among Feuerbach's ideas were that all human actions spring from and are based on love; love creates and destroys; it gives life and takes it away; it is being and not-being as one. Wagner's dedication reads, 'Only you can be this work's dedicatee, and I merely return to you what has been yours all along.' Meanwhile, the Wagner household had been re-established, for in September 1849 Minna, Natalie, dog Peps and parrot Papo joined Richard in Zurich.

Two further prose works date from Wagner's next year in Switzerland, one enchanting, the other infamous. *Wieland der Schmied* (Wieland the Smith) is a prose sketch for an opera in three acts. Like his creator, Wieland follows illusory ideals, but finds and fulfils his true destiny. *Das Judentum in der Musik* (Judaism in Music), written in August 1850, presents Jews as unsightly, jabbering schemers who, as artists, can excel only in a reproductive, not in a creative capacity. The one hope Wagner offers members of the unloved race is to 'stop being a Jew'. He does not say, however, whether this may be achieved through baptism or by more unconventional means.

The high drama of the year 1850 was Wagner's discovery of Jessie Laussot, the first of his extra-marital beloveds. At the age of sixteen she had heard *Tannhäuser* at Dresden. Now, eight years on, having married a wine merchant in Bordeaux, she wanted to support the revered composer financially, and persuaded her husband to invite Wagner to Bordeaux. Fate had fettered both Jessie and Wagner to the wrong spouses, and when they met and fell deeply in love, they glimpsed an opportunity for their chains to be broken. Minna had to be informed first, gently and artfully. On 2 March Wagner wrote: 'It is inconceivable that anyone could be more kind-hearted, noble-minded and sensitive than our friend Jessie Laussot. I think you would be truly surprised, my dear wife, if you were to witness the deep impact which your husband's works are making on healthy, unspoilt, generous minds.'

The lovers planned to meet in Marseilles and escape together into Asia Minor. The wine merchant came to hear of it, locked up his wife and told Wagner he was going to shoot him. Wagner accepted the invitation, but by the time he arrived at the house the couple had left, without giving a forwarding address. He wrote to Liszt in July, 'My proposed journey has come to nothing. There were too many obstacles. If I could have my way, I should prefer to leave this world altogether.'

For a time Wagner felt numb and tormented. He confided to Julie Ritter, his maternal friend, 'I shall never feel ashamed of this love ... but the woman who wanted to bring me salvation, has proved herself a child ... She was all love and we had consecrated our lives to the goddess of love ... the depth of her fall breaks my heart. Farewell, my beautiful, blessed Jessie! You have been dearer to me than anything in the world, and I shall never forget you.' To his friend Uhlig he intimated, 'If I could only tell you how much has died for me with that little creature.' He was referring, however, not to his separation from Jessie but to the loss of Papo, his parrot.

After her husband's death, Jessie married the historian Karl Hillebrand. Almost two decades later, in 1869, she broke her silence and wrote to Wagner. Cosima reported in her diary, 'A silly letter from Mme Laussot who wishes to explain to Richard what had happened twenty years ago. This irritates him, since it is so utterly pointless.'

With Jessie out of sight, Wagner returned to Minna. 'I shall not impose any conditions for coming back to you, since I am aware of your state of health. I have therefore decided to return unconditionally' (early July 1850). How did Minna receive the generous offer? She scribbled at the bottom of the page, 'this is full of untrue assertions, but our reunion is due to my love, which is far too deep not to make me forget and forgive.'

Oper und Drama (1851), the most extensive of Wagner's prose works of the Zurich period, deals with the development of opera from Gluck to Meyerbeer, and with contemporary social conditions which influenced operatic customs and standards. Wagner postulates a fundamental reform of our society as the only guarantor for an overdue reform of our art. Little did he know how deeply he had wounded Meyerbeer, his former patron and protector, when he derided his achievements and denied his importance in the history of opera. Meyerbeer noted in his diary, 'I am really hurt by Wagner's violent attacks.'

The year 1851 was an astonishingly productive one for Wagner. Not only did he begin to sketch out the contents of *Rheingold* and *Walküre*, but he also produced his autobiographical *Eine Mitteilung an meine Freunde* (A Communication to my Friends). He explains how *Der fliegende Holländer*, *Tannhäuser* and *Lohengrin* conformed to the principles set forth in *Oper und Drama*, and he accounts for his own progress as a creative artist. He also reveals his plans for the projected *Ring* cycle.

After these literary enterprises he felt in need of therapeutic reconditioning. At that time he believed in the restorative powers of a water cure. In November he wrote to Uhlig from Albisbrunn:

> This is my daily programme: early in the morning a cold pack, from half past five to seven, followed by a cold bath and a walk. At eight o'clock I have breakfast which consists of dry bread, with milk or water. This is followed by a first and a second enema. Then another walk, then a cold compress on the abdomen. At midday I get a cold massage and another compress. Then lunch in my room ... followed by a long two-hour walk. Approximately five o'clock another wet massage and a short walk. At six a hip-bath of fifteen minutes, followed by a short walk. Then another compress. Dinner at seven consists of dry bread and water. Then two more enemas.

After nine watery weeks Wagner returned to Zurich, where he conducted a series of enthusiastically received Beethoven symphonies. Among the listeners were Otto Wesendonck, wealthy silk merchant, and Mathilde, his 23-year-old wife.

The beloved muse Mathilde Wesendonck with her son Guido; painting by E. B. Kietz (1856)

In the spring of 1852 Wagner conducted four performances of *Der fliegende Holländer*, in the small Zurich theatre which seated only 500. The performances established Wagner's name throughout Switzerland and were noted, with mixed feelings, in Germany. The rest of the year was devoted to intensive work on the *Ring*, and in December the text of the whole *Ring* was complete.

Wagner's first encounter with Mathilde Wesendonck, his future beloved muse, was as brief as his encounter with the fifteen-year-old Cosima Liszt. In October 1853 he gave a reading of his *Ring* poem, with Cosima and her father, Liszt, among the listeners. A week later the Wesendoncks arrived in Paris, where they met Wagner. To complete destiny's roundelay, Minna joined him the next day. A week later the Wagners were back in Zurich, she looking after their new, grander home, he completing the composition draft of *Rheingold* in a mere nine weeks.

While the *Ring* was progressing well, a regular income on which to base his artistic plans – and to cover his considerable daily expenses – was still beyond Wagner's reach. Sympathetic friends, headed by Julie Ritter, were convinced that they owed such a regular income, in the form of a monthly pension, to Wagner's genius. They managed to raise a subscription of 800 thaler (£5,000 in 1990s value), not enough, of course, but it comforted Minna a little. She was aghast, however, when most of the first year's pension went to pay some, though not all, of the creditors. A confidential report of the Zurich police to their Dresden colleagues in March 1854 claimed that Wagner was leading a luxurious life, that in all likelihood he was receiving secret funds from undisclosed German sources, and that it was known that Wagner himself had burnt down the costume department of the Dresden Opera in 1849. The report ended: 'People's faith in his music of the future is evaporating. The conviction is growing that his music, though brilliantly orchestrated, possesses neither soul nor melody. What little there is of the latter, he is thought to have stolen.'

The chief event of the year was Wagner's discovery of the philosophy of Arthur Schopenhauer (1788–1860). So deep was this impact that he read the philosopher's *Die Welt als Wille und Vorstellung* four times. 'Only then did I fully understand my Wotan' (*Mein Leben*). Schopenhauer's negation of the Will, his pessimism and his sceptical attitude accorded well with Wagner's mood at the time and with the essence of Wotan, although the god is first seen as the pure embodiment of the Will. But in the course of the tetralogy Wagner endowed Wotan with that kind of resignation that made him yield his power to Siegfried. It was not so much a matter of Schopenhauer influencing Wagner, but of the two minds meeting at the right moment. In 1854 Wagner was ready for Schopenhauer, as he was ready, a little later, for the composition of *Tristan und Isolde*, which in turn meant that he was ready for Mathilde Wesendonck.

Notwithstanding his mood of resignation and lack of expectation, he completed the score of *Rheingold* in September 1854. The opera ends in an optimistic blaze of C major, as the gods enter into Walhall. Such are the freakish incongruities that exerted their force upon Wagner's life and his works.

The next year, 1855, Wagner was in London, but this time not as a petitioner, as in 1839, but as the conductor of a series of eight concerts. With the orchestra of the Philharmonic Society he performed Haydn, Mozart, Beethoven, Weber and Mendelssohn, as well as the overture to *Tannhäuser* and excerpts from *Lohengrin*. The press loathed it all: 'Music is not his special birthgift' (*Sunday Times*); 'Herr Wagner is a necessary evil' (*Morning Post*); 'So much incessant noise, so uninterrupted an exhibition of pure cacophony' (*The Times*). Wagner, in turn, did not think much of either the orchestra or his public. 'These Englishmen are crude fellows. They play everything at the same dynamic level,' he wrote to Minna; and to Otto Wesendonck, 'Your typical Englishman is your typical sheep.' But he loved the Zoological Gardens at Regents Park, and there he observed both animals and humans. 'In Paris, the businessmen look like people taking a walk. In London, people taking a walk look like businessmen,' as Cosima quoted him nearly twenty years later in her diaries. Liszt, as always, boosted his friend's morale. He advised him to disregard the hostile press and pointed out that English philistines were no more unpleasant than their German counterparts. He also urged him to continue his work on the *Ring* and to 'be content with living as an immortal'.

Thus fortified, Wagner was elated when Queen Victoria received him, having applauded the overture to *Tannhäuser*. What impressed him most was the queen's eagerness to talk to him while the German police were still hounding him 'like a highway robber. Greetings from your Knight of the Garter' (to Minna, June 1855). With fond memories of this meeting, and a net profit of £40, he returned home.

Wagner had not journeyed to London with great expectations. He now faced the future with equanimity, as his mentor Schopenhauer would have advised him. He also had for some time been thinking Buddhist thoughts. Nirvana, leaving the inadequacies of life behind, together with the Schopenhauerian denial of the Will, created the propitious soil for his next operatic enterprise. Simultaneously with his work on the *Ring*, he wrote a scenario for an opera in three acts, *Die Sieger* (The Victors). This deals with Buddha's teachings of withdrawal from worldly affairs, renunciation, the migration of souls and redemption. Wagner decided against composing this Indian opera, but much of its substance found its way into the *Ring*, *Tristan* and *Parsifal*.

Having spent one more summer month in another water-cure establishment – he was suffering from erysipelas – Wagner turned to the composition of the first act of *Siegfried*. But only two days later Liszt and his entourage arrived for a five-week stay. Liszt played his 'Faust' Symphony and the 'Dante' Symphony on the piano, for his friend's assessment. Wagner suggested a few alterations which Liszt did not adopt. In return, Wagner incorporated some of Liszt's more daring harmonic progressions in his later score of *Tristan und Isolde*. To celebrate Liszt's fifty-fifth birthday, they gave a private performance of *Die Walküre*, Act I, with the composer as Siegmund and Hunding, and his friend at the piano. (Oh for a video of that occasion!)

Another musical soirée took place at the Wesendoncks' house, but the climax of this mutually inspiring reunion was reached when both composers gave a public concert at St Gallen, in November 1856. Liszt conducted the first half, with his own *Orpheus* and *Les Préludes*, and after the interval Wagner conducted Beethoven's 'Eroica' Symphony. Three days after Liszt's departure Wagner resumed his work on *Siegfried.*

In 1857 the Wesendoncks provided Wagner with a house on their new opulent Zurich property. In *Mein Leben* we read that Wagner wrote the first prose sketch of *Parsifal* there, significantly on Good Friday, 20 April. In fact, the Wagners did not move into their new home until 28 April, while Good Friday that year fell on 10 April, but when Wagner ordained a day to be Good Friday, the calendar knew better than to object. On Mathilde's suggestion Wagner called his new home 'Asyl' (resting place). It was there that he interrupted his work on the *Ring* and switched to the composition of *Tristan und Isolde.*

The fifth day of September 1857 was a portentous day in the Wagner biography. Seated around his table were his wife Minna, Mathilde the newly beloved, and Cosima and Hans von Bülow who had interrupted their honeymoon to be with Wagner. Thirteen years later Cosima was to divorce Bülow, in order to marry their present host. Wagner played and sang to them passages from *Siegfried.* Mathilde was enthralled and Cosima wept. Perhaps they had been listening to Siegfried's last words:

She is for ever, always mine,
my wealth, my world,
my one and all.
Living in love,
triumphant in death.

Was Mathilde wondering? Cosima day-dreaming? For Minna there could have been nothing but care.

The day before Christmas Eve, Wagner and eight instrumentalists played *Träume* (Dreams), one of five songs he wrote to Mathilde's verses, to celebrate her birthday. Thirteen years later, on Christmas Day 1870, Wagner was to perform his *Siegfried Idyll* on the staircase of the villa 'Tribschen', to celebrate Cosima's birthday.

Mathilde was Wagner's *Tristan* muse. Her receptive, intoxicating femininity coaxed his susceptible nature to a hitherto unattained level of fervent creativity. She well deserved the tribute which Wagner paid her on the last day of the year:

Hochbeglückt,	Blissful pair,
schmerzentrückt,	freed from care,
frei und rein,	pure, sublime,
ewig Dein –	ever Thine –
was sie sich klagten	their sighing,

und versagten,	their denying,
Tristan und Isolde,	Tristan and Isold,
in keuscher Töne Golde,	in notes of chastest gold,
ihr Weinen und ihr Küssen	their kisses and their tears
leg ich zu Deinen Füssen,	are for Mathilde's ears,
dass sie den Engel loben,	placed at the angel's door
der mich so hoch erhoben.	who gave me wings to soar
R.W.	R.W.

How do husbands and wives cope with their partners' suspected infidelities? Otto Wesendonck coped by having Wagner's portrait painted as a present to Mathilde, that it might comfort her once the sitter was gone. Minna, on the other hand, intercepted her husband's letter to Mathilde in which she read, 'When I look into your eyes, there is nothing more to say ... Blind is he who, gazing into your eyes, would not find his soul in them.' Intended for one pair of eyes, this letter now met three, for Minna created a dramatic scene in Otto and Mathilde's villa. Poor Minna. How could she be expected to take her husband's epistle for what it was – not a love letter but an exercise in maintaining his *Tristan* mood.

For many years Wagner would reiterate, by word of mouth and in letters, that Mathilde had been his one and only love, that he would never cease loving her. Yet, thirteen years later, he told Cosima that he had never been really serious about that relationship. As for Mathilde, she was right in citing *Tristan* against Wagner when she reminisced, long after his death: 'Richard Wagner loved his Asyl. Why did he leave it? Idle question. *Tristan und Isolde* was created at that time. The rest is silence and humble reverence' (*Allgemeine Musikzeitung*, February 1896).

In July 1858 Hans and Cosima visited Asyl once more. A month later Wagner left for Venice, while Minna returned to Germany. There was an extraordinary episode at that time. Julie Ritter's son Karl, a composer and poet, undertook a boat trip with Cosima on Lake Geneva. There they made a suicide pact. Karl was to kill first Cosima, then himself. In the end they decided to live on. What had happened? Both were tied, like Wagner, to unsuitable marriage partners. But was that all? Were they in love? Was Cosima secretly in love with Wagner? His letter of 4 September to Mathilde provides a clue: 'On her return Cosima was overwrought. This showed itself in her frenzied tenderness towards me. Next day, when they were about to leave, she fell at my feet and covered my hands with tears and kisses.'

Towards *Tristan*

Two artistic enterprises dominated Wagner's next two years, his work on *Tristan und Isolde* and preparations for launching a reconstructed *Tannhäuser* in Paris. The miraculous *Tristan* score, with its unheard-of vast, chromatic canvas, was completed in August 1859. Meanwhile Wagner, whose petition for an amnesty had been rejected by the King of Saxony, sought and found revitalizing comfort in the philosophy of Schopenhauer. Much of it made its way into his *Venice Diary* (*Tagebuch seit meiner Flucht aus dem Asyl*), a collection of unposted letters to Mathilde.

To finance his renewed assault on Paris, he sold the publication rights of the unfinished *Ring* to Otto Wesendonck, and in September he established himself and a hired valet in the French capital once again. To Minna he wrote that he was confidently expecting a great success with *Tannhäuser*. Unaffected by Schopenhauerian pessimism, he sold *Rheingold* (which Wesendonck had already bought) to the firm of Schotts, after

Wagner photographed in Paris by Pierre Petit, 1861

phoria blunted unexpected blows concerning *Tristan*: the opera had been rejected as too difficult and too advanced by the opera houses in Karlsruhe, Dresden, Hanover and Strasbourg.

Wagner's renewed attempt to impress the Parisians seemed a success. In January and February 1860 he conducted three concerts with excerpts from *Der fliegende Holländer*, *Tannhäuser*, *Lohengrin* and *Tristan*. In the audience were Meyerbeer, Gounod, Berlioz, Auber, Saint-Saëns, Baudelaire, the painter Gustave Doré and the writer Catulle Mendès. A month later Napoleon III ordered the Paris opera director to prepare the French première of *Tannhäuser*.

When news of a partial amnesty reached Wagner, he went on a Rhine cruise with Minna. How did his nationalist heart respond? 'Alas, I felt not a trace of emotion,' he wrote to Otto Wesendonck; and to Liszt, 'Believe me, we have no fatherland. The Germany I know is the Germany that lives within me.'

Rehearsals for *Tannhäuser* began in September, and during the next few months Wagner revised the first act, and considered how to accommodate the wishes of the influential members of the Jockey Club, who demanded a ballet no earlier than the second act. Rehearsals and revisions, however, came to a standstill when Wagner was taken ill with typhoid fever. But by the end of the year he had completed the new Venus–Tannhäuser scene, while his ballet, the Bacchanale, remained in its rightful place, in Act I.

After a total of 164 rehearsals, orchestra and cast really knew their music. Unfortunately, a poor conductor – Bülow called him 'a shabby ass, decrepit and deaf' – was in charge of the fine orchestra. The first performance in March 1861 was interrupted when whistling and shouting broke out and continued right to the end. Those powerful socialites, the members of the Jockey Club, had succeeded in their protest against the unprecedented inclusion of a ballet in the first instead of the second act, which deprived them of their customary dinner, followed by their visit to the opera in time for the second-act ballet, when they could enjoy the dancing of their mistresses in post-prandial serenity. Nor did subsequent performances fare any better. Catcalls dominated the proceedings, Wagner recalling in *Mein Leben*:

> Bülow embraced Minna after the performance, sobbing; she herself had not been spared insults from her neighbours, when she had been recognized as my wife. Our faithful servant girl, the Swabian Therese, had been jeered by one of those raging hooligans, but when she noticed that he understood German, she silenced him with a resounding 'Schweinehund'.

The third performance saw the most damaging disturbances, with fighting between Wagner's friends and enemies, and lengthy stoppages between acts. Baudelaire sighed that a handful of barbarians had besmirched the French name throughout the world. Wagner withdrew his score, and Minna, who still remembered her husband's success with *Tannhäuser* in Dresden back in 1845, now complained to her daughter Natalie:

> It is due to Richard's pigheadedness that *Tannhäuser* was only performed three times. Had he only composed a ballet for the second act, perhaps before the contest of the minstrels, this opera would have become a source of fame and of money.

Poor Minna once again revealed the lack of artistic perception and human sympathy which constituted the chief cause of the breakdown of their marriage.

Wagner's resilience enabled him to emerge from his Parisian defeat and to bask in the triumphant reception of *Lohengrin* in Vienna in May 1861. The audience called him from his box to the stage, where he said, 'Your acclaim is my sweet burden. I must go on and on.' Before the year was out, Wagner had gone on. To *Die Meistersinger von Nürnberg*.

He informed Mathilde Wesendonck in February 1862 that he was going to look for a nest by the Rhine, to hatch his *Meistersinger* egg. But first he gave a virtuoso reading of the text to friends, in Schott's residence in Mainz. An eye-witness called it an unforgettable experience, convinced that the listeners had met with an epoch-making work.

Wagner found his nest in Biebrich, but his peace was soon shattered. Minna had crossed Germany, from Dresden to the Rhine, and she stayed for what *Mein Leben* called 'ten days of hell'. Her letter to Natalie of 6 March 1862 reveals the unbridgeable chasm between the spouses:

> At breakfast he received a letter from that Wesendonck woman, and he raged and roared, that it was no concern of mine ... Another bulky letter arrived from that Wesendonck hussy ... Next day a box arrived ... I had the little case opened, assuming that it contained some music, but it was again from that bitch: an embroidered cushion, tea, eau de cologne and pressed violets. Of course this provoked another outburst, but I do not care to repeat his words.

How the unfortunate woman must have ground her husband's nerves close to breaking point. For a long time now neither of them had been able to bring out anything but the worst in each other.

To conjure up the mood for *Meistersinger*, a new muse was required. Blue-eyed, flaxen-haired Mathilde Maier, a lawyer's daughter, was twenty-nine, highly intelligent and beautiful. In his first letter (May 1862) Wagner addressed her, 'Dear Mathilde, that is what I call you,' and she replied, 'Dear, highly respected sir, that is what you are to me.' The 'respected sir' soon became a 'beloved Master', and the 'dear' grew into 'dearest'. *Meistersinger* was in good hands.

At the end of March 1862 Wagner at last received an unconditional amnesty, and he was able to travel and reside anywhere on German soil. But he preferred to hatch his *Meistersinger* egg in Biebrich. Two Mathildes enriched his forty-ninth birthday. To the Swiss one, the erstwhile *Tristan* muse, he wrote about his present work, 'this will become my most complete masterpiece.' The new one, Mathilde Maier, was among his birthday guests. In July the Biebrich nest was overcrowded with birds of passage. Hans and Cosima von Bülow called, as did the singers Herr and Frau Schnorr von Carolsfeld, his future Tristan and Isolde. Another guest was August Röckel, his former fellow revolutionary.

In November Wagner stayed for a few days in Dresden with Minna – their last meeting. He went on to conduct excerpts from *Meistersinger* and the *Ring* in front of an enthusiastic audience in Vienna. The year ended with an exercise in Wagnerian clairvoyance. In his preface to the text of the *Ring* in 1863 he outlined his plans for a festival theatre in which to perform the work, in a small German town which was not accustomed to operatic repertory conditions. This theatre would feature an auditorium shaped like an amphitheatre and a sunken orchestra pit. In one special festival season, nothing but the *Ring* would be performed, and the most accomplished and dedicated artists would answer Wagner's summons to realize the drama of the future. But only a prince or a princely person could call this dream forth. 'Will this prince be found?' Eighteen months later he was.

During the next twelve months Wagner experienced his artistic and material zenith, swiftly followed by financial shipwreck and near-imprisonment.

Triumphant concert tours took him to Prague, Vienna and to St Petersburg, where he donated his fee, with Wagnerian relevance, to the inmates of the local debtors' prison. Further concerts, all richly rewarded, were arranged in Moscow, Budapest, Prague, Karlsruhe, Breslau and Vienna. The programmes featured excerpts from his operas and, often, his acclaimed interpretations of Beethoven's symphonies. From the proceeds he intended to buy himself a new residence. But where, and with whom? In January 1863 he addressed his second Mathilde from Vienna: 'Oh for heaven's sake! You people know how to make life difficult. You know full well that I shall have to leave the Rhine if you cannot find me a cosy nest. Fine sweethearts I have, God knows. Adieu, wicked child!' *Meistersinger* was probably in his mind, for this is Hans Sachs's grumbling way of telling someone he loves her.

In subsequent letters to Mathilde Maier we find several utterances which reveal, in a flash, the Wagner behind his customary mask: 'Pity us [artists] – we are the raw material of the world spirit.' 'Look after your little dog. These animals were given to us by a benevolent power, to make amends for our fellow men.' 'That I am a mystery to you, my treasure, does not surprise me. I am the greatest mystery to myself.'

Unaided, Wagner found a domicile in Penzing, near Vienna. He rented a substantial apartment, furnished it luxuriously, hired a married couple as cook and housekeeper, and bought himself an entirely new wardrobe, with velvet and silk as the predominant textiles. He then asked Mathilde Maier to come and live with him. She replied that he had better first divorce his wife, whereupon Wagner dropped the matter. He engaged a young girl instead, 'to make tea, keep my clothes in order and look nice and amicable'.

In November 1863, after so many months of travelling, Wagner visited his past, present and future, all in one week. In Zurich he stayed, for the last time, in the Wesendoncks' house. Then he called on Mathilde Maier and her family, who put him up for the night; the next day he went to see the Bülows in Berlin. There he took Cosima for a drive, and the two sealed their love with a vow to face the future together, come what may, and as soon as possible.

Shortly after his return to Penzing his funds had run out, and he issued a number of uncovered cheques. Detection, disgrace and arrest were imminent. Wagner's last hopes for moral and material rehabilitation were shattered by the news that the Vienna Opera had, after innumerable rehearsals, decided that *Tristan* was unsingable, unplayable and unperformable.

At the end of his tether, Wagner penned his own epitaph:

Hier liegt Wagner,	Here lies he
der nichts geworden,	whom the world forsook.
nicht einmal Ritter	Universities
vom lumpigsten Orden;	forswear him,
nicht einen Hund	Bestowers of titles
hinter'm Ofen entlockt er,	cannot bear him.
Universitäten nicht mal	In short, he tempted
'nen Dokter.	no dog from his nook.

To escape his creditors, he fled from Vienna on 23 March 1864 to Munich, and from there to friends in Switzerland, and from there to Stuttgart. On 3 May, four days after his arrival, a letter from the newly crowned King Ludwig II, aged eighteen, summoned him to the court in Munich. Wagner wrote to Eliza Wille:

> I should be the most ungrateful person alive, were I not to tell you immediately of my infinite good fortune! ... The King knows everything about me and understands me like my own soul. He wants me always to be near him, to work, to rest, to perform my works, and he will give me all I need for that. I am to complete the 'Nibelungen', and he will have it performed my way ... I am to have whatever I need. What do you say to that? Is it not beyond belief? Can it be anything but a dream?

As so often in Wagner's life, historical events and artistic insights have a way of crossing his path when he is equipped to meet them. The readiness is all.

King Ludwig and the *Ring*

They were unequal. Ludwig was a boy of eighteen and Wagner was fifty-one. Ludwig was a monarch, Wagner a commoner. Ludwig commanded immense power and worldly means, Wagner owned nothing but debts. But where their paths converged, the crossing became a flash-point that was to illuminate their lives.

King Ludwig regarded himself as the divine agent of salvation, a Lohengrin, a Siegfried, a Parsifal. He paid Wagner's debts, heaped presents upon him, accommodated him in a villa by Lake Starnberg, and arranged a regular salary and pension. All this to enable his protégé to complete his *Ring* and all his future works in peace. No patron of the arts had ever done anything so sane as this king whom the doctors later declared insane.

In the course of the next nineteen years, until Wagner's death, they wrote 449 letters to each other, as well as 143 telegrams. Ludwig called him 'Basis of my existence, delight of my life, dearly beloved Friend', and Wagner responded with 'My Champion and Protector, most beloved Friend, my sweet Lord'.

To Wagner, who had thus escaped shipwreck and drowning, Haus Pellet, his new sanctuary by Lake Starnberg, must have seemed like a desert island, with Wagner – discounting servants and assorted pets – as sole occupier. Searching for a prospective cohabitee, he again solicited the second Mathilde for domestic and related services. 'I live here on two floors,' he wrote in June 1864, 'I below and you, if you came, above. O my God! Always those wretched petty bourgeois considerations, and yet so much love!' A week later the matter had resolved

Richard Wagner with his patron King Ludwig II of Bavaria; a twentieth-century portrait by Fritz Berger

itself. Cosima, together with her daughters by Bülow, Daniela and Blandine, arrived at Haus Pellet, and less than ten months later she was to give birth to Isolde, her and Wagner's first child. To keep Mathilde Maier up to date Wagner informed her that 'Your coming to me now would have the opposite effect to the one I previously desired.'

Was Wagner devious? Or was the artist who had created harrowing predicaments for his protagonists – the Dutchman, Tannhäuser, Wotan, Tristan and Parsifal – now being visited by a bewildering predicament of his own? In the operas, his characters' nature determined their dilemmas. So it was with Wagner, and in his self-provoked dilemmas we may perceive the man's own nature.

Meanwhile the King was impatiently awaiting performances of Wagner's future works. Wagner obliged with an optimistic timetable: he planned to perform *Tristan* and *Meistersinger* in 1865, the complete *Ring* in 1867–8, *Die Sieger* in 1869–70 and *Parsifal* in 1871–2. Wagner was correct only about *Tristan. Meistersinger* was three years behind schedule, the *Ring* nine years and *Parsifal* eleven. *Die Sieger* was never composed.

King Ludwig also asked Wagner whether he had changed his mind about politics and religious matters since his flight into Switzerland. Wagner replied with his essay *Über Staat und Religion* (On the State and Religion, 1864). Its calm tone, free from polemics, reflects the writer's stable life and peace of mind at that time. Leaning on Schopenhauer, he acknowledges the value of the monarchic principle and the benevolent monarch; in place of patriotism, which he identifies with 'Wahn' (illusion), he points to religion as the *sine qua non* of human dignity, but he rejects ecclesiastic dogmatism in favour of practical religion – a theme which he was to substantiate in *Parsifal.*

Wagner also expressed his gratitude to the King in his *Huldigungsmarsch* (March of Homage), and its synthetic pathos reveals his dexterity in manufacturing to order, as does his deferential poem to Ludwig of 16 September 1864:

To My King
My royal liege, my patron and my keeper
Whose gentle mildness fills my heart with joy,
O let me plummet deep and ever deeper
In quest for words of praise without alloy!
Then let me mount up where the path grows steeper,
And grant me strength such wisdom to employ
That I may find true words of acclamation,
Expressing my most humble veneration.

To be close to the King, Wagner moved into an elegant house in Munich, again rented for him by the monarch. Here he made the momentous decision to take up the *Ring* once more, after it had lain dormant for seven years. Ludwig showed his delight by purchasing the whole work, incomplete as it was, for 30,000 florins (approximately £100,000). The fact that he had already sold the *Ring* twice, to Wesendonck and to Schotts, did not inconvenience the enterprising composer.

Three notable events brought the year to an end. The King made Hans von Bülow his court pianist, and Cosima rejoined her husband in their new Munich home. In December *Der fliegende Holländer* had its Munich première, but on the same day a thunder-cloud threatened Wagner's peace of mind: the king appointed Von der Pfordten as prime minister, a man who had been minister of education in Saxony during Wagner's Dresden days and who was Wagner's implacable enemy.

It was not just a single event, such as the appointment of Von der Pfordten as prime minister, that led to Wagner's downfall, but an accumulation of actions, projects, opinions and innuendos. The King had plans for a Wagner Theatre to be built by Gottfried Semper, architect of the Dresden Opera House. The royal exchequer frowned on the expense, and the press recalled the architect's – and Wagner's – involvement in the 1849 uprising. Furthermore, Wagner presented his newly painted portrait to King Ludwig and discreetly asked the treasury to pay for it. The press loved that story. They took the opportunity of reporting on Wagner's luxurious furnishings, his never-ending demands for further subsidies and his political influence on their young monarch. They announced gleefully that Wagner had dared to call the King 'mein Junge' (my dear boy). The Munich papers and journals also ran frequent gossip columns on the Bülow–Cosima–Wagner triangle. Nor did the prodigiously successful première of *Tristan und Isolde* in June 1865 succeed in silencing the press, for Ludwig Schnorr von Carolsfeld, Wagner's young Tristan, died a month after the first performance, and the press attributed his sudden demise to the composer's ruinous demands on his singers' vocal and physical strength.

The combined persuasive powers of press and cabinet induced the King to request his friend's withdrawal from Bavaria 'for the present', and Wagner became an exile once more. In December 1865 he left for Switzerland. It had been a good year, just the same. In April Isolde was born, and in July Wagner

The royal palace of King Ludwig in Munich, with the court theatre and opera house on the right

began his autobiography, *Mein Leben*, which Cosima took down from his dictation and which runs from his birth to his rescue by King Ludwig.

Wagner's overpowering personality was the cause of a great deal of confusion and conflict in the lives of those nearest to him. Cosima's conviction that it was her destiny to be handmaiden to genius brought much grief to Bülow, to Liszt, to Wagner and to herself. Ludwig's royal status encouraged his self-indulgent nature, with the result that he issued and countermanded orders concerning Wagner, while his credulity made him listen to smooth operators. Where such diverse characters share the same stage, there must be much ambivalence and little stability. Thus Cosima came to stay once more with Wagner, in his new house 'Tribschen' by Lake Lucerne, only to leave him again for Bülow. The pattern was repeated several times, until she joined Wagner for good in November 1868. Meanwhile Minna had died in January 1866, and Cosima and Wagner's second child, Eva, was born in February 1867. King Ludwig became engaged to his cousin, the Duchess Sophie Charlotte, at the beginning of 1867, but broke the engagement nine months later. His relations with Wagner were subject to similar irresolution. He would beg his friend to return to Munich, only to refuse him an audience when he arrived. The only certain factor in the lives of Ludwig, Cosima and Wagner was uncertainty.

It would be wrong to assume that the Wagner of the mid 1860s, the King's protégé, had shed his former republican convictions. His *Deutsche Kunst und deutsche Politik* (German Art and Politics, 1867), a series of fifteen newspaper articles, was meant for Ludwig's eyes. Wagner hails the emergence of the German soul in Goethe, Schiller, Mozart and Beethoven. He assigns to German art a decisive influence on the nation's health. The King's predecessors, he maintains, had failed to nurture genuine art, and in his section on a monarch's responsibilities he reveals his continued republican faith to such an extent that Ludwig's cabinet ordered the newspaper to discontinue the series.

The pivotal event in 1868 was Wagner's encounter with Friedrich Nietzsche. The summer had begun most auspiciously with the première of *Die Meistersinger* at the Munich Opera. Wagner had shared the King's ceremonial box and was celebrated by the audience. Thus elated, Wagner was in the right frame of mind for finding a truly congenial thinker. In November 1868 they met in Leipzig. The 24-year-old Nietzsche had been appointed professor of philology in Basle, and was delighted to speak to his idol – he had studied and succumbed to the score of *Tristan und Isolde* in his school days. His route to Wagner was therefore on a somewhat more esoteric level than that of King Ludwig, who had discovered Wagner through

Lohengrin. Their first encounter was followed by an exchange of letters and by a total of twenty-three visits by Nietzsche, who was given two rooms at Tribschen, Wagner's villa, for his own use; in between visits, he did a good deal of shopping in Basle for both Wagners, errands which he never resented. Their mutual veneration of Schopenhauer established an important link, while their copious discussions about the aesthetics of art and about the philosophy of music revealed a closeness of thought which levelled the discrepancy in years. Nietzsche's *Die Geburt der Tragödie* (Birth of Tragedy, 1872), influenced by Wagner's *Oper und Drama*, advocates the 'art-work of the future'.

The friendship between these two of the most eminent men of their century was to run into several crises, until it turned into heavy-hearted animosity. In *Richard Wagner in Bayreuth* (1876), Nietzsche's enthusiastic endorsement of the festival's ideal of redemption through art already contained critical undertones. But when Nietzsche attended the actual Bayreuth performances of the *Ring* in 1876, he became disillusioned; in his eyes, Wagner the creative genius had turned into a master of ceremonies. The audience, 'unmusical as alley cats', cared less for the acts than for the intervals in between, and the regenerative aspect of the work was trivialized, he felt, by the attendance of its bejewelled and bemedalled spectators. He felt he was the more genuine upholder of Wagner's aims than Wagner himself. So he fled.

In Nietzsche's subsequent works, *Menschliches, Allzumenschliches* (Human, All Too Human, 1878), *Der Fall Wagner* (The Case of Wagner), *Nietzsche contra Wagner*, *Ecce Homo* (all 1888), he revealed the reasons for his change of allegiance. Wagner's philosophy of life seemed to have turned into a philosophy of the good life, with his craving for luxury, both personal and domestic. The crowd of largely anti-Semitic sycophants, the new 'Wagnerians', impaired his integrity. Some of the *Ring*'s dramatic stage climaxes Nietzsche took for cheap showmanship. Where Wagner aligned his music to dramatic needs, Nietzsche like Schopenhauer would favour music's supremacy alone. He also read into *Parsifal* Wagner's apologetic return to Christianity, his genuflexion before the Cross, before Rome. Above all, it was the Wagner as he appears on many pages of Cosima's diaries whom he resented – the Wagner who, together with Cosima, would often belittle other people's achievements, the Wagner who could be ungrateful and ungracious, the Wagner who dropped friends and benefactors who had outstayed their usefulness, in short the masked, not the real Wagner. Nietzsche relinquished the poseur, to keep faith with the original. In his *Die fröhliche Wissenschaft* (Joyful Science) he described their relationship:

We former friends have grown apart. We are two ships, each steering its own course ... It was our destiny that we should become strangers. But the memory of our former friendship should make us revere it ... Let us keep faith with our celestial friendship, even though we may have to be mortal enemies.

At the beginning of 1869 King Ludwig told Wagner of his plans for a performance of *Rheingold*. The idea of isolating *Rheingold* from the rest of the *Ring* was anathema to Wagner, and his refusal to co-operate provoked a crisis. But before this came to an acrimonious exchange of letters and telegrams, the Bülow–Cosima–Wagner consanguinity was to be disentangled. Bülow at last agreed to a divorce, a week after his wife had given birth to Siegfried, Wagner's child. However, neither Bülow's compliance nor the happy event was able to exorcise Cosima's guilt-ridden dreams. 'Good night, Hans, whom I have made so unhappy. I dream of a world in which we shall all be united and love one another,' Cosima wrote in her diary on 8 July 1869; and five years later, 'I dreamed Hans was calling to me, "Cosima, Cosima, I am going to die this night."'

In spite of Wagner's protests, rehearsals for the première of *Rheingold* were under way, and Wagner's future *Parsifal* muse, Judith Gautier, was among the spectators. Conductor Franz Wüllner received a telegram in which Wagner warned him, 'Hands off my score, sir, or go to hell!' But Ludwig was adamant. He instructed his cabinet secretary that 'Wagner must not get away with his abominable intrigues.' Ludwig had demonstrated that he could live without Wagner, though not without his music. Like Nietzsche. Like Bülow. Meanwhile Wagner found solace in his work. In October 1869 he began his first draft of *Götterdämmerung*, although *Siegfried* was still unfinished. He was to require another five years to complete the *Ring*, a quarter of a century after its inception. In November Wagner asked his king, 'Do you wish to perform my works the way I want them performed or do you not?' The question is as pertinent today as it was then.

King Ludwig had been unable to wait any longer for *Die Walküre*, so he commanded a series of performances, again in spite of Wagner's protest. Judith, daughter of the French poet and novelist Théophile Gautier, and Wagner's future beloved, shared Ludwig's longing and attended a performance in July 1870, where she was joined by Brahms, Saint-Saëns and Liszt. Judith and two companions stayed with the Wagners on their way home to Paris. Cosima was in high spirits, for on 18 July she had obtained her divorce from Bülow. 'Germany is united, may God bless its arms!' she wrote in her diary, which was more tactful than saying it out aloud – whereas Wagner was unable to keep his sentiments to himself any longer. He begged his French guests to appreciate the extent of the loathing which

Richard and Cosima Wagner, photographed in 1872 by Fritz Luckhardt

he and Cosima felt for the French. Judith commented later that Wagner's passionate reaction to the events of the day was understandable and that she would have liked him less had he shown no enthusiasm for the German cause. She thus revealed her character and, possibly, her enchantment with what she saw as the real Wagner, an enchantment which made her condone his bouts of irrationality. On one of Judith's last days at Tribschen, Nietzsche and his sister arrived, and the event was celebrated with music from *Götterdämmerung* and *Tristan*. At the end of July the French visitors returned to their threatened homeland.

25 August 1870 was Judith's birthday, King Ludwig's birthday, and the wedding of Wagner and Cosima. Judith had been invited but the war prevented her from travelling.

Paris capitulated in January 1871, shortly after Wilhelm I had been proclaimed Kaiser. The ensuing French civil war resulted in the burning of parts of Paris, but Wagner provided comfort for his friends, sending them the vocal score of his newly finished *Siegfried*, with the dedication 'For Judith and Catulle, my dear friends'. Judith reported, 'I kissed the writing.'

The year 1870 was the centenary of Beethoven's birth, and Wagner marked the occasion with an important essay, *Beethoven*. The man who brings happiness to the world, Wagner wrote, is greater than he who conquers the world. In *Beethoven* Wagner bases his philosophy of music on the metaphysics of Schopenhauer, and concludes that his own earlier works, especially *Oper und Drama*, were in need of a reappraisal. He now advocated the supremacy of music over the spoken word, and he stated that Beethoven's *Leonora* Overture was a self-sufficient entity, which contained the whole of the drama within the music alone. He was to translate this proposition into practice four years later, when he concluded *Götterdämmerung* with a musical leitmotif which was to express the wordless hope for renewal and redemption.

The year ended with a birthday greeting to the 33-year-old Cosima. Wagner assembled a group of instrumentalists on the staircase in Tribschen, where they played the *Siegfried Idyll* to his slumbering wife. 'A sound awoke me which grew ever stronger; I knew I was no longer dreaming, there was music, and what music! When it had died away, R. came into my room with the five children and gave me the score of his 'Symphonic Birthday Greeting'. I was in tears, so was everybody in the house.'

The defeat of the French army by the Prussians and the subsequent establishment of the German Reich provoked a display of patriotism throughout the country which made Wagner forget, for a while, his republican principles. Apart from his unworthy satire on the French in defeat, *Eine Kapitulation* (A Capitulation), he composed the *Kaisermarsch*, 'For Large Orchestra and People's Chorus'. Both text and music discredit the creator of the *Ring* and *Tristan und Isolde*. Wagner had hoped for his march to be played at the official victory celebrations, but the Berlin authorities wisely declined the offer. Undismayed, he considered sending the march to the London Exhibition, and changing Luther's hymn 'Ein' feste Burg' (A Stronghold Sure) to 'God Save the King'.

Bayreuth, and Wagner's Final Years

Wagner's temporary coquetry with the Reich, hastened by King Ludwig's growing coolness, resulted in a perfunctory audience with Chancellor Bismarck and, more importantly, in a concert before the new emperor and his empress in Berlin. Wagner conducted Beethoven's Fifth Symphony and, why not, his *Kaisermarsch*. But the rest of the year 1871 was devoted to pursuing the completion and eventual performance of the *Ring* cycle. With Cosima he inspected the beautiful baroque opera house in Bayreuth, but found it too small for his purpose. The little town, however, appealed to them, and Wagner readily agreed when the town council offered him a suitable plot for erecting his Festspielhaus (Festival Theatre). Bayreuth was far away from all tourist routes and thus required a special effort on the part of future audiences. This was in accord with Wagner's concept of an ideal audience: not visitors but 'pilgrims' who, like the ancient Greeks, would congregate in an amphitheatre, eagerly awaiting their regeneration through art. Wagner had found the tabernacle but not yet the treasure house.

Promising events, as well as depressing ones, marked the road to the Bayreuth Festival. The newly formed Patrons' Association, created to provide financial support for the enterprise, was a dismal failure. The new Festival Council, however, consisting largely of prominent and wisely benevolent Bayreuthers, proved a great asset. Their efforts resulted in an immediate start to the building operations. On 22 May 1872, his fifty-ninth birthday, Wagner laid the foundation stone. King Ludwig had stopped sulking and sent a cordial telegram ('More than ever I am one with you in my thoughts'), and Wagner buried these verses underneath the foundation stone:

Hier schliess' ich ein Geheimnis ein,
A secret I enclose herein;

Da ruh' es viele hundert Jahr':
may it repose for many a day.

So lange es verwahrt der Stein,
So long this stone preserves my words,

mach es der Welt sich offenbar.
the world will fathom what I say.

To find the right kind of singers for the *Ring*, Wagner and Cosima undertook an extensive tour of inspection which lasted from November 1872 to April 1873. They attended most of the important German opera houses, nineteen in all. The journey proved worthwhile, and the Festspielhaus began to rise, Richard Wagner's own Franconian Walhall.

In his pamphlet *Das Bühnenfestspielhaus zu Bayreuth* (The Stage Festival Theatre at Bayreuth, May 1873), Wagner described the ceremonies that accompanied the laying of the foundation stone. He also disclosed the special features which were to make the interior of the Festspielhaus unique – the sunken orchestra, the amphitheatrical auditorium, the absence of intersecting gangways. To convince doubting readers of the practicality of such arrangements, he appended six architectural blueprints. Two days after issuing the pamphlet, Wagner began the composition of *Götterdämmerung*.

In August 1873, in the presence of Franz Liszt, Wagner presided over the 'topping-out' celebrations; he was however forced to postpone the opening to the summer of 1875, a forecast which fell short of reality by another year. Escalating financial problems had slowed the building operations and were now threatening a total standstill. King Ludwig, still disenchanted with Wagner's obstinacy over his staging of *Rheingold* and *Walküre*, refused to help.

Since the cash flow from Munich had dried up, Wagner considered approaching the Kaiser. But in February 1874 King Ludwig had an unexpected change of heart. He could not visualize a future without Wagner's works, so he authorized a credit of 100,000 thalers (approximately £400,000 in 1990s money). 'Our enterprise must not fail!' he announced. This generous subsidy paid for the *Ring* decorations, for the complicated machinery, and for the installation of gas lighting. Every penny of the loan was repaid, though not entirely in Wagner's lifetime, but certainly by his heirs. The King's munificence went further. He donated 75,000 marks (approximately £100,000) towards the building costs of Wagner's splendid new town house, 'Wahnfried' (peace from delusion). This bounteous injection of cash made it possible for Wagner to hold a series of rehearsals with the first batch of singers who had arrived at Bayreuth.

The most important day in Wagner's artistic life was probably 21 November 1874, for the *Ring* was completed on that day, after almost twenty-six years.

The cost of the Bayreuth undertaking kept rising, in spite of loans and subsidies. Wagner was forced once again to dissipate his energies in order to provide further funds, by conducting in Vienna, Budapest and Berlin. The summer of 1875 was to be devoted to preparatory rehearsals. In January 1875 he invited his singers to Bayreuth for six weeks, offering them free travel and board and lodging. So great was Wagner's magnetism that the artists gave up their summer vacations and undertook laborious study and lengthy journeys, all to serve Wagner, unpaid. It must have been the final sentence in their new Master's letter of invitation that clinched the deal: 'Join us in realizing a hitherto undreamt-of ideal.'

It must be open to doubt whether, in the entire history of operatic productions, one single person had ever been required to undertake, practically single-handed, so many tasks. Having conceived the salient features of the Festspielhaus, Wagner procured the means for its erection. He journeyed throughout Germany to audition suitable singers. When they arrived in Bayreuth, he coached them until they had mastered a musical style which was quite alien to them. He instructed scenery painters and costume makers. He combined the offices of stage manager, stage hand, prompter, conductor, singer and actor. He smoothed ruffled feathers, and solved the technical problems posed by flying horses, swimming nixies, a rainbow bridge, conflagration and flood, invisibility, transmutation, dwarfs, rams, ravens, woodbird, bear, serpent, dragon and toad. Nowhere may the reciprocity of Wagner and his works be observed more clearly than here. The man had created the *Ring*, and its inherent driving force tapped a hitherto unavailable flow of energy in the man. This gave him, at the age of sixty-two, supreme vigour.

As he reviewed the year's achievements, he was cheerfully exhausted, and he presented a copy of the privately printed *Mein Leben* to King Ludwig 'for his exclusive use'. He failed to mention the existence of a further twelve copies.

Trivia before the storm. That is how 1876, the *Ring* year, began. Wagner had received a commission from America to write music for the centenary celebrations of the Declaration of Independence, and he responded with the *Centennial March* (*Grosser Festmarsch*). This work, which might be described as the child of an automatic pilot and a dollar princess, featured passages from *Rienzi* and *Tristan*, and Cosima remarked that Wagner had been unable to think of anything while composing but the promised fee of 5,000 dollars. The music bears this out.

On 13 August 1876, after six weeks of intensive rehearsals, the Bayreuth Festival opened with the first *Ring* cycle. King Ludwig had attended the general rehearsals, but left before Kaiser Wilhelm arrived for the opening. 'I will not receive other royal personages, loathsome as they are, and listen to their empty chatter ... Have a partition installed to screen me from other royalty and ensure, if necessary with the help of the police, that they stay away from me in the intervals' (King Ludwig to Wagner). Other guests included the Emperor of Brazil, assorted kings, queens, princes, dukes, Liszt, Tchaikovsky, Bruckner, Mathilde Wesendonck and Mathilde Maier. King Ludwig attended a subsequent cycle, as did Nietzsche and Judith Gautier.

The artistic triumph was colossal. The 'art-work of the future' had arrived. But Wagner felt empty. Being able to relax for the first time in two years, he only saw and fretted over technical shortcomings and minor flaws in the production. The *Ring* of his creation, seen with his own mind's eye, differed vastly from the staged *Ring*, seen through the opera glass. This depressed him, and he told Cosima that he wanted to die.

> Must it be for the last time that I embraced you this morning? No, I shall see you again. I want to, because I love you. Adieu. Be good to me.

Wagner wrote this to Judith Gautier after she had left Bayreuth on 2 September 1876. She had attended two cycles of the *Ring*, and during that time she had seen Wagner daily, either at Wahnfried, or secretly at her lodgings. He took her to the Festspielhaus and showed her the hidden orchestra pit, the complex *Ring* scenery, the machines needed for producing steam, flood and fire, the multifarious fauna and flora. He demonstrated the swimming cradles which kept the Rhinemaidens afloat. Judith noted that Wagner had lost none of his youthful elasticity, as he leapt across pieces of scenery and introduced her to the realizations of his dramatic vision. And every day he became dearer to her, and she to him. At one of the performances he held Judith in his arms and whispered, 'This is how I would love to hear all my music from now on.'

To keep in touch, Wagner arranged a clandestine correspondence with Judith. Herr Schnappauf, his aptly named barber ('schnappauf' means 'snap up'), was to act as postmaster and intercept Judith's letters which are, alas, no longer extant. Wagner, in his copious notes, recalled their moments of intim-

Das Rheingold at Bayreuth in 1876; in this contemporary drawing the acoustic cover is incorrectly drawn in relation to stage and orchestra.

acy. 'I still love you,' he wrote, 'Your embraces live in my soul,' and he called her 'You beautiful abundance of my life'.

A few days after Judith's departure, Wagner said farewell to Mathilde Maier, his *Meistersinger* muse, 'his last woman friend', as Cosima called her, optimistically, in her diary. Ready for a complete change, he took Cosima to Italy for the next three months, where the past, however, would not leave him alone. Letters from Bayreuth informed him of a catastrophic festival deficit. In October he met Nietzsche for the last time, and in December he saw Jessie Laussot in Florence, twenty-six years after their cancelled flight into the Orient.

A second festival season in 1877 was out of the question. Once again, Wagner had to to look for ways of raising funds to save the Festspiele. His second series of concerts in London – the first took place in 1855 – consisted of eight performances at the Albert Hall (7–29 May 1877), with himself and Hans Richter as conductors. He presented copious excerpts from most of his operas. This time the press showed greater perception than they had twenty-two years previously. *The Times* wrote: 'A very large audience greeted him with a cordiality not to be mistaken. Everybody was glad to see the man about whom all musical Europe had been talking.' From the *Musical Times*: 'Nothing like this can be found in the entire range of Music.' George Bernard Shaw reported in *The Hornet*: 'At each concert Herr Wagner was received with tempestuous applause. On 19 May he was presented with an address, and a laurel wreath was placed on his brow, which latter distinction was probably more gratifying to his feelings than favourable to the dignity of his appearance.' On two particular days, 16 and 17 May, Wagner demonstrated his undiminished vitality. He conducted his fifth concert, had an audience with Queen Victoria, and gave a reading of *Parsifal*, all within forty-eight hours.

In between concerts Wagner and Cosima went sightseeing. Dover impressed them as much as London. They loved the Zoological Gardens, Crystal Palace, the British Museum and Westminster Abbey, where the organist played them music from *Tannhäuser*. They met George Eliot, her partner George Henry Lewes and the painter Edward Burne-Jones.

After five strenuous weeks they left England, moved by the genuine enthusiasm of their audiences. But the Bayreuth deficit remained. Wagner took home just one tenth of the required total. No wonder that he began to search for a radical solution to his problem – how to pay off all festival debts, how to put future festivals on a sound financial basis, and how to provide a regular, ample income for himself and his family. The answer was America.

The previous year's *Centennial March* had led to offers for Wagner and his family to settle in the United States. He informed King Ludwig of this, who immediately implored him to abandon 'this dreadful plan', warning him, wisely, that living in America would most likely result in artistic sterility, and holding out hopes for a rosy future in the vicinity of his royal patron, who would guarantee the survival of the Bayreuth Festival. Wagner joyfully accepted and told Ludwig that the composition of *Parsifal* was in hand.

Judith Gautier now became Wagner's proxy muse. In his letters to her in Paris he told her she was in his thoughts when he was working. He asked her to send him a yellow sofa cover of satin which he was to name 'Judith', 'for those good mornings with *Parsifal*'. Further letters contained further requests for Parisian merchandise, cold creams, silk brocade and perfumes ('my bathroom is underneath my study, and I like to smell the aroma'). He then informed her that his next three years were to be devoted exclusively to *Parsifal*, and that nothing (nobody?) must be allowed to divert his attention. Judith was to experience the law governing the muses in Wagner's life: their value

The Bayreuth battlefield; caricature by Karl Klie (1876)

decreases as the work they inspired prospers. In mid February 1878 Judith opened a letter from Bayreuth: 'I have asked Cosima to discuss with you those Parisian purchases ... Be good to Cosima and write to her kindly and at length. I shall then always share your news. Love me forever. Thus you will often see me in your mind, and perhaps we shall really meet again one day.'

In return for King Ludwig's rescue act in wiping out the festival deficit, Wagner agreed to allow *Parsifal* to be performed in Munich. Taking a little time off, he wrote the essay *Publikum und Popularität* (Public and Popularity, 1878). The mystical atmosphere of *Parsifal* pervades this hazy piece, in which he criticizes modern audiences, journalists, professors, students, Nietzsche and the Jews. The year 1878 ended, as the next began, with complete performances of the *Ring*, first in Munich, then in Leipzig. Vienna was next in presenting the cycle (May 1879). Apart from some further essays of secondary significance, *Parsifal* ruled this and the next two years. But not exclusively. Throughout his life Wagner insisted on solving social, political, artistic and philosophical problems, in the form of books, essays, pamphlets and articles. Once he had taught the world what was right and what was wrong, he was able to give his undivided attention to what really mattered to the world, his music.

Interspersed with his work on *Parsifal* were several essays: *Zur Einführung in das Jahr 1880* (Introduction to the Year 1880, written in December 1879). From 1880, when little work was done on *Parsifal*, there appeared three essays: *Religion und Kunst* (Religion and Art); *Was nützt diese Erkenntnis?* (What Use is this Knowledge?) and *Zur Mitteilung an die geehrten Patrone der Bühnenfestspiele in Bayreuth* (To the Honoured Patrons of the Bayreuth Festival). In April 1881 Wagner completed the score of *Parsifal* (Act I), and wrote the essay *Zur Einführung der Arbeit des Grafen Gobineau* (Introduction to Count Gobineau's 'Ethnological Review of the Present State of the World'). In June he began the score of Act II, and in August wrote the essay *Heldentum und Christentum* (Heroism and Christianity). In October the score of *Parsifal* (Act II) was completed, and in November he began Act III. In January 1882 *Parsifal* was accomplished.

In January 1880 Wagner discussed costumes and scenery for *Parsifal* with the Russian painter Paul von Joukovsky, but in February he suddenly revived his emigration plans. Having promised King Ludwig the first option for staging the new work in Munich, he was now going to offer it to a promoter in America. He intended to settle in Minnesota, with Cosima and the five children, and establish an academy for singers of Wagnerian roles. For one million dollars, he stipulated, the Americans could purchase him, together with all his present and future works, and that without any additional fees. The price was too high, and Wagner serenely informed the King that he had changed his mind, and that *Parsifal* was to be performed at Bayreuth alone. Ludwig was tired of quarrelling with his 'beloved friend' and gave his consent. He also put the Munich orchestra and chorus at Wagner's disposal. But a minor crisis arose when Ludwig asked Wagner to conduct for him a private performance of the prelude to *Parsifal*. At the end the King asked for the prelude to *Lohengrin*, to enable him to compare the two. Not an unreasonable request, but to Wagner this amounted to asking for a glass of beer after the Eucharist. He stalked off the rostrum and handed the baton to another conductor. It is unfortunate that this their last meeting was to end in discord.

In September 1881 Judith once more stayed at Wahnfried. Turning to Cosima's diary of that time, one learns that Liszt had come to see his daughter and his old friend, that they had all spent 'a strange evening with Mme Gautier', that Cosima was not sure whether Wagner regarded the meeting with his former muse and postal shopper as 'pleasing or just embarrassing'. Cosima herself seemed to have been ill at ease. 'When I came downstairs,' she wrote, 'I discovered R. at the piano and our friend Judith in rich, rather revealing finery.' Why this all-round unease? Had word of Judith's racial descent reached Wahnfried at last?

In *Richard Wagner et son oeuvre poétique*, which she published in 1882, Judith wrote:

> There is no trace in him of the egoistic insensitivity which great men frequently exhibit after they have attained some degree of public acclaim. He is, if anything, too sensitive. He allows his mood to lead him into momentary bouts of severity ... Sometimes he can forget and completely change his opinion. He can love what a short while ago he did not, and always with the same sincerity.

Judith probably wrote that last sentence with a heavy heart. In pronouncing Wagner capable of loving what a short while ago he did not love, she conveys the dismal truth that he could also love no longer what a short while ago he did.

It is ironic that most of the men who were good to Wagner in the last years of his life were Jews. Their unselfish assistance reflected their loftiness of purpose, for both Richard and Cosima tested their loyalty with wanton anti-Semitic remarks; yet their devotion to the cause made them impervious. Hermann Levi (1839–1900), a rabbi's son, was King Ludwig's court conductor. The first conductor of *Parsifal*, he was for a time a house guest at Wahnfried. Both Wagners teased him about his Jewishness, and he endured their scurrilities with tender forbearance, since Wagner was also capable of pro-Semitic sentiments. 'Levi moves Richard to pity,' Cosima wrote in her diary in July 1878, 'because he regards himself as an anachronism, being a Jew. Richard assures him that the Catholics may think themselves more aristocratic than the Protestants, but that the Jews were, after all, the most aristocratic race.' Levi told his father that Wagner was the best and noblest of men and that he, Levi, was thanking God for the privilege of being allowed to serve him.

Angelo Neumann (1838–1910), a singer turned opera director, toured extensively with Wagner's operas, always amiably agreeing to the composer's stipulations. In the season 1882–3 he gave 135 performances of the *Ring* operas, in addition to fifty-eight concerts of Wagner's music. Heinrich Porges (1837–1900) was Wagner's musical assistant at Bayreuth for the 1876 and 1882 festivals. He made detailed notes of Wagner's rehearsal instructions to his singers and players, which give us a vivid picture of Wagner as a producer. Josef Rubinstein (1847–84), a brilliant pianist, caught Wagner's attention with his written introduction, 'I am a Jew. That is all you need to know about me.' Wagner invited him to Bayreuth, and the young Russian became a fixture at Wahnfried, where he combined the functions of house pianist and uncomplaining listener to Wagner's soliloquies. The year after Wagner's death he committed suicide.

Wagner conducts; a cartoon by Willi Bithorn (1876)

All of them endured, revered, rejoiced. More to the point, they furnished Wagner with the warmth of their intelligent presence and with the serenity he needed for his works. This was the atmosphere in which *Parsifal* could flourish, and on another lengthy Italian holiday his last opera was completed in Palermo.

One year was left to Wagner. In May 1882 he returned to Bayreuth, in time for the rehearsals of *Parsifal*. Time enough also for a final meeting with Judith. She shared Wagner's box at the opening of the second Bayreuth Festival, as she had done in 1876, to see 'their' *Parsifal*. Premonitions of farewell and finality clouded those days, and Wagner was in tears throughout the performance. He was not alone. Hermann Levi wrote to his father that after the last, triumphant performance, Wagner made a speech and 'everybody was in tears'.

In September all the Wagners left for their final holiday in Italy. Liszt and Levi stayed with them in Venice, where they discussed Wagner's plans for the future. He was going to revise *Tannhäuser*, and then no more operas, only symphonies.

Levi left Venice on 12 February 1883. The next day Wagner suffered a fatal heart attack, while working on his essay *Über das Weibliche im Menschlichen* (On the Feminine Element in Humanity). After the words 'Liebe – Tragik' the pen slipped from his hand.

Levi wrote to his father on 15 February:

> In my dreadful, indescribable grief you are in my loving thoughts. Future generations will realize what he was to the world and what the world has lost in him. It was my good fortune to see him twenty-four hours before his death ... He was in a most cheerful mood, as we strolled in the procession of masked revellers on the piazza at midnight. He led the way with his daughter Isolde, striding with the liveliness of a young man ... It was a glorious night, and at one o'clock we drove home ... At midday on Monday I left Venice, the Master accompanied me to the stairs, kissed me several times – I was much moved – and twenty-four hours later!!

Journey towards the *Ring*

Year	Age	
1813		Wilhelm Richard Wagner born in Leipzig on 22 May. His father, police official Friedrich Wagner, dies on 23 November of the same year.
1814	1	Wagner's mother, Johanna Rosine, marries Ludwig Geyer, a poet, actor and painter.
1817	4	Richard attends infant school in Dresden.
1821	8	Ludwig Geyer dies. Richard boards with Geyer's brother, a goldsmith in Eisleben.
1822	9	He attends school in Dresden, as 'Wilhelm Richard Geyer'.
1823	10	His fascination with ancient mythology begins.
1825	12	Richard performs Weber's *Der Freischütz* at home with friends.
1826	13	Translates first three books of Homer's *Odyssey* into German.
1827	14	Begins his tragedy *Leubald*. Drops the name Geyer and settles with family in Leipzig.
1828	15	Attends Nikolai Gymnasium in Leipzig, as Richard Wagner. *Leubald* completed. Composition lessons with Gottlieb Müller.
1829	16	Composes Piano Sonata in D minor, String Quartet in D major, Piano Sonata in F minor.
1830	17	Copies and makes piano arrangement of Beethoven's Ninth Symphony. Attends Thomas-Schule in Leipzig. Composes Overture in B flat major, Overture in C major, Overture to *Die Braut von Messina* (all lost). First performance of Overture in B flat major in Leipzig.

1831	18	Studies music at Leipzig University, but neglects and terminates his study. Composition lessons with Theodor Weinlig. Composes incidental music to Goethe's *Faust*, Piano Sonata in B flat major, Piano Fantasia in F sharp minor, Concert Overture in D minor.
1832	19	Composes Piano Sonata in A major, *König Enzio* Overture, Concert Overture in C major, Symphony in C major. First performances of *König Enzio* Overture and Concert Overture in C major in Leipzig. First performance of his Symphony in Prague.
1833	20	Becomes chorus master in Würzburg.
1834	21	Completes his first opera, *Die Feen*. Becomes musical director in Lauchstädt, where he meets his future wife, the actress Minna Planer. Becomes musical director at Magdeburg.
1835	22	Composes *Columbus* Overture.
1836	23	Completes his second opera, *Das Liebesverbot*. Composes *Polonia* Overture. Marries Minna at Königsberg.
1837	24	Composes *Rule Britannia* Overture. Becomes musical director at Königsberg.
1838	25	Begins composition of *Rienzi*, his third opera.
1839	26	Flees with Minna to Paris, via London, to escape creditors.
1840	27	Composes 'Faust' Overture. *Rienzi* completed.
1841	28	*Der fliegende Holländer* completed.
1842	29	Leaves Paris for Dresden. First performance of *Rienzi* in Dresden.
1843	30	First performance of *Der fliegende Holländer*, in Dresden. Becomes Royal Saxon Court Conductor.
1844	31	Conducts *Holländer* in Berlin to great public acclaim but hostile press.

1845 32 *Tannhäuser* completed. Conducts first performance of *Tannhäuser* at Dresden Court Theatre (Wagner's niece, Johanna, sings the part of Elisabeth).

1846 33 Growing volume of debts. Conducts Beethoven's Ninth Symphony in Dresden.

1847 34 Conducts *Rienzi* in Berlin.

1848 35 *Lohengrin* completed. Writes verse draft of *Siegfrieds Tod.* The theatre director Eduard Devrient notes in his diary: 'Wagner read to us from his compilation of the Siegfried sagas ... wants to turn it into an opera, but I fear this will come to nothing.'

1849 36 Writes essays *Man and Existing Society*, *The Revolution*, *The Art-Work of the Future*, *Art and Revolution.* Participates in Dresden uprising. Police issue warrant for his arrest: he escapes into exile in Switzerland.

1850 37 Romantic entanglement with Jessie Laussot in Bordeaux: plans to elope with her. Musical sketches for *Siegfrieds Tod.* First performance, under Liszt, of *Lohengrin* at Weimar.

1851 38 Writes book *Oper und Drama*, prose and verse draft of *Der junge Siegfried* and prose sketches for *Rheingold* and *Walküre.*

1852 39 Prose drafts of *Rheingold* and *Walküre*; verse drafts of *Walküre* and *Rheingold.* Wagner reads the four poems of *Der Ring des Nibelungen* to friends. Writes to Uhlig: 'I am shameless enough to proclaim: this is the greatest thing I have ever written. Your Nibelung Prince, Alberich.

1853 40 Composes piano sonata for Mathilde Wesendonck. The complete *Ring* poem is privately printed and published. Writes to Liszt: 'Mark well my new poem – it contains the beginning of the world and its end.' Begins composition of *Rheingold.*

1854 41 *Rheingold* completed. Begins composition of *Walküre.* Discovers Schopenhauer's *Die Welt als Wille und Vorstellung.* Writes optimistically to Wilhelm Fischer: '*Walküre* in summer, then *Der junge Siegfried* next spring, and *Siegfrieds Tod* in winter. By Easter 1856 the whole thing will be complete. Then comes the impossible – my own theatre.'

1855	42	Revises *Faust* overture. Conducts eight concerts in London and is received by Queen Victoria.
1856	43	*Walküre* completed. Begins composition of *Siegfried*. Writes to Fischer: 'Next year I shall perform the whole cycle. Your seats are reserved. Now find me a decent tenor.' *Der junge Siegfried* renamed *Siegfried*, *Siegfrieds Tod* renamed *Götterdämmerung*. 'It is only during the actual composition that the true nature of my text is revealed to me. Everywhere I discover secrets which had previously been hidden from me.'
1857	44	Moves to 'Asyl', a villa on the Wesendoncks' property near Zurich. Interrupts work on *Siegfried* to write and compose *Tristan und Isolde* and *Meistersinger*. Close relationship with Mathilde Wesendonck. Poem (first version) of *Tristan und Isolde* completed, and composition begun. Composes three *Wesendonck-Lieder* (to poems by Mathilde).
1858	45	Composes two more *Wesendonck-Lieder*.
1859	46	*Tristan und Isolde* completed.
1860	47	Partial amnesty: Wagner may enter Germany, with the exception of Saxony.
1861	48	Paris Opera performs *Tannhäuser*, but owing to hostile reception Wagner withdraws it after three performances. Reads his poem of *Meistersinger* to friends in Mainz.
1862	49	King of Saxony grants full amnesty. Continues work on *Meistersinger*.
1863	50	Extensive conducting tours (Vienna, Prague, Moscow, St Petersburg, Budapest).
1864	51	Issues uncovered cheques and escapes creditors and likely imprisonment. King Ludwig II summons Wagner to his court, offering friendship, cancellation of debts, special allowances, free housing and a regular salary. King Ludwig commissions *Der Ring des Nibelungen* for 30,000 florins.

1865	52	Isolde, Wagner and Cosima's first child, is born. First performance of *Tristan und Isolde* in Munich. Banished from Munich, Wagner departs for Switzerland.
1866	53	Settles in his house 'Tribschen' by Lake Lucerne, financed by King Ludwig.
1867	54	Eva, Wagner and Cosima's second child, is born. *Meistersinger* completed.
1868	55	First performance of *Meistersinger* in Munich.
1869	56	After gap of twelve years resumes composition of *Siegfried.* Siegfried, Wagner and Cosima's third child, is born. First performance of *Rheingold* in Munich. Begins composition of *Götterdämmerung.*
1870	57	Wagner to Judith Gautier: 'Yesterday Siegfried drank Gutrune's fatal potion. I bet this will result in some mischief which I shall have to put into music.' First performance of *Walküre* in Munich. Wagner and Cosima are married. Writes essay *Beethoven* and composes *Siegfried Idyll.*
1871	58	*Siegfried* completed.
1872	59	Settles in Bayreuth. Cosima notes in her diary: 'I lack the strength to describe the emotion that gripped me when R. called me to say that he had completed his sketch [of *Götterdämmerung*]. He plays the ending for me, and I cannot tell which moved me more, the noble music or the noble achievement. I feel my goal has been attained and I can now close my eyes.'
1873	60	Reads poem of *Götterdämmerung* in Berlin.
1874	61	*Götterdämmerung* completed.
1875	62	Rehearsals for the following year's *Ring* at Bayreuth.
1876	63	Three complete cycles of *Der Ring des Nibelungen* performed at the opening of the Bayreuth Festspielhaus.
1882	69	*Parsifal* completed.
1883	70	Wagner dies in Venice on 13 February.

Sigmund and the Beast, an episode from the *Volsunga Saga*; illustration by Patten Wilson

Wagner's Sources for the *Ring*

Wagner's Sources for the *Ring*

In basing the *Ring* predominantly on ancient Norse mythology, Wagner ensured its enduring allure, since myths are for all time. The myth seeks to interpret the world, and Wagner integrates the arts for that purpose.

When Wagner began to study the mythological raw material for the *Ring*, the ancient tales gripped him to such an extent that he felt born again, as he put it in *Mein Leben*. He thought the myths were addressing him, saying, 'know us, unravel us, interpret us'. So when he read medieval texts, such as the *Nibelungenlied* and the *Volsunga Saga*, he encountered puzzling fragments which needed decoding. In joining the pieces, discarding the impenetrable, stripping away disturbing veils, he devised a coherent tale which could be taken for the long-lost original text on which narrators and scribes had based their own tales.

The myths taught Wagner that modern man may be more sophisticated than mythological man, but that he is not necessarily wiser, more understanding or morally superior. In delving into myths we gain, as Wagner did, a deeper insight into human behaviour. In *Oper und Drama* Wagner suggested that myths are significant throughout the ages, but that every age needs to expound them anew. He believed that myth and music were made for one another and that his *Ring* was a nineteenth-century equivalent of an ancient myth. Hence his frequent transcriptions of mythological events into pure music, excluding the need for textual clarification.

Literary Sources

Wagner's chief literary sources for the *Ring* are:

1. Aeschylus (*Oresteia*, *Prometheus Bound*)
2. The Poetic (or Elder) Edda
3. The Prose Edda
4. *Das Nibelungenlied*
5. The *Volsunga Saga*
6. The *Thidrek Saga*
7. *Das Lied vom hürnen Seyfrid*
8. The *Märchen* of Jacob and Wilhelm Grimm
9. *Die deutsche Heldensage* of Wilhelm Grimm
10. The *Deutsche Mythologie* of Jacob Grimm

Aeschylus

Wagner admired the works of Aeschylus, especially the *Oresteia* and *Prometheus Bound.* Of particular importance to Wagner was the reconstruction of what was originally a *Prometheus* trilogy (with *The Theft of the Fire* and *Prometheus Unbound*) by Johann Gustav Droysen, who translated it into German. In his writings Wagner often acknowledged his indebtedness to Aeschylus, whose works had moulded his perception of music drama. Aeschylus taught Wagner five maxims:

1. A dramatic presentation is not meant to 'entertain', but to contribute to the spectator's knowledge of himself.
2. Dramatic art, music, dance and choreography create a unity of all the arts.
3. The amphitheatrical structure promotes a transformation of an audience into a congregation.
4. The nature of the Aeschylean drama, with its interaction of divine and human characters, helps to turn a theatrical event into a festival.
5. The author of a drama should also be responsible for its staging.

Wagner assimilated not only Aeschylus' principles of dramatic art, but also a wealth of details that found their way into the *Ring*. The Greek chorus comments, reflects and forecasts: in the *Ring* this role is taken over by the orchestral web of leitmotifs. Wagner's original title for *Das Rheingold* was *The Theft of the Rhinegold*, analogous to Aeschylus' *The Theft of the Fire*, which reports the building of a castle (Wagner's Walhall) for the young god Zeus. Aeschylus also mentions a helmet that gives invisibility (Wagner's Tarnhelm), and takes us to the smithy of Hephaistus (Wagner's Nibelheim) where, with the help of fire, metal chains are fashioned. Zeus, in *Prometheus Bound*, lives in fear of losing his power, which is founded on trespasses against the law of nature (Wagner's Wotan). The priestess Io, pursued by Zeus's wife Hera, is directed by Prometheus to Egypt, where she is to give birth to a son (Wagner's Brünnhilde, pursued by Wotan, directs Sieglinde to a forest, to give birth to Siegfried). Zeus causes Prometheus to be chained to a rock, because he had aided the mortals by bringing them fire (Wagner's Brünnhilde is put to sleep on a rock, for aiding the mortals Siegmund and Sieglinde). Prometheus will be set free by a hero of mortal descent, Hercules (Brünnhilde is set free by Siegfried).

On the day before his death Wagner said that his admiration for Aeschylus was still growing.

Facing page, the Norns; illustration by C. Ehrenberg

The Poetic Edda

This Icelandic collection by anonymous poets, written between 1150 and 1250, contains nineteen strophic poems, probably meant to be sung. The poems deal with gods and heroes, among them Sigurd (Wagner's Siegfried), Gunnar (Gunther) and Högni (Hagen). In the Edda Wagner found the story of Sigurd and his foster father, the dwarf Regin (Mime in the *Ring*), Sigurd's slaying of Fafnir, and his awakening of Sigrdrifa, an early incarnation of Brünnhilde. Strangely, the poems also feature a 'Brynhild', who receives a golden ring from Sigurd. Sigurd is later ensnared into marrying Gudrun (Gutrune) and, in the guise of Gunnar, obtains Brynhild for him. The betrayed Brynhild has Sigurd killed, not by Högni, but by Gunnar's brother, Guttorm. Wagner modelled his use of alliteration in the *Ring* on the Edda's technique of *Stabreim*, the use of two or more words within one or two lines which begin with the same initial sound, such as 'kith and kin', 'be true, trusty hero', or 'Brünnhild brings you her life'.

The Prose Edda

Snorri Sturluson (c. 1178–1241) compiled this series of myths of the ancient Scandinavian gods in around 1225. Being in prose, they actually facilitate our appreciation of some of the obscurities in the older Poetic Edda. Here Wagner found much material for *Rheingold*. The Prose Edda was written some 200 years after the Christianization of Iceland, and Snorri Sturluson reveals a degree of moral sophistication which presented a challenge to Wagner. In this section (one of Wagner's sources for the beginning of *Götterdämmerung*) the Edda discusses the Norns:

> The Norns determine men's fate, but they are hardly impartial. To some they allot a good, comfortable life, while others have preciously little to chew. Some live long, others die early. Why? Because some Norns are good, and they grant a good life. But there are also some wicked Norns, and they create bad luck.

Such post-pagan subtlety was not for Wagner. His Norns, like his gods and humans, are all subject to Necessity, a condition which had been proclaimed by Aeschylus. Consequently, Wagner's Wotan informs Erda:

> In thrall to the world
> Norns do their weaving,
> unable to alter what must be.
> (*Siegfried* III, 1)

Das Nibelungenlied

An anonymous author wrote this epic poem in Austria, at the beginning of the thirteenth century. He overlaid earlier sources with a veneer of medieval chivalry and Christian customs. In selecting, rejecting and fusing such material he was, in fact, setting a precedent for Wagner's own method of constructing one myth from many.

The *Nibelungenlied* consists of two sections. The epic's first part presents Siegfried's arrival at King Gunther's court; his conquest of Brunhild (Wagner's Brünnhilde) on Gunther's behalf, in exchange for the hand of Kriemhild (Gutrune), the king's sister; the quarrel between the brides, Brunhild and Kriemhild; and Hagen's murder of Siegfried. The second part, which was of no concern to Wagner, tells of Kriemhild's next marriage and her revenge for Siegfried's death.

Although Kriemhild is the central character of the *Nibelungenlied*, Wagner casts her (in his Gutrune) in a minor role. He also saw his Siegfried differently from the well-born, well-bred hero of the *Nibelungenlied*. But he was indebted to the medieval poem for many details of Siegfried's life and, particularly, of his death. He also used the *Nibelungenlied*'s account of Hagen being branded as Siegfried's murderer, although in *Götterdämmerung* the dead Siegfried's hand rises menacingly, whereas in the *Nibelungenlied* his wounds begin to bleed. This Wagner discarded as being less theatrically effective.

Where the *Nibelungenlied* indulges in drollery and extravagance, Wagner condenses days and nights of turmoil into a few summarizing lines. In the epic poem Siegfried dons his magic cloak and aids Gunther in his athletic contest with Brunhild. They throw the javelin (at each other!), they hurl a rock and

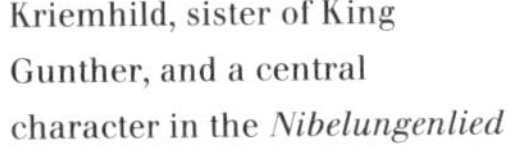

Kriemhild, sister of King Gunther, and a central character in the *Nibelungenlied*

they exceed twenty-four yards in the long jump (thus almost trebling the current Olympic record). Gunther's victory makes Brunhild his wife, but in their first night together she refuses to consummate the marriage. Unaided by Siegfried, the hapless king is bound hand and foot by his spouse, who suspends him from a nail in the wall. Next night Siegfried once more comes to his aid. In the dark he changes places with Gunther in the bridal bed and, after a lengthy struggle, he subdues the amazon maid. He draws a golden ring from her finger and takes away her girdle, then smuggles Gunther into the chamber and swiftly steals away. Wagner rightly rejected the ghoulish humour of the situation, but gave Brünnhilde these telling lines at the end of *Götterdämmerung* (Act II):

> You timid man,
> treacherous spouse!
> Rotten is the wondrous race
> that breeds such weaklings as you.

When it first appeared in print, in 1757, the art-loving King Frederick II of Prussia dismissed the *Nibelungenlied* as 'stuff and nonsense', but the author and philosopher Friedrich Theodor Vischer wrote in 1844, 'I recommend the *Nibelungenlied* as the text for a grand opera.' Wagner, in his own way, complied.

The *Volsunga Saga*

This prose epic, based on a long oral tradition, was compiled by an anonymous Icelandic author in the first half of the thirteenth century. It presents the history of the race of the Volsungen (Wagner's Wälsungs) from Odin (Wotan) to Aslaug, daughter of Sigurd (Siegfried). It is Wagner's principal *Ring* source, and it inspired William Morris's magnificent translation and, closer to our time, yielded a great deal of subject matter for Tolkien's *The Lord of the Rings.* Since the *Volsunga Saga* contains material from both Eddas, it throws light on problem areas in those works and fills in gaps where the Eddas present us with fragmentary sections. Since the *Volsunga Saga*'s scope is wider than Wagner's, several fine portions remained unused, such as Sigurd's choosing of a suitable horse: he made his selection from twelve excellent stallions which he drove into a deep river; only one was courageous enough to swim across, and Sigurd's mind was made up. Another story concerns King Gunnar (Wagner's Gunther):

> They threw him into a snake pit and bound his hands. Gudrun sent him a harp and he plucked its strings with his toes. He played so beautifully that all the snakes were lulled to sleep, except for one venomous adder which crept up to him and struck his heart.

Maybe the adder was deaf. At any rate, Wagner designed a less spectacular but more heroic end for his feeble King Gunther, when he perishes at Hagen's hands.

The *Thidrek Saga*

Norway is the home of this saga written between 1260 and 1270, although it probably originated in what is now northern Germany. Thidrek of Bern (Verona) was the Ostrogothic conqueror Theodoric who died in 526. The saga's chief importance for Wagner lay in its detailed description of Siegfried's early life.

In the saga Queen Sisibe, who had given birth to a baby boy in a forest, placed the child in a glass casket which fell into a river. There it later burst against a rock, the child fell out and was taken by a hind to its lair. The hind suckled it, together with its own fawns. Mimir (Wagner's Mime) found the boy in the forest, took him into his smithy and named him – Sigfrid. The boy grew into an immensely strong and intractable lad who split Mimir's anvil in two. To get rid of the troublemaker, Mimir gave Sigfrid food and drink for nine days and sent him away to burn charcoal for him. Mimir also sent word to his brother Regin, the dragon, encouraging him to swallow the lad. When Sigfrid came across the dragon, he clubbed him to death with a blazing tree trunk. This made him so hungry and thirsty that he consumed his nine days' provisions. Bathing in the dragon's blood made him invulnerable, except between his shoulders, where he could not reach. On Sigfrid's return to the smithy, Mimir presented him with a sword and advised him to 'go to Brynhild and ask her for the horse Grani'. To show his gratitude, Sigfrid cut off Mimir's head, set out for Brynhild's palace and killed fourteen watchmen, before setting eyes on Brynhild. She told Sigfrid about his parents and provided him with her horse, Grani.

Wagner seemed to have been fascinated by the tale, details of which are echoed in concise observations, such as Mime's comments in *Siegfried* (Act I, scene I):

> I tinker and clinker away,
> just to humour the boy,
> one blow, he breaks it in bits.
>
> I'll fetch some flesh I have roasted;
> I'll bring you a bowl of broth,
> a brave, succulent brew.

Wagner's Siegfried, whose breaking of Mime's anvil mirrors the *Thidrek Saga*, is like Sigfrid curious about his parentage, asking 'Who are my father and mother?' and later:

What was my mother like?
A roe-dear, maybe, lucid and light,
has such eyes, when they sparkle.
(*Siegfried* II, 2)

Although written later than the *Nibelungenlied*, the *Thidrek Saga* had a special appeal for Wagner, since it preserves the pre-Christian tone of the various tales, and dispenses with the *Nibelungenlied*'s veneer of courtly custom and knightly niceties.

Das Lied vom hürnen Seyfrid

The early sixteenth-century 'Song of Seyfrid of the Horny Skin' mixes several earlier sources. The anonymous author was somewhat careless in disdaining to explain several contradictions, but nevertheless provides much information about giants, dwarfs and about their rivalries. The account generally agrees with the *Thidrek Saga* in its telling of the hero's upbringing: he is apprenticed to a smith; he kills a dragon and, when he bathes in the dragon's blood, acquires a horny skin so impregnable that no man's weapon could harm him. Later we hear of a winged dragon who had abducted a beautiful maiden. Seyfrid despatches the dragon and marries the maiden. It is possible that when Wagner read about this, the wife–dragon connection lodged itself so firmly in his mind that it influenced his astonishing use of the Dragon motif at Brünnhilde's awakening in *Siegfried* (Act III, scene 3).

The *Märchen* of Jacob and Wilhelm Grimm

Surreal phenomena such as invisibility, humans changing into animals and vice versa, speaking birds, dragons both winged and earthbound, magic potions, enchantments and disenchantments, the slumbering maiden awakened by her deliverer – these are some of the elements that occur in the Grimms' collection of 'Fairy-Tales for Children and Home' (1812–15).

The fairy-tale is cousin to the myth. Both discuss and attempt to unravel life's enigmas. Since this is also a central theme of the *Ring*, Wagner makes ample use of the Grimms' offerings. The Sleeping Beauty's slumber, induced by a spindle prick, corresponds to Brünnhilde's sleep (*Walküre*, Act III, scene 3), induced by Wotan's kiss, while the prince's crossing through the thorny hedge is recalled in Siegfried's crossing of the wall of fire (*Siegfried*, Act III, scene 3). Puss-in-boots, the tricky adviser, goads the magician into turning himself first into an elephant, then into a lion and finally into a mouse, which causes his death by consumption. Similarly, Loge provokes Alberich's transformation into serpent and toad (*Rheingold*, Scene 3) which leads to his downfall. 'The Youth who Left Home to Learn Fear' is reflected in Siegfried's analogous quest.

Dornröschen (Sleeping Beauty); an illustration from Heinrich Lefler and Joseph Urban's 'Märchen-Kalender'

Gold in the water (*Rheingold*, Scene 1) occurs in 'The Frog Prince'. The 'wishing-hat' in 'Crystal Ball' anticipates Alberich's Tarnhelm (*Rheingold*, Scene 3). 'The Golden Bird' features a tree that bears golden apples, as does *Rheingold* (Scene 2). A dead body's arm raises itself in 'The Stubborn Child', as in *Götterdämmerung* (Act III, scene 3). Grimm's Young Giant breaks all the iron rods given to him, and Siegfried performs similar tricks with Mime's swords (*Siegfried*, Act I, scene 1). The Grimms wrote in the introduction to the *Märchen* that their collection contained 'thoughts about the spiritual aspects of life'. Not unlike Wagner's *Ring*.

Die deutsche Heldensage of Wilhelm Grimm

This superbly researched work (1829) presents a history of German heroic sagas from the sixth to the sixteenth century. Grimm investigates both connections and changes of emphasis and substance which the heroic saga experienced in the course of a thousand years. His detailed examination of the characters in the *Nibelungenlied* and in the *Thidrek Saga* must have been helpful to Wagner, who shared Grimm's fascination with the interrelationship of different sagas. Another attraction to Wagner was Grimm's discussion of the miraculous in epic poetry, an area of great significance in the *Ring*: the curse, the power of the ring and the Tarnhelm, flying horses, rainbow bridge, the appearance of Erda, the reading of secret thoughts, the rope of destiny, spells and charms.

Wagner diverges from Grimm when he feels that even the miraculous needs human assistance to become fully effective. In the German saga tradition, for example, Siegfried kills the dragon and dips his finger in the monster's fatty substance which 'runs like a river'. Smearing the stuff all over himself, Siegfried's skin becomes horny, like the dragon's, except between his shoulder blades. Wagner dislikes this. We hear in *Götterdämmerung* (Act II, scene 5) that Brünnhilde's love for Siegfried had made her weave spells of invulnerability on his body, but that she omitted to cast such spells on his back, because 'never would he turn his back in battle, and there my spells do not guard him.' In attaching a flaw (Brünnhilde's neglect) to the miraculous, Wagner adds plausibility and establishes a connection between the supernatural and reality.

The *Deutsche Mythologie* of Jacob Grimm

The 'German Mythology' (1835), an outstanding contribution to scholarship, retraces and reconstructs pagan customs and beliefs of the German past. Its source material ranges from the Romans to the late Middle Ages. Wagner, in common with many of his contemporaries, eagerly absorbed information about his own distant ancestors, together with corroborative details about the gods and heroes who were to appear in his

Ring. In *Deutsche Mythologie* Wagner read about Norns winding the threads of destiny, and made good use of this material in *Götterdämmerung*. He also learned from Jacob Grimm about the old German custom of swearing an oath on a sword. For dramatic reasons, however, he replaced the sword with a spear in *Götterdämmerung* (Act II, scene 4), where Siegfried swears his oath on Hagen's spear, the weapon that was later to kill him. So great was the impact of this work on Wagner that he wrote in *Mein Leben*:

> I was captivated by a wondrous magic. The baldest legends spoke to me as though they came from my own homeland of long ago ... The effect of all this on the state of my mind I can only describe as a complete rebirth.

Man, Myth and Music

The Autobiographical Source

Wagner displays his constant need for self-revelation not only in *Mein Leben*, but also in his earlier *Eine Mitteilung an meine Freunde* (A Communication to my Friends, 1851), which gives an account of his artistic development and tries to explain his complex nature. Thousands of lengthy letters, and his huge appetite for soliloquizing in company, provide further evidence of the superabundant storehouse of his mind, whose capriciousness matched the man's outer appearance. His stepdaughter Natalie described him: 'Snow-white pantaloons, sky-blue tail coat with huge gold buttons, cuffs, an immensely tall top hat with a narrow brim, a walking stick as high as himself, with a huge gold knob, and very bright, sulphur yellow kid gloves.' This is Wagner the extrovert, the actor, the stage manager. It would be surprising if aspects of such a personality had not coloured, influenced and even determined certain aspects of his *Ring* characters. Wagner's perpetual craving for wealth is mirrored in Alberich's identical lust:

> Hurry below!
> In the new-made shafts
> go gather new gold!
> (*Rheingold*, Scene 3)

The Ring reveals love's various manifestations, from the lecherous to the exalted. The former is Alberich's preserve:

> O let me fondle your neck, let me nudge it.
> My clamorous blood bids me cling to your billowing bosom.
> (*Rheingold*, Scene 1)

Wagner's choice of words is uninfluenced by any external sources. It emanates from a sexual attitude that is not altogether alien to him.

On a more austere level, Wagner originally designed Siegfried as the hero who was to redeem Wotan and the whole world, a role not unlike the one which Wagner himself had assumed in seeing his own works as vehicles for the regeneration of mankind. Wagner, the political and artistic revolutionary, believed in destroying defective matter, not for the sake of destruction, but to create something better from the remains: a republican monarchy, or Nothung, forged by Siegfried from the pulverized fragments. Wagner expressed this attitude in a letter of November 1851 to Theodor Uhlig:

> The revolution alone can provide me with artists and audiences, for the coming revolution is bound to put an end to our muddled theatrical institutions. It is inevitable that they will all come crushing down. From the ruins I shall reclaim what I need.

Whoever sees characters in the *Ring* as projections of persons around Wagner, or of Wagner himself, steps into a minefield of bias and conjecture. The affinity, however, of Wagner with Wotan and of Minna with Fricka is inescapable. Wagner wrote to Minna (April 1850): 'I have broken with everything old, and I fight it with all my strength. You cling to somebody, I to something; you to individuals, I to mankind.' Wotan tells Fricka (*Walküre*, Act II, scene 1):

> You will not learn what I would teach you,
> to think or to dream of a deed,
> before you see it yourself.
> Common places will please you alone;
> but what is yet to come,
> I smile on and uphold.

Minna wrote to Mathilde Schiffner (July 1852): 'I am so tired of wandering and living out of a suitcase. How I envy everybody who has a cosy home.' Fricka tells Wotan (*Rheingold*, Scene 2):

> My concern for Wotan's faithfulness
> forces me to consider
> how to keep him beside me,
> lest he slipped loose from his spouse.
> Handsome our palace, precious our household,
> such as to charm you to cherish our home.

In the same scene Wotan tells Fricka:

> Ranging and changing, life's own law –
> that thrill I cannot relinquish.

Similarly, Wagner wrote to Minna (May 1850): 'I must write to you once more before going far away ... to Malta, then on to Greece and Asia Minor ... The world of today no longer exists for me.'

The relationship between Wagner and his works is reciprocal.

Processing the Sources

> Those layers of garments with which later authors had shrouded [the ancient myths], I was able to strip off, one by one, until I could see it at last in all its chaste beauty.
> (*Eine Mitteilung an meine Freunde*)

Left, Freya and her chariot; *above*, Odin; illustration by Edward Burne-Jones. Odin is Wagner's Wotan, the composer's sporadic role-model; Freya is Wagner's Fricka, who similarly relates to Minna Wagner

How did it all begin? Who were the first humans? Who made them? What keeps the universe together? Will the world come to an end one day, and why and when? What happens afterwards? Is there an afterwards? Will the gods survive? These are some of the questions which are posed in the ancient myths. They are also discussed in the *Ring*, together with such mythological themes as fate, free will, extremes of human behaviour and emotion, oaths, the power of a curse, lust, broken faith, revenge and murder; but also trust, love, honour, courage, generosity and the golden age of innocence.

In the course of his intensive study of the source material, Wagner had to select, reject, combine and modify. He fused myth, epic, legend, history, gods and humans, and in the process he fashioned a new myth for our time. Into the mixture he blended features of his own invention, such as the Rhinemaidens as guardians of the gold, Alberich's stealing of the gold, Wotan's creation of a free hero, and Wotan's fathering of Brünnhilde with Erda.

When it suited his purpose, Wagner did not hesitate to combine features from different sources. In the *Nibelungenlied* he read about a golden wand which *might* bestow command of the whole world to the man who *could* find its secret. Wagner gave this power to the golden ring, which he took in turn from the *Volsunga Saga*, and he gave the *Nibelungenlied*'s conditional forecast about command of the world to Wellgunde, who informed Alberich (in *Rheingold*, Scene 1), that if a man *were* to able to fashion a ring from the gold, he *might* gain immense power.

Myth into Music

Before there was anything, there was nothing. Wagner learned from the *Voluspa*, in Snorri's Prose Edda, that at first there was a vast void. Then rivers began to spring up. An age of ice gave way to an age of thaw, and the giant Ymir came into existence. Then the first gods had their being, followed by the earth, the sky, the sun, the moon and the stars. Man was made, and woman, and night and day.

Wagner, too, began the *Ring* at the beginning. But, instead of staging what he had read, he translated the process of creation, as reported in the Edda, into music.

At the very beginning of *Rheingold* one is hardly aware of that deep note which the double basses are playing, the bottom E flat. It has already persisted for four bars, but all eight double basses are going to sound their note for another 132 bars. In the fifteenth bar three bassoons enter, on B flat. The fundamental tonic is joined by its dominant. Life has begun. Then eight horns weave their canonic web, entering one after the other. The world is being shaped and peopled. Where the Edda specifies, Wagner universalizes, creating his own world.

The Rhinemaidens

The titan Oceanus, in Greek mythology, married his sister (as did Wagner's Siegmund and Sieglinde), and they brought forth three thousand Oceanids, spirits of the rivers. Aeschylus, in his *Prometheus Bound*, includes a number of Oceanids as the Chorus. They show compassion for Prometheus, the archetypal outsider, much as Wagner's Rhinemaidens initially treat the outsider Alberich with forbearance.

A different kind of water-dweller appears in the Poetic Edda. Aegir, god of the sea, had nine daughters who represent the billows of the deep. One of them, Wave, was inclined to mischief and would occasionally cause ships to sink. This may have been in Wagner's mind when he made the Rhinemaidens Woglinde and Wellgunde drown Hagen. In the *Nibelungenlied*, the nymphs are less aggressive. Hagen converses with some mermaids who were bathing in the Danube. They warn him of his imminent death. In *Götterdämmerung*, the equally prophetic Rhinemaidens tell Siegfried:

> As you slew the dragon,
> shall you be slain,
> and here, today.

Aegir, god of the sea, with Ran, one of his daughters

Wagner drastically reduced the 3,000 Oceanids of Greek mythology to a more manageable three. He blended their good-hearted nature, as displayed in *Prometheus Bound*, with the austerity of the daughters of Aegir in the Poetic Edda. Wave (in German 'Welle') he turned into Wellgunde, while the river Danube of the *Nibelungenlied* became the river Rhine.

Golden Apples

In Greek mythology, the Hesperides were personifications of clouds illuminated by the sun. They were the guardians of golden apples. Hercules, on his quest for this treasure, crossed the sea in a golden ship. He killed a guardian dragon and obtained the golden apples, which were later returned to the Hesperides. Wagner transferred the dragon to the second act of *Siegfried*, making Freia the guardian of the golden apples instead.

Wagner was familiar with 'The Theft of Idun's Apples' in the Prose Edda. Idun, goddess of beauty and everlasting youth, provided the gods with a daily ration of golden apples that kept the immortals young and healthy. The mischievous Loki (Wagner's Loge) started a quarrel with the giant Thiazi who, in the shape of a mighty eagle, snatched Loki in his claws and gave him a most uncomfortable ride. In exchange for his freedom, Loki promised to bring the giant Idun and her golden apples. Loki was released, and tricked Idun into following him to a tree bearing golden apples just like hers, which he pretended to have discovered. He persuaded her to take her own apples along, for comparison. Thiazi was waiting; again in the form of

The giant Thiazi, in the shape of an eagle, catches Loki.

an eagle, he swooped down and carried Idun and her apples away. The gods began to grow old, and they forced Loki to rescue Idun and her apples. Donning a falcon skin, he flew to Thiazi's hall, where he found Idun alone. Murmuring a magic formula, he turned her into a nut and flew away, carrying her in his beak. The giant pursued the falcon, but was caught by the gods. Thor (Wagner's Donner) threw the giant's eyes into the sky where they still shine as stars. Another incantation by Loki turned the nut back into Idun who, with her golden apples, restored youth everlasting to the gods.

In 'Skirnir's Journey' (also in the Prose Edda) Freyr, the god of fertility, bade his messenger Skirnir bring him Gerd, the beautiful frost giantess with whom Freyr had fallen in love from afar. To reach her, Skirnir had to pass through a wall of flames guarding her halls. He presented Gerd with eleven golden apples of youth which she rejected, together with other offerings, such as a golden ring which every ninth night produces a further eight rings, and a magic sword that fights by itself. Gerd finally assented and promised to give herself to Freyr. This rich story provided material for *Rheingold* (the golden apples and the ring), *Walküre* (the wall of flames) and *Siegfried* (the sword).

Fricka

Frigg, as both Eddas call her, was the guardian of wedlock. Whereas her husband Wotan would admit fallen heroes to Walhall, Frigg welcomed virtuous and devoted couples, after their death, to her hall. In *Walküre* (Act II, scene I) Fricka defines her role:

I have heard Hunding's call,
demanding cruel amends,
and wedlock's guardian answered him.

In Norse mythology Frigg is by no means an immaculate deity. Like Wotan and all other gods, she has her weaknesses. She is fond of anointing her body, she indulges in frequent baths, she carefully grooms her golden tresses, she adorns her white robe with golden brooches and wears precious ear-rings, all of which pleases her husband mightily. Wagner illustrated Fricka's penchant for gold, when she arrives (in the above scene) in her ram-drawn chariot, brandishing a golden whip. He also made her charmingly human when, in *Rheingold*, Scene 2, Loge assures her:

No husband would forsake his own wife,
were she to choose some dazzling charm,
which dwarfs below are forging.

Fricka swallows the bait, soliciting her husband: 'Perchance my dear husband / would harvest the gold?'

In both Homer and the Poetic Edda the chief god and his spouse supported rival parties. In the Eddic 'Grimnismál', Odin (Wotan) sides with Geirrod, a wicked king, while Frigg champions Agnar, Geirrod's brother. In the *Iliad*, Zeus and Hera quarrel over the proposed sacking of Troy, one deity helping the Trojans, the other the Greeks. Wagner acknowledged this intriguing feature which attributed human qualities to the gods, when Fricka challenges Wotan who intends to aid Siegmund, the Wälsung, in his forthcoming fight with Hunding: 'The Wälsung falls to my honour! / Will Wotan now pledge me his oath?' (*Walküre*, Act II, scene I). Notwithstanding their essential differences, Fricka is always anxious about her husband's well-being. In the 'Lay of Vafthrudnir' (from the Poetic Edda), Odin sets out on a precarious expedition, and Frigg is unwilling to let him go. But then she bids him: 'Go forth unharmed, unharmed return / to those who are waiting for you.' In *Rheingold* (Scene 3) Wotan resolves to face Alberich in Nibelheim and wrest the gold from him. Fricka solicits: 'O soon return to your worried wife!'

Wagner's sources present Fricka as the embodiment of motherly and wifely care, and the composer continued that theme. As Minna's husband, however, he was unable to resist the occasional innuendo which served the dual purpose of adding another dimension to Fricka's nature and of displaying Wagner's brand of rhyming slang. When Fricka confronts Wotan (*Walküre*, Act II, scene I), he sighs: 'The daily storm, the daily strife!'

Frigg spinning the clouds; illustration by J. C. Dollman

Die Walküre and the *Volsunga Saga*

Many details from the saga are used in *Die Walküre*, although sometimes particular details are transferred to different characters in the drama. This table points out some of the differences and similarities:

Volsunga Saga	*Die Walküre*
King Volsung is descended from the chief god, Odin.	Siegmund is descended from the chief god, Wotan.
Volsung has eleven children, including Sigmund and Signy.	Wotan has eleven children, including Siegmund and Sieglinde.
Volsung's dwelling is built around a tree whose branches cover the roof.	Hunding's dwelling is built around a tree whose branches cover the roof.
Signy marries King Siggeir against her will.	Sieglinde marries Hunding against her will.
At the wedding feast an old, one-eyed stranger enters the hall and plunges a sword into the tree trunk, bequeathing it to him who could extract it. Many tried and failed, but Sigmund succeeds.	At the wedding feast an old, one-eyed stranger enters the hall and plunges a sword into the tree trunk, bequeathing it to him who could extract it. Many tried and failed, but Siegmund succeeds.
Sigmund refuses Siggeir's offer of three times its weight in gold for the sword.	This detail is not used in *Die Walküre.*
Siggeir kills Volsung and all his sons, except Sigmund.	Hunding kills Siegmund.
Sigmund lives alone in the forest.	Siegmund lives alone in the forest.
Signy leaves Siggeir for her brother Sigmund.	Sieglinde leaves Hunding for her brother Siegmund.
Signy bears her brother's son, Sinfjotli.	Sieglinde bears her brother's son, Siegfried.
Sigmund and his son Sinfjotli live many years as outcasts in the forest.	Wälse (Wotan) and his son Siegmund live many years as outcasts in the forest.

The Twin Lovers

It is difficult to come to terms with the fact that the lovers Siegmund and Sieglinde are also brother and sister. It should be remembered that Wagner's drama is located in mythological times and that, as children of Wotan and a mortal woman, the two are demigods. Modern convention and modern morality does not necessarily apply to the age when the gods walked on earth.

Osiris, the judge of the dead in Egyptian mythology, married his sister Isis. The later Pharaohs, rulers of Egypt, married their sisters, in order to procreate sons of noblest stock. Niörd, the Scandinavian spirit of water and air, married his sister Nerthus. Kronos, father of Zeus, had his sister Rhea for wife. Zeus himself married his own sister, Hera. In the *Volsunga Saga*, Signy changes shapes with a witch and visits her brother Sigmund for three nights, unrecognized by him, so that she can bear him a son. In Wagner's drama, Sieglinde yields unquestioningly to her brother's life-giving embrace, Wagner substituting love for trickery. This ethical evolution was not easily achieved. In his *Nibelungensage (Mythus)* of 1848, Wagner wrote:

> A childless couple of the race of the Wälsungs was impregnated by Wotan, by means of one of Holda's apples. A pair of twins, Siegmund and Sieglinde, is born. Siegmund takes a wife, and Sieglinde weds Hunding. Both marriages remain childless. In order to beget a true Wälsung, brother and sister cohabit.

Holda (Idun) the kind protectoress, who guarded the golden apples of youth

Wagner's prose sketch of 1852 is more explicit. The first act ends: 'Siegmund (beside himself) ... Sister and wife – as the twins had clung to each other in their mother's womb, so the blissful couple are now conjoined. Let the blood of the Wälsungs blaze on!' Siegmund, outcast and outsider, defies convention in the name of all-conquering love.

Opera-goers are not alone in being provoked into a sympathetic or hostile response to the situation of the twin-lovers. Critics, too, have sometimes wished for the first act curtain to fall a little earlier. The theatrical journal *The Era* reported on a performance of *Walküre* in 1882:

> The story is so revolting, indecent and impure that it ought never to have been tolerated on the English stage ... A composer must have lost all sense of decency and all respect for the dignity of human nature who could thus employ his genius and skill.

Brünnhilde's Awakening

Ancient Greek, Scandinavian and Teutonic sources influenced Brünnhilde's awakening in the final scene of *Siegfried*. Both Prometheus and Brünnhilde were punished by being confined to a mountain side. Both are rescued by a hero, Hercules and Siegfried respectively, heroes of divine descent who are also the sons of mortal mothers, Alkmene and Sieglinde. In Aeschylus' *Prometheus Bound* the captive calls to the elements:

> Brightness of day,
> swift-sailing winds,
> earth mother of life
> and you, bright sun!

In *Siegfried* (Act III, scene 3) Brünnhilde awakes:

> Hail, my sunlight!
> Hail, my sky!
> Hail, my radiant day!

There are other parallels between the drama and the opera. Fire is present in both – Prometheus bestowed it on the human race for comfort and protection, and in the opera it guards the slumbering maid. A like fate is shared by Hercules and Siegfried. The Greek hero's death was caused by his wife, who went on to take her own life. Siegfried's death was caused by his wife, who likewise took her own life.

The Poetic Edda provided Wagner with a proliferation of details for his scene. 'The Lay of Sigrdrífa' tells of Sigurd riding towards a blazing fire which died down at his approach. Wagner's Siegfried says, 'Through a violent fire I ventured to you.' The Edda reports that after penetrating a circle of shields, Sigurd found a man in armour, asleep on the ground. He removed the helmet, saw it was a woman, cut open her armour and awakened her. Wagner adopted this sequence, but let Siegfried waken Brünnhilde with a kiss. In the Edda poem, the maid's first words are:

Who slit my breast-plate, who broke my sleep?
Who freed me from my sheltering mail?

Likewise, Brünnhilde says:

And there is my breast-plate's shimmering steel;
a keen-edged sword sundered its chain.

But then Wagner opens a psychological dimension. Brünnhilde realizes her vulnerability and becomes fearful:

I am without sheltering shield,
without help, a hapless maid.

We have already compared Brünnhilde's 'Hail, my sunlight! Hail, my sky! Hail, my radiant day!' with the corresponding passage in *Prometheus Bound.* In the Edda the maid exclaims, 'Hail, my day! Hail, sons of day! Hail, my night! Hail, child of night!' The latter invocation, cryptic though it may be, is ominous. She names herself 'Sigrdrífa' (bestower of victories) and relates the cause of her long slumber. She had once disobeyed Odin by aiding a warrior whom Odin had marked out for death. The god then pricked her with a sleep-thorn and decreed that she was to surrender to the man who would wake her. She then vowed she would only marry a fearless hero. Wagner adopted the account, detail by detail.

The second half of the Edda poem mentions the runes of wisdom which Sigrdrífa teaches Sigurd. They pledge their love, Sigurd vowing:

I shall abide by your loving advice,
and swear you shall be my wife,
and you shall ever live in my heart.

This whole encounter is missing in the *Nibelungenlied,* although it is implied. The poet either did not know, or he did not want to know. Perhaps he felt that Siegfried's later renunciation of Brunhild was incompatible with a hero's conduct. Wagner, of course, solved that problem by having his hero drink a potion of forgetfulness.

The *Volsunga Saga*'s account of Brynhild's awakening mirrors that of the Poetic Edda, and offered Wagner nothing new. The *Thidrek Saga*, however, contained new details. Mimir presents a helmet, full armour, shield and sword to Sigfrid, before sending him to Brynhild. He also advises Sigfrid to ask Brynhild for a horse. Sigfrid accepts gifts and advice, and then tests the quality of the sword by decapitating its donor. Arriving at Brynhild's castle, he bursts through the iron gate and kills seven watchmen. Wagner, too, introduced an obstacle which Siegfried had to overcome on his way to Brünnhilde, namely Wotan. Where the saga tends to be crude, Wagner is perspicacious in fusing Siegfried's fight with an unidentified mountain guard and that guard's (Wotan's) defeat and abdication. In the saga, Brynhild welcomes the intruder and tells him his par-

The awakening of Brünnhilde; illustration from the *Sporting and Dramatic News*, 1880

ents' names, Sigmund and Sisibe. Sigfrid then asks her for a horse, Grani, which she willingly presents to him. Grani, however, refuses to be caught by the twelve men she had sent out. But when the horse sees Sigfrid it trots towards him and welcomes its new master, whereupon Sigfrid thanks Brynhild and rides away. Grani's empathy with Sigfrid found its way not into the 'awakening' scene, but into the Prologue of *Götterdämmerung*, where Brünnhilde assures Siegfried:

The course you command,
be it through fire,
fearlessly Grane will follow.
Take care of him. He cares for you.

Wagner did not use any of the the *Thidrek Saga*'s bloodier details, but found several gentler ones in the fairy-tale *The Sleeping Beauty*. Here too, horse and fire have a role to play, albeit a passive one, for both share the princess's slumber. Most important, however, is the kiss which awakens the princess. This appealed to Wagner, who wished to distance himself from some of his older sources' lack of refinement. The sight of Brünnhilde that prompted Siegfried's kiss gave Wagner the opportunity to combine an aesthetically appealing manner of awakening Brünnhilde with the precise moment of Siegfried's first experience of fear. Furthermore, the kiss as an experience central to the drama found its way into Wagner's final work, *Parsifal* (as did the fairy-tale's thorny hedge, which turned into beautiful flowers to welcome the prince). Substituting the matter-of-factness of his Northern sources with the delicacy of his own treatment, Wagner achieved in this scene a passage of outstanding poetic and emotional appeal:

How waken the maid,
to see her eyes look at my eyes?
Will not their blaze strike me blind?
Dare I the deed?
O craven, my heart!
O coward, my hand!
Timorous fellow,
is this what fear is?
O mother, mother!
A woman folded in sleep
has taught me the meaning of fear.
How conquer my fear?
How calm my heart?
Awaken, awaken,
maiden divine!
She hears me not.
New life I must drink

from those lips, those adored ones,
what though I die in a kiss.

Mime and the Wanderer

Contests of knowledge are as old as man. There were the riddles of the Sphinx to Oedipus, and, in the *Ring*, the contest of knowledge between Wotan and Mime. The Poetic Edda contains several such contests, and it is Odin who usually emerges magnanimously victorious, sparing the loser's life, as Wotan is to spare Mime's. Early man seems to have assumed that familiarity with events of the past conferred foresight of those of the future. Therefore, when Odin asks his questions, he first delves into events of the past, but eventually probes his opponent's knowledge of events to come, such as the fate of the gods. Such questions then assume cosmic significance.

The Eddic 'Lay of Vafthrudnir' presents the contest between Odin, disguised as Gagnrad (on-the-move), and the giant Vafthrudnir. There are many similarities between this encounter and the contest of Wotan (disguised as the Wanderer) and Mime in *Siegfried* (Act I, scene 2):

ODIN
I have travelled far,
I have learned much.

THE WANDERER
Far, far have I fared;
on the earth's vast surface
much have I moved.

Both 'wanderers' get a defiant reception, and both ask for shelter:

VAFTHRUDNIR
Who dares to taunt me?
You shall not leave here alive,
unless your knowledge is greater than mine.

MIME
Who is it that tracks me in my retreat?
I have wit to spare, I want no more;
so, wise man, there lies your way!

GAGNRAD
I am in need of food and drink;
I have travelled far, so grant me welcome.

THE WANDERER
A way-weary guest seeks to rest,
so grant him repose.

In the Edda, the giant asks four questions, but the god asks seventeen. They fall into three categories – name, origin and degree. Alternatively, what is it called, where does it come from, and what is its status? (One might recall Lohengrin's injunction: 'Dare never to enquire, / nor ever to aspire / to ask me whence I came, / nor for my birth and name.')

As the present contests proceed, both visitors are identified:

VAFTHRUDNIR
I staked my wit against Odin's;
Odin, the wisest of all.

MIME
Wotan's eye quite blinds me;
my cave is exposed to its blaze.

Both giant and smith are allowed to keep their heads; indeed, it is questionable whether we were meant to take the threatened outcome literally. Early man believed in the interrelation of knowledge and power. He whose knowledge was exposed as deficient also lost his power – sufficient punishment and longer lasting than instant decapitation.

Wotan Calling Erda

In the poem 'Baldur's Dreams' from the Poetic Edda, Odin visits the underworld and wakens a dead prophetess whom he compels to foretell the fate of the gods. A comparison between several lines of the poem and Wagner's Wanderer–Erda scene reveals the composer's indebtedness to this source:

'Baldur's Dreams'	*Siegfried*
He chanted runes, runes of power.	The songs I utter, are lordly rousers.
Who breaks into Hel, who calls me up, who adds to my grief?	Who haunts my sleep, my clear-sighted sleep? Who dares to break my dream?
Wayfarer am I, Valtam's son, speak of Hel, speak of the day.	The wide world ranging, wandering far, searching for knowledge.
You forced me to speak, now let me go.	Let me vanish below; sleep again seal my wisdom.

Wayfarer you are not.	You are not what you assume.
Not seeress are you, nor woman all-wise.	Wisdom of ages lasts no longer.

Siegfried's Overpowering of Brünnhilde

Wagner's sources yielded conflicting material for this crucial scene. In the *Nibelungenlied* Brunhild is shown to possess superhuman strength which she does not hesitate to use, whatever the outcome. She puts her wooers to death; she can throw mighty rocks and the javelin to deadly effect; she humiliates King Gunther by suspending him from a nail in their wedding chamber. Wagner preserved the martial aspect of his heroine, but he emphasized her mental rather than her physical bellicosity, as she defies Wotan and, at the end of the second act of *Götterdämmerung*, as she turns into an avenging fury. On the crucial question of the previous relationship between Siegfried and Brunhild, the *Nibelungenlied* is vague. Siegfried seems to know the way to Brunhild's castle. On his arrival, the virgin warrior greets him before King Gunther. Later, seeing that Siegfried is married to Kriemhild (Wagner's Gutrune), she weeps. When questioned, she explains that Siegfried's manifest status as a liegeman – he had been helping the king into the saddle – was degrading for Kriemhild, her sister-in-law. On the other hand, she seems to be jealous of Kriemhild, perhaps as a cover for the love she feels for Siegfried:

> Again and again Brunhild shot sidelong glances at Kriemhild who was indeed very beautiful to look at.
>
> ———
>
> She was still so fond of him, that her only wish was to see him alive.

Wagner felt what many readers of the *Nibelungenlied* would have felt: that Brunhild's distress over Siegfried's inferior status masked her true feelings. He therefore motivated her anguish through her discovery of the ring on Siegfried's finger. Two final, remarkable points must be mentioned. Brunhild bears Gunther a son, and they name him Siegfried (!); after Hagen has killed Kriemhild's husband, Brunhild completely fades from the narrative. Clearly, Wagner had to look elsewhere for more substantial information.

In 'The Short Lay of Sigurd' in the Poetic Edda, Wagner found that Brynhild was conquered by Sigurd (Wagner's Siegfried) who handed her over, untouched, to Gunnar (Wagner's Gunther). But Brynhild had fallen in love with her conqueror, for she vowed:

I shall hold him, Sigurd,
the young hero, in my arms,
though it be his end.

This extreme passion for the man who vanquished and relinquished her is exemplified in her statement (as Brünnhilde, in *Götterdämmerung*, Act II, scene 5):

Confined in bondage, I am his booty:
the pitiful, lowly prize
Siegfried has given away.

And when Hagen offers himself as her instrument of vengeance, she mocks:

One single flash from the eyes of the traitor,
which Tarnhelm's disguise could not hide,
and your manliness turns into terror.

Another poem from the Poetic Edda, 'The Prophecy of Gripir', contains a key to the Siegfried–Brünnhilde drama. Sigurd visits Gripir, his mother's brother, who can foresee the future. He learns that he is to avenge his father's death by killing Hunding's sons. He will kill the dragon and obtain its treasure. He will waken Brynhild and she will teach him runes of wisdom and healing. He will love her and leave her. He will promise Gunnar to help him win Brynhild, and he will marry Gunnar's sister, Gudrun. Sigurd listens attentively and prompts Gripir to tell more, by recalling each stage of the prophecy as though he were a commentator as well as a participant.

Gripir said:
'Queen Grimhild will offer you
her own fair daughter.'
Sigurd said:
'Little foresight has Sigurd, I fear,
conquering for another man
the maid so much beloved.'

Commenting on his own folly, Sigurd abandons, at least temporarily, his own identity – a grievous loss, but a precondition for turning traitor. Gripir then foretells Sigurd's oath of fidelity with Gunnar, and his conquest of Brynhild by stealth. This shocks the young hero:

Siegfried, Brünnhilde and Grane, accompanied by Brünnhilde's leitmotif

Sigurd said:
'How can this be?'
Gripir said:
'You will stand in Gunnar's bearing and form,
but you will keep your own voice and your spirit.'

Wagner probably found it too discreditable for his Siegfried to betray his beloved while in full control of his own senses. He therefore made Siegfried propose to Gunther, in *Siegfrieds Tod* (the first draft of *Götterdämmerung*), 'As we exchange our physical shapes, let us also exchange our hearts.' This deviation from the Eddic poem found its way into Wagner's stage direction in *Götterdämmerung* (Act I, scene 3): 'After a violent struggle he draws the ring from her finger. She shrieks, sinks into his arms, and her eyes meet his.' At that very moment, clarinets sound the Liebesglück motif, the same motif that had accompanied Siegfried's earlier wooing of Brünnhilde in *Siegfried* (Act III, scene 3), when Brünnhilde gently checked his stormy advance:

O Siegfried, leave and forbear!
Do not come close with your feverish frenzy.
Master me not with your resolute might.
Destroy not your own heart's delight.

It is bitterly ironic that both situations, the treacherous and the amorous, share identical music and physical closeness. One precedes the couple's joyful union and brief bliss, the other supplants it. Where the mythological source is almost brutal in its revelation of Sigurd's corruptibility, Wagner shifts the emphasis by partly exonerating his Siegfried, thus turning him, and therefore Brünnhilde as well, into truly tragic characters.

The *Thidrek Saga* was not much used by Wagner for this scene, although its account is noteworthy. We learn that after the slaying of the dragon, the birds warned Sigfrid to beware of Mimir, the dragon's brother. Mimir, however, treated Sigfrid kindly, presented him with a sword and a suit of armour and advised him to go to Brynhild's castle. To gain access to her, Sigfrid killed seven knights and seven watchmen. Brynhild received him graciously and presented him with the horse Grani. The story then preserves silence about any amorous consequences. When, much later, Sigfrid visited Brynhild for a second time, he came as Gunther's brother-in-arms. This time Brynhild did not welcome Sigfrid, since he had taken Grimhild (Wagner's Gutrune) to wife. She accused him of having broken his vows to her. This comes as a surprise to the reader, but not to Sigfrid who explained that a marriage to Brynhild would have been disadvantageous to him, since Brynhild had no brother, whereas Grimhild's brother was a mighty king. Brynhild agreed to wed Gunther, but refused to consummate the marriage. So, dressed in Gunther's clothes, Sigfrid overcame her and took her virginity. Later, when Hagen killed Sigfrid, Brynhild ordered the body to be thrown into Grimhild's bed. None of those stark, merciless events showed Sigfrid in a becoming light. The only detail which Wagner accepted from the *Thidrek Saga* was a figure of speech. In the saga Hagen informed the widow that a wild boar had killed her husband. In *Götterdämmerung* (Act III, scene 3) Gunther urges his sister:

> Call down no curse on me!
> Call down your curse on Hagen!
> He is the accursed boar
> who has savaged Siegfried to death.

It was from the *Volsunga Saga* that Wagner obtained further valuable material for the *Ring*. From the Poetic Edda he had learned that Brynhild had taught Sigurd runes of wisdom and of healing. The *Volsunga Saga* is more specific:

> Brynhild said: Do not trifle with a maiden's love, nor with another man's wife. When you see beautiful women, do not let them beguile you, lest you lose your sleep over them. Neither entice them with kisses or other tokens of love. Do not

argue with a drunkard; it may result in great trouble and even in loss of life. Never swear a false oath; bitter vengeance follows the breaking of plighted troth. Be meticulous with the corpses of men drowned, diseased or slain, and prepare their bodies with care. Above all, beware of treacherous friends.

Wagner adopted Brynhild's runes, though in an 'inverted' fashion. No, Siegfried did not heed her words. He did trifle with a maiden's love. He did let a beautiful woman beguile him. He did swear a false oath and he failed to beware of false friends.

Of even greater importance to Wagner was a later chapter in the *Volsunga Saga* where, after Brynhild's and Sigurd's marriage to their respective spouses, Brynhild calls Sigurd 'the foremost and dearest of all men'. Sigurd replies that he had loved her better than his own life, but that he had been enticed away from her. When Brynhild reminds him that she had sworn to marry only the man who had crossed her circle of flames, and that she would keep that oath or die, Sigurd answered, 'You shall not die. I will put away Gudrun and marry you.' But Brynhild said, 'I will not have you, nor any other man.' At that, the author says, 'Sigurd's heart swelled so that the rings of his armour burst.' Essence and tenor of this rueful but fervent colloquy permeate Brünnhilde's address at the end of *Götterdämmerung*:

GUTRUNE
Brünnhilde, black with envy
you brought this harm to our house.
You goaded all these men against him.
Woe came in when you came in.

BRÜNNHILDE
Be still, poor wretch!
You never were his true wife.
His paramour, never his spouse.
His wife, his sworn wife am I.

———

I, Brünnhild, betrayed by my lover,
yet understanding it all:
what must be, let it be.
All things, all I know now,
all is clear to my eyes.

———

Heiajoho, Grane! Ride we to greet him!
Siegfried, Siegfried, see! Brünnhild brings you her life.

The final bars of the *Ring* score with the composer's postscript: 'Completed in Wahnfried on 21 November 1874. I say no more!!'

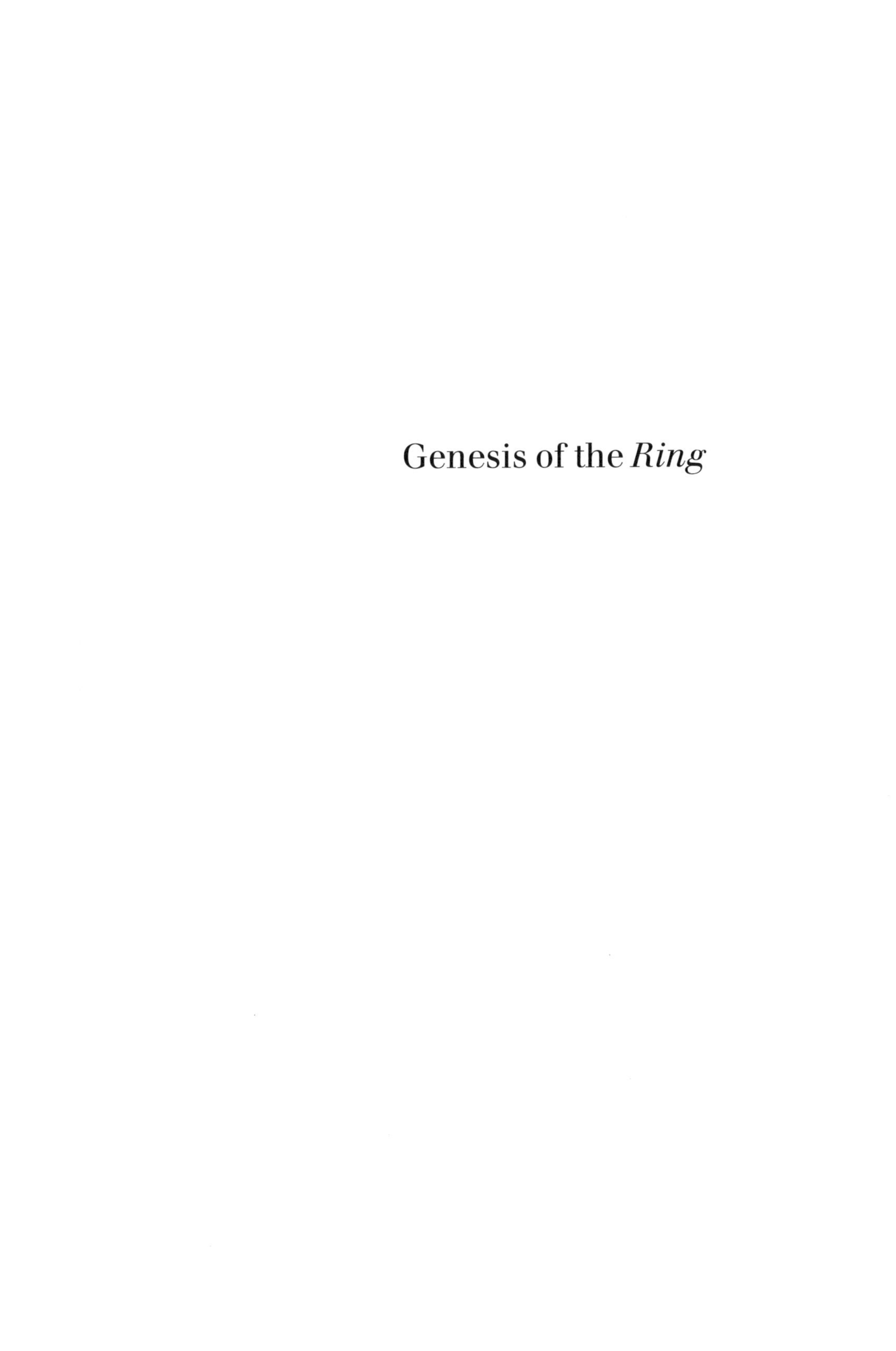

Genesis of the *Ring*

Genesis of the *Ring*

Wagner began the *Ring* in 1848, and completed it twenty-six years later with the last note of *Götterdämmerung*. He wrote in the margin of his manuscript, 'Vollendet in Wahnfried am 21. November 1874. Ich sage nichts weiter!! RW.' (Completed on 21 November 1874 in Wahnfried. I say no more!!).

After a quarter of a century of saying, Wagner now says no more, and draws our attention to the fact by appending two exclamation marks. Why? Brünnhilde's last words, which had vexed Wagner for so long, are the end of the end:

Sacred fever lays hold of my heart –
him to embrace, and embraced but by him –
our love is eternal – our love, it is now!
Heiajoho! Grane, ride we to greet him!
Siegfried! Siegfried, see!
Brünnhild brings you her life!

From 1848 onwards Wagner had penned numerous versions of the final page, only to reject them all. He concluded that there was to be no conclusion. In order to understand the meaning of the end of *Götterdämmerung*, it is necessary to accompany Wagner on his 26-year odyssey towards the final section of the *Ring*.

Political Parallels

The late 1840s were a turbulent time in Europe, in Germany and in Wagner's Dresden. In his *Autobiographische Skizze* (Autobiographical Sketch, 1842/3) we read: 'At once I became a revolutionary and I was convinced that no reasonably alert person could help occupying himself exclusively with politics.' Apart from being the supreme artist, Wagner was a political person with a nagging social conscience. He knew of Pierre-Joseph Proudhon's *Qu'est-ce que la propriéte?* (What is Property?); Proudhon's answer, 'property is theft', moulded Wagner's political thinking at the time. Even more familiar to him were the fiercely anti-Christian writings of Ludwig Feuerbach, who wrote: 'Once religion and gods cease to exist, man will be emancipated.'

Love was Feuerbach's motto, as it was Wagner's in his early sketches for the *Ring*. 'Love,' wrote Feuerbach, 'can create and annihilate, can give life and take life. All the dealings of man are determined by love.' The philosopher's *Das Wesen des Christentums* (Essence of Christianity), with its message of a new religion of humanity, affected Wagner's thinking for a long time.

Another revolutionary thinker who influenced Wagner was Mikhail Bakunin, a leading protagonist of the Dresden uprising of 1849. Wagner was for a while his friend and collaborator. Bakunin's teachings of anarchism and his hopes for a totally destructive revolution are mirrored in a letter from that time that Wagner wrote to Theodor Uhlig, his violinist friend in Dresden. 'Paris,' wrote Wagner, 'is a great city, and as such it must be burned to the ground. Other great cities shall follow, and then we should at last be able to breathe fresh air again.'

Wagner's journey towards the *Ring* was marked by indecision and procrastination, and noteworthy for what appear to be many false starts. In fact, all these were essential in a process of mind-clearing and of trying to find the forms in which his thoughts could find their definitive expression. An early marker on this journey was Wagner's revolutionary article for the *Dresdener Anzeiger* of 16 June 1848. Wagner, then Royal Court Conductor, signed his article 'A member of the Fatherland Association'. He also read it to a large gathering of that society. The article demanded, amongst other things, every citizen's right to the vote, the establishment of a single legislative chamber in Saxony instead of a two-tier system, the abolition of privileges for the aristocracy, a standing army and free trade throughout the kingdom of Saxony. In return, Wagner promised the unhindered survival of the monarchy. He envisaged the king as leader and guarantor of all republican ambitions. Wagner, the Royal Court Conductor, submitted these aims to an enthusiastically receptive audience that was eagerly awaiting a performance the next day of *Rienzi*, with its significant finale, the burning of Rome. The authorities responded by cancelling the performance. And what had Wagner expected? In his article he had asked the aristocracy to 'give up, unconditionally, your positions at a court which keeps you all in pampered insolence'. He also harangued the financial world and demanded that their representatives must no longer 'be slaves of that inert, unproductive fruit of nature, that pale metal called gold'.

Risking his own position, Wagner displayed his typical crusading spirit which was an amalgam of altruism, naivety and bravado. In his notebook (the *Rote Brieftasche*), he wrote: 'Republican essay in *Anzeiger* – dreadful effect – *Rienzi* cancelled – alarm at Court.' On the day that *Rienzi* should have been performed, 18 June 1848, Wagner drew on his well-practised custom – to snatch victory from the jaws of bafflement, writing a letter to his director, Freiherr von Lüttichau:

> I humbly beg Your Excellency to grant me a fortnight's leave of absence ... I do not wish to be misunderstood, least of all by Your Excellency ... Nowadays even the most uneducated are entitled to express their opinions. As for an educated person, it is his duty to exercise that right ... Although the future belongs to the Progressives, that party needs men whose intelligence and peaceful disposition prevents crude excesses. I have only rarely attended their meetings, and then only as an observer ... The monarchy itself has never stood in the way of republican aspirations. In fact, our aims could be realized in accord with the monarchy ... I am deeply shocked to find that I have been grievously misunderstood ... If I should have offended any person, I sincerely crave his forgiveness.

The king, Friedrich August II of Saxony, was apparently pacified, but Lüttichau never trusted his Kapellmeister again. Politically cornered, Wagner decided to withdraw, temporarily, from debating and from meddling in internal affairs, and to search for different ways of publicizing his republican aspirations: he decided to *compose* his revolution. Instead of writing tracts about the regeneration of mankind, he wrote and composed a cycle of music dramas on just that theme, convinced that the operatic stage was the right, and indeed the only worthy place for securing his audience's attention and for firing their imagination.

In the revolutionary outbreaks in the European capitals, although the loudest cry was for liberal freedoms (as expressed by Wagner's article), the voice of a more radical socialism was also beginning to be heard. This development found expression in Wagner's first prose draft for the *Ring*, *Die Nibelungensage* (*Mythus*) of October 1848. Here the gods do not perish; there is no final conflagration; love is not cursed; the Nibelungs are set free from slavery; and even Alberich is redeemed. In *Mein Leben* Wagner recalled that he had been pondering, on his solitary walks, how to bring about a new kind of society, how to build on and improve socialist and communist ideas, and how to realize his own dreams of regeneration through artistic means. His *Ring* offered such a regeneration and the *Nibelungensage* contained striking parallels between political and mythological themes:

a. The working classes likened to the Nibelungs:
The race of the Nibelungs dwells in Nibelheim, land of mists. Nimbly and tirelessly they dig into the bowels of the earth, like worms in a dead body; they smelt and forge hard metals.

b. The capitalist proprietor likened to Alberich:
Alberich seizes the pure and noble Rhinegold from the depth of the river, and cunningly he forges from it a ring that makes him master of the whole Nibelung tribe.

c. Upper classes likened to the giants:
The giants are alarmed by the progress of the Nibelungs in producing awesome weapons. Used to brutish inactivity and ease, they fear that their naivety might no longer protect them from Alberich and his crafty plans for conquest.

d. Pragmatism as practised by Wotan:
The gods take advantage of this conflict. Wotan hires the giants to build a fortress for the gods, from where he can rule the world in peace and order. The giants demand the Nibelung hoard as payment, and the gods, using skill and cunning, succeed in outwitting Alberich.

e. Idle wealth exemplified by Fafner:
The giants' hoard and ring are guarded by a monstrous dragon. The ring serves to keep Alberich and all his Nibelungs under control. But since the giants do not know how to use their power, the dragon lies inert on the hoard in brutish sloth.

f. The new society visualized in Wotan's grand thought:
A free agent, independent of the gods, is needed to atone for the gods' guilt. In man the gods perceive an innate ability for this purpose. So they bring him up to fulfil his destiny, to atone for their trespasses.

g. Demolition of existing power structure as pursued by Siegfried:
Siegfried sets out to avenge his father's murder. He falls upon Hunding and kills him. Only then does he follow Mime's advice to slay the dragon ... and Mime also. He then takes the ring and the Tarnhelm from the hoard.

h. Wotan as Republican King:
One only shall rule, glorious Father, you! I escort this man to your presence, a pledge of your eternal might. Receive him with the grace which is his due.

Over the next year Wagner wrote further 'revolutionary' or 'political' works: he toyed with a plan for a drama on Friedrich I (Barbarossa) in which we find such themes as the nature of wealth, the place of the church in our society and the desirability of a benevolent monarchy. Wagner also worked on a spoken drama, *Jesus von Nazareth* (1849), in which a secularized Jesus appears as a revolutionary leader. Some of the drama's themes – that property law is responsible for crimes against property, and that stealing from a needy neighbour is a greater sin than taking from the rich – are of greater relevance to the problems of the time than to the planned *Ring*. But there are also signposts towards the *Ring* and further ahead: the idea that loveless marriage is the root of much evil (Wotan and Fricka, Hunding and Sieglinde, Siegfried and Gutrune); and that universal love abolishes all sin, a theme central to *Parsifal*. A further apparent diversion was Wagner's sketch for a drama about Achilles. He wishes to be greater than the gods; Achilles' mother, Thetis, proclaims that the gods will reach their perfection in man; Achilles, thus, is a precursor of Siegfried.

Also in 1849 Wagner wrote the essay *Die Wibelungen*. He clearly felt in need of more extensive study of the historical and mythological background to his *Siegfried* project, and he constructed a plot which was to influence not only *Siegfried* and the whole Nibelung sphere, but also his final work, *Parsifal*. Wagner established a Wibelung–Nibelung connection with a prodigious sleight of hand. The Wibelungs, he tells us, were really the Ghibellines, who supported the Hohenstaufen emperors in their incessant conflicts with the Welfs, supporters of the Pope. The Wibelungs' forefathers were the Nibelungs. The changed initial letter was due to their liking for alliteration, as in their slogan 'Wibelungen und Welfen'. Another Wagnerian revelation was the supposed descent of Friedrich Barbarossa from the Trojans. Wagner also established links between Jesus and Siegfried, and between the Nibelung hoard and the Holy Grail. Siegfried's slaying of the dragon is interpreted as the sun ousting darkness. The essay ends:

> The great emperor himself had lodged the Nibelung hoard inside a mountain, like the one from which Siegfried had originally obtained it. There he now sits in Mount Kyffhäuser, old Redbeard Friedrich, surrounded by the hoard of the Nibelungs, and by his side the sharp sword that once had slain the fearsome dragon.

Again, Wagner was not satisfied with his endings. He revised this one, and it now reads:

> Two ravens fly around my mountain. They grow fat from the spoils of my empire. One of the ravens pecks from south east [Wagner means Austria], the other from the north east [Russia]. Chase away the ravens, and the hoard will be yours!

Astonishingly, Wagner also found time in 1849 to publish an article *Die Revolution* (The Goddess Revolution speaks):

I shall destroy this existing order, which separates one mankind into hostile nations, into the strong and the weak, into rich and poor. The millions, the children of the revolution, shall proclaim to the world the new gospel of happiness.

It is tempting to deplore Wagner's apparent procrastination. In reality, his revolutionary writings, his *Friedrich I*, his *Wibelungen*, all turned out to be essential studies for a worthier object. His vision of the coming revolution, with its cleansing conflagration heralding a new age, was shortly to be realized in the ending of *Siegfrieds Tod*.

Alternative Endings

The *Nibelungensage* of 1848 saw in Siegfried the prototype for a new society, where actions are not determined by custom, law or force, but by self-determination and universal love. Instead of the final conflagration in *Götterdämmerung*, Wagner designed this dramatically and ethically agreeable ending:

> Hear then, you mighty gods. Your guilt is abolished; the hero has taken it upon himself. The Nibelungs' slavery is ended, and Alberich shall be free again. This ring I give to you, wise sisters of the watery deep. Melt it down and keep it free from harm.

For the final scene, Wagner designed an apotheosis which recalls the ending of *Der fliegende Holländer*:

> The flames meet across Brünnhilde and Siegfried. Suddenly a dazzling light is seen. Above the margin of a leaden cloud the light streams up, showing Brünnhilde, armed as a Valkyrie on horseback, leading Siegfried by the hand.

Wagner completed *Siegfrieds Tod*, the prose draft of what later became *Götterdämmerung*, only a fortnight after the *Nibelungensage (Mythus)*, on 20 October 1848. The ending of *Siegfrieds Tod*, modelled on that of the *Mythus*, describes Brünnhilde's actions in the final scene: she thanks Hagen, for he had not murdered Siegfried, but rather 'had marked him out for Wotan'. She then asks for a funeral pyre to be erected for Siegfried and herself. Having put the ring on her finger, she proclaims the freedom of the Nibelungs and of Alberich, and restores the ring to the 'wise sisters of the water', predicting that the flames which are about to consume her shall cleanse the ring of the curse.

She bids the nymphs melt down the golden ring, and proclaims Wotan as sole ruler and guardian of the universe, inviting him to rejoice in Siegfried's imminent appearance in

Walhall: 'Receive him graciously. He shall be the guardian of your eternal power!' Wagner appended an intriguing stage direction to the final immolation: 'Solemn chanting by the vassals and their women accompany the action.'

It took Wagner five weeks to turn his prose into a verse draft. He also converted the final stage direction into the lines:

WOMEN
Where are you bearing this hero so solemnly?

MEN
Siegfried we bear to the fire.

WOMEN
Was he slain or died he at home?

MEN
He was slain, but not defeated.
Walhall waits for him.

WOMEN
Who follows him?

MEN
His wife and his horse follow through the flames.

MEN and WOMEN
Wotan, ruler of gods, bless these flames!
Burn hero, burn bride, burn faithful horse.
Let them enter Walhall in joy,
hale and purified, united for all time.

Although Wotan has, for the present, been reprieved, it is Siegfried who is the central character of the 1848 version. Wagner knew Hegel's opinion that new historical periods were set in motion by 'heroes'. In 1848 Wagner's sympathies were certainly with Siegfried, and he later confided to August Röckel that in the gods' rapport with the heroes he had created a 'Hellenistic-optimistic' ending.

On 12 August 1850 Wagner began the first musical sketches for *Siegfrieds Tod*. He realized that an excess of narrative concerning previous events would lumber the drama with much undesirable ballast. He therefore decided to precede *Siegfrieds Tod* with *Der junge Siegfried* (Young Siegfried). Similar deliberations convinced him that even *Der junge Siegfried* would carry too much reported action, and he resolved on the Nibelungen tetralogy of *Rheingold – Die Walküre – Der junge Siegfried* (later *Siegfried*) – *Siegfrieds Tod* (later *Götterdämmerung*).

In 1851 he wrote both a prose and a verse draft of *Der junge Siegfried*, and at some time before the summer of 1851 he changed his previous ending. In 1848 he had written:

One only shall rule!
Glorious Father, you!
Rejoice
in the freest of heroes:
Siegfried I escort to your presence.
Receive him graciously:
he is the guardian of your everlasting rule.

These seven lines he now crossed out, replacing them with eight rather different ones:

Blessed atonement
I announce
to the glorious,
hallowed, eternal gods.
Rejoice
in the freest of heroes!
His own bride escorts him
to receive the brotherly greetings of the gods.

For the present, the gods survive. Walhall is not yet for burning.

Soon after the previous, revised ending, Wagner revised it once more. Brünnhilde now promises the gods redemption through death, *Todeserlösung*. The term has been misunderstood by several translators. It does not mean redemption from death, but *in* death, which is the very opposite:

Depart and relinquish your power,
and your guilt shall be no more.

———

Fade away in bliss
before the deed of man,
of the hero whom you created.
I proclaim to you freedom from fear,
through blessed redemption in death.

These are by no means Wagner's last words on Brünnhilde's last words. More was to come.

In November 1851 Wagner wrote a momentous letter. He informed Liszt that it would take him at least three years to complete the whole *Ring*. In reality, he needed another twenty-three. In December 1852 Wagner revised his ending once again:

Nor goods nor gold,
nor glitter of gods,
nor house nor hall,
nor splendid display,
nor treacherous treaties,
nor broken bonds,
nor arrogant custom's
adamant law:
blissful in gladness and gloom –
love alone shall endure.

This new ending contains two themes, the sovereignty of love, and the irrelevance of authority, conventions and law. Here Wagner was anticipating *Tristan und Isolde*, which he conceived a little later, in 1854. Both themes are the central concern of that drama. We shall call the above passage the 'Tristan' ending.

By the end of 1852 Wagner had completed the verse drafts of both *Rheingold* and *Walküre*, and in February 1853 he had fifty copies of the complete *Ring* poem printed. He then assembled a company of eager listeners to whom he read the whole enterprise. Only eighteen months later, in September 1854, the full score of *Rheingold* was finished.

During the next eighteen months Wagner completed *Walküre*. On 23 August 1856 he sent a revealing letter to his friend Röckel who, though in prison, took a lively interest in the ever-changing development of the *Ring*. In that letter Wagner paid tribute to Schopenhauer, whom he credited with the inspiration for yet another ending. In place of his 'Hellenistic–optimistic' slant of 1848, he now saw 'the essence of the world and its nothingness'. The former theme, 'Love alone shall endure,' he informed Röckel, had to be sacrificed on Schopenhauer's pessimistic altar. This was the new 'Schopenhauer' ending:

I depart from Wunschheim [home of desire],
Wahnheim [home of delusion] I flee forever;
the open gates
of birth and rebirth
I close behind me.

Sorrowing love's
deepest distress
opened my eyes:
I have seen the end of the world.

At the end of his letter to Röckel, Wagner encouraged him to remain cheerful, using a key phrase which we shall examine a little later, 'suit your philosophy to your needs'. In Wagner's diary for 1856 we read: 'Buddhism ... *Die Sieger* [The Victors] conceived, after Buddhist legend ... new ending for *Götterdämmerung*, conceived on sick bed.' In May 1856 Wagner sketched a scenario for a projected opera, *Die Sieger*. Its main theme is the Buddhist teaching that you are reborn as the creature that you had harmed in your previous existence. A maiden falls in love with a young disciple of Buddha. She begs the Buddha's permission for their union. But Buddha discloses that, in a previous incarnation, she had rejected a deserving suitor, and now she must atone by undergoing the pangs of unrequited love. Wagner soon laid the project aside, but it had helped him in clearing his mind about the new *Ring* ending and, beyond that, about *Tristan* and *Parsifal*.

The same notebook that Wagner used for his sketch of *Die Sieger* also contains a hitherto largely neglected stage direction, headed 'Ending for *Siegfried*':

> Brünnhilde lights the funeral pyre and turns round to the others. For those now dead she wishes no rebirth. To Hagen she predicts a series of rebirths which are to end in redemption. She herself is to meet her own redemption, since she knows that she will not be born again. To those still living she offers a choice between her fate and Hagen's: 'If you love life, then look not at me but at him!' She approaches her horse and for a long time she speaks quietly to him. The chorus voices its growing sympathy with her. They all watch intently, as she mounts her horse and rides triumphantly into the flames.

We are no longer surprised to find Wagner once again revising the final page of *Götterdämmerung*. He now considered a 'Buddhist' ending:

> Sorrowing love's
> deepest compassion
> opened the gates for me:
> if you prize life
> above everything else,
> avert your eyes from me!
> If you gaze with pity
> at me, as I depart,
> then you may attain
> redemption, as I do.
> Thus I greet the world
> and leave it.

In September 1856 Wagner began composing *Siegfried*, but eleven months later broke it off. He was not in the mood, at the time, to involve himself in the third act of *Siegfried*, with its jubilant glorification of Siegfried and Brünnhilde's love. So he finished the second act, and then waited for almost twelve years before resuming work on the *Ring*.

Wagner's frame of mind in the late 1850s, sombre, saturnine, Schopenhauerian, eased him into seeing out his melancholy love-tangle with Mathilde Wesendonck, and into tackling *Tristan und Isolde*. He informed Mathilde that, after reading Schopenhauer's work *Die Welt als Wille und Vorstellung*, he arrived at quite new insights. Some of these even amended and partially supplanted the philosopher's teachings. Complete pacification of the will, he told Mathilde, was not attainable through resignation, as Schopenhauer maintains, but through love, and that 'not as an abstract love of the world, but the love between man and woman'.

For his protracted, rueful farewell from Mathilde, and for his work on *Tristan*, Wagner sustained himself with his own brand of 'improved' Schopenhauer. In other words, he did what he had advised the prisoner August Röckel to do: he suited his philosophy to his needs. Sooner or later Wagner had to assert his independence as a thinker, by exchanging the disciple's cap for the master's beret. Schopenhauer and Wagner agreed that life was a prison from which we long to escape. They disagreed over the means for escaping. For Schopenhauer it was death, for Wagner it was love; and neither the Schopenhauer, nor the 'Buddhist' endings to the *Ring*, were likely to survive this Wagnerian realignment.

In *Der Fall Wagner* (The Case of Wagner), Nietzsche maintained that Wagner had a fundamental change of heart, when the encounter with Schopenhauer made him rethink the meaning of the *Ring*. Nietzsche asserted that the Wagnerian vessel had been running merrily under the flag of universal love, when it hit the reef of Schopenhauer's philosophy. In fact, Nietzsche was wrong. The first edition of *Siegfrieds Tod* (1853) shows Schopenhauerian traits, a year before Wagner had heard of the philosopher. If Wagner had not been thinking thoughts similar to Schopenhauer's in 1853, he would not have been able to appreciate Schopenhauer in 1854.

In August 1857 Wagner broke off the composition of the *Ring*. He proceeded to compose *Tristan und Isolde* (August 1857 to August 1859) and *Meistersinger* (November 1861 to October 1867). In March 1869 he resumed work on the *Ring*, which he completed, at last, on 21 November 1874.

The final and perhaps most intractable problem which Wagner had to solve he deferred to the very end: which of the numerous endings was to be the definitive one? He eliminated six of his nine versions and was left with three: the 1852 'Tristan' ending, the 1853 private printing and the 1856 'Schopenhauer' ending. Wagner finally decided that the second of the three versions, the 1853 private printing, contained everything all the other versions had to offer. He composed it, but had the other two endings printed as well, and added in explanation, 'These lines would be omitted in a live performance, since their meaning would be quite clearly expressed by the music.' The opera now ended:

Sacred fever lays hold of my heart –
him to embrace,
and embraced but by him –
our love is eternal,
our love, it is now!
Heiajojo, Grane, ride we to greet him!
Siegfried, Siegfried, see:
Brünnhild brings you her life.

Wagner declined to compose the 'Schopenhauer' ending, and in so doing he paid the philosopher a great compliment. Schopenhauer, unlike Wagner, always maintained that music alone can express clearly what words may only convey dimly. Words would appeal to the intellect, music to the emotions. The listeners' intellect may persuade them that the universal destruction at the end of the *Ring* is unequivocal. Their emotions, however, perceive the positive message of the final bars, which is reinforced by the Assurance motif.

Wotan, hungry for power, and Brünnhilde, all love, both perish in the cosmic catastrophe, but the timeless power of love survives. The very title of the fourth part of the *Ring* discloses Wagner's thoughts: (Götter)dämmerung means both 'dusk' and 'dawn'. A new beginning is not ruled out.

The *Ring* and *Lohengrin*

In 1844 Wagner borrowed some books from the Royal Library in Dresden; they constituted part of his source material for the *Ring*. A year later he began *Lohengrin*, which he completed in 1848. Also in 1848 he wrote the verse draft of *Siegfrieds Tod* (later renamed *Götterdämmerung*). The next year the unsuccessful Dresden uprising drove Wagner into Switzerland. In 1852 the poem (libretto) of *Siegfrieds Tod* was completed. Wagner informed his friend Theodor Uhlig that the *Ring* would have to wait until 'after the revolution', for only then would the world understand the revolutionary content of that work.

Common Aspects

The production, in close proximity, of a complete opera (*Lohengrin*) and the poem for an opera (*Siegfrieds Tod*) resulted in the sharing of a number of dramatic themes in the two works. But the chief theme that knitted them firmly together stemmed from the composer's own life: revolution. The way in which Wagner fused music, drama and text in *Lohengrin* was indeed revolutionary, both for the composer of *Rienzi*, *Holländer* and *Tannhäuser*, and for the state of operatic practice at the time. But the political revolution that turned Wagner into a refugee determined much of the content and motivation of the *Ring*. Having failed in 1849, the revolution was to take place, a quarter of a century later, on the stage of the Bayreuth Festspielhaus. Wagner, the self-assured, self-centred, self-sufficient genius, had been a revolutionary from the outset. The task, achievement and eventual failure of the title hero in *Lohengrin* toughened Wagner's desire for a cataclysmic change of the artistic and political climate in the mid nineteenth century. Thus, one work influences another, and both influence their creator. There are a number of interesting parallels between the two works:

Lohengrin	The *Ring*
Requisites: horn, sword, ring.	Requisites: horn, sword, ring.
Magic property of ring: none.	Magic property of ring: makes its wearer, reputedly, lord of the world.
Lohengrin's sword defeats his enemy.	Siegfried's sword cleaves an anvil, destroys a dragon and kills Siegfried's enemy.
Anonymity bestows invincibility; when no longer nameless, the hero must depart.	Golden apples bestow eternal youth; when no longer available, the gods grow old.
Forbidden question: Lohengrin will not disclose his identity to Elsa.	Forbidden question: Siegmund will not disclose his identity to Hunding.
Elsa awakes from her reverie, beholds her future husband and willingly surrenders.	Brünnhilde awakes from her slumber, beholds her future husband, and recoils.

Two Second Acts

The structure of any single act in Wagner's output was of such strength and inevitability that its architectural features remained lodged in the composer's mind and could be reworked. The second acts of *Lohengrin* and *Götterdämmerung* demonstrate this to an astonishing degree. Both orchestral preludes are sombre and eerie. Both acts begin with a scene of nocturnal plotting (Ortrud and Telramund in *Lohengrin*, Alberich and Hagen in *Götterdämmerung*). Both contain a discussion about a forthcoming wedding. In both acts there is a summoning of warriors. Brides are welcomed and their reception is interrupted in *Lohengrin* as well as in *Götterdämmerung*. There is an invocation of pagan gods in both works. Ortrud brings charges of deceit in *Lohengrin*, as does Brünnhilde in *Götterdämmerung*. Two malefactors, Telramund in *Lohengrin* and Hagen in *Götterdämmerung*, plot the hero's downfall. Both acts end with a bridal procession, against a background of gloom and foreboding.

In *Lohengrin*, horn, sword, ring, the forbidden question and the heroine's awakening are prerequisites of the story-line; in *Götterdämmerung* Wagner elevates these dramatic features to prime components of the cosmic catastrophe.

The Golden Ring

An incomplete circle, a flawed ring. We shall follow this musical symbol through the tetralogy, and see why Wagner did not round the circle, and whether he meant the ring to be all-powerful or not.

In the first scene of *Rheingold* the Rhinemaidens inform Alberich that before forging a ring from the Rhinegold, he must renounce love. Alberich accepts, but does not heed Wellgunde's conditional promise: 'The world's riches a man *could* inherit ...' So he seizes the gold and pronounces his curse on love. He will soon learn how rash was his assumption of the ring's omnipotence.

In the second scene Loge reports the theft and Alberich's renunciation of love. The gold, he says, 'now *seems* more worthy to him than woman's grace.' Loge is well aware of the ring's doubtful qualities, but to whet Wotan's appetite for its conquest, he adds that once the ring has been forged from the gold it will *help* its owner to gain the whole world. Help, of course, does not mean guarantee, and Loge, like all successful soothsayers, covers his tracks. The ring's unsubstantiated properties cause different people to expect different benefits from it. For Wotan it is a symbol of rule, for Fricka it is no more than an ornament:

Do you think such golden garnish,
dainty delight,
be fit for the wife of my lord?

Wotan chooses to disregard Loge's warning that forging the ring would entail renouncing love, and believes Froh's reckless remark that stealing the ring exempts the thief from the penalty for forging it. Having aroused Wotan's desire for the ring, Loge immediately checks it by reminding him that it belongs to the Rhinemaidens and that Wotan would, of course, have to return it to them. To Fafner, the ring means possessing eternal youth, though it is unclear how he could have thought this, unless the mere thought of possessing the ring produced hallucinations. Fafner agrees to accept the ring in place of Freia, but Wotan refuses contemptuously:

Are you insane?
The gold is not mine yet.
Shame on your greedy ambition!

The law-maker is about to turn law-breaker. When the giants take Freia hostage, the gods grow visibly old, a verification of Fafner's earlier surmise, 'Eternal youth would be ours, were the magic gold in our grasp.' Wotan, led by Loge, invades Nibelheim in quest of the ring.

In the third scene, Mime relates that Alberich has succeeded in forging the ring, the properties of which seem to be twofold. It has turned all Nibelungs, including Mime, into Alberich's slaves, and it divines ever new locations for mining more gold. Mime, however, harbours thoughts of depriving his brother of the ring. When we meet Alberich, he appears as a ruthless bully:

Back to your burrows!
Hurry below!
In the new-made shafts
go gather new gold!
This whip shall greet you,
if you go slow!

His next pronouncement is awe-inspiring. He gives notice of his ambition to rule the world by terror:

Your menfolk first shall bow to my might,
then your winsome women – how they trifled with me! –
they all shall answer my lust, though love be no more.
Beware of my legions of night!
For soon the Nibelung gold
shall rise and ravish the world!

The Rhinemaidens' taunting has produced terrifying results. Such threats can be countered only by subterfuge. Loge, therefore, suggests to Alberich that someone could steal the ring when its owner was asleep, whereupon Alberich parts with the secret of the Tarnhelm, which makes him invisible or transforms him into any shape of his choice. He succumbs to Loge's wheedling requests for a demonstration, and his resultant capture must cast doubts on the ring's effectiveness.

Alberich ransoms his life with the ring, which will soon pass to Wotan who now reminds his victim of his original sin, the theft of the Rhinegold. Alberich counters with a powerful moral argument:

If I have sinned,
my sins shall be mine alone;
but on all that shall be, is and was,
falls your sin for all time,
if you should ravish the ring.

But Wotan is oblivious to Alberich's warning, and the ring fascinates him to such an extent that he also forgets its purpose, namely to ransom Freia:

I hold what makes me supreme,
of lords the omnipotent lord.

He overlooks that, by virtue of his having obtained the lordly spear and sacrificed one eye for gaining wisdom, he had already established his rulership over the world, without any need for the ring. But he succumbs to the temptation of compounding wealth with more wealth. Here Alberich utters his second curse. Having cursed love, he now puts a curse on the ring and on all its future owners:

Having the ring means having ill fortune,
and not to have it means living in hell.
Now is it yours: keep it with care,
but my curse none shall escape!

Should not the supposed omnipotence of the ring invalidate such a curse?

When Fafner demands the ring from Wotan, Loge precipitates the god's reply. He informs the giants, mischievously, that Wotan intends to return the ring to the Rhinemaidens. Wotan asserts his firm intention to hold the ring for himself. This prompts Erda to appear with her dire warning of the impending end of the world. She does not give Wotan the option of bartering ring for survival, she merely states the inevitable:

A day of doom seeks the immortals.
Be counselled, flee from the ring!

Ironically, the ring is not only incapable of averting the gods' demise, but, according to Erda, it should be shunned, while surrendering it would make no difference to the outcome. Perplexed, Wotan gives the ring to the giants in exchange for Freia, and witnesses the power of Alberich's curse which seems to be more effective than the power of the ring itself: Fafner kills his brother for possession of the ring. *Rheingold* ends with the Rhinemaidens lamenting the loss of their 'guiltless gold', while Loge turns the knife in their wound:

Bask no more in forfeited gold,
but in Wotan's brave new glory
bask forever in bliss!

The next music drama, *Die Walküre*, concerns itself with aspects of love (Brünnhilde's, Siegmund's, Sieglinde's, and the thwarted love of Wotan) – not the territory for the ring, symbol of power, to flourish. Wotan mentions the ring in his colloquy with Brünnhilde, when he recounts its early history. He contrasts Alberich's successful venture in purchasing love with his own efforts to create a free hero, now that Siegmund is doomed. In the first act of *Siegfried*, the ring haunts Mime's thoughts. Fafner, its present owner, has turned himself into a dragon and sleeps on his golden hoard. If he, Mime, could only forge a sword sharp enough for Siegfried to kill the dragon, then the guileless boy would obtain the ring, after which Mime could easily talk him out of it. But the task of forging such a sword is beyond Mime. In the course of the battle of wits between Mime and his unbidden guest, Wotan the Wanderer, Wotan recounts Alberich's former control of his Nibelung slaves by virtue of the ring, and its eventual passing to Fafner. Mime knows all this, and he takes little delight in the retelling. But when he witnesses Siegfried's adroit reforging of the splintered sword Nothung, he takes heart:

With the selfsame sword that now he is forging,
he shall be sent to his doom,
and mine will be ring and gold.

In the second act, Alberich repeats to the Wanderer his earlier forecast of world domination by the first and future lord of the ring. Alberich has stationed himself close to Fafner's lair, to await the outcome of the fight between Siegfried and Fafner, the passing of the ring from Fafner to Siegfried and, hopefully, from Siegfried to Alberich. The Wanderer informs Alberich, 'Fafner falls, the ring shall pass to a new master.' To make his own prophecy come true, Alberich resorts to a plan that has failure written all over it. He tells Fafner of Siegfried's approach and proposes to persuade Siegfried to leave the dragon alone. All he wants in return is the ring. Fafner's reply is somewhat discouraging: 'I hold what I have. Let me slumber!'

Siegfried duly despatches the dragon, but shows no interest in the golden hoard. He retrieves the ring and the Tarnhelm only at the Woodbird's prompting:

The ring awaits its new master,
and he shall be lord of the world.

To be lord of the world is meaningless to Siegfried, and he has already forgotten the bird's prognosis as he views both ring and Tarnhelm: 'What shall I do with these things?' He calls them 'trinkets' and intends to keep them as battle trophies. In contrast, both Alberich and Mime are trying to establish their respective rightful ownership of the ring. Alberich claims his title to the ring, since he first obtained its raw material from the Rhinemaidens. Mime counters with the assertion that Alberich had allowed the ring to be taken from him, and was thus no longer fit to command it. Mime, however, had brought up Siegfried, and ring and Tarnhelm were due to him as payment for the boy's board, lodging and education. Alberich's answer does not exhibit much brotherly love:

The scurviest cur
has better claim than you to the ring.

Both resolve to obtain it, Mime by killing Siegfried, and Alberich, as we shall learn in *Götterdämmerung*, by creating a hero son, Hagen. Thus, the adversaries Wotan and Alberich have transferred their contest for world dominion to their offspring, Siegfried and Hagen.

It soon becomes plain that Mime is out of the running. The dragon's blood has enabled Siegfried to hear Mime's secret thoughts:

With your glorious sword,
child, will I chop
your head right off.

Mime does not survive, and the last reference to the ring in *Siegfried* occurs in the final act, when the Wanderer optimistically informs Erda that Siegfried is now the ring's new lord, and that Alberich's curse cannot affect the hero, since he knows no fear. Here is a vital clue to the ring's presumed omnipotence.

The Norns, however, are greatly concerned about the curse that rests on the ring. In *Götterdämmerung* they complain that the ring's curse gnaws at the strands of their rope of destiny. When in the next scene Siegfried gives the ring to Brünnhilde, it is as a symbolic gift, of sentimental rather than practical value:

All the tasks I have performed,
reside within this ring.
Now make its virtue your strength,
a sacred vow of my troth.

When Siegfried arrives at King Gunther's court, Hagen wants to know what it was that Siegfried obtained from the dead Fafner's cave. 'Just one ring,' answers Siegfried, adding that 'a woman guards it with care.' With utter determination Hagen now launches his campaign for the conquest of the ring. He engineers Siegfried's union with Gutrune, and he despatches Siegfried and Gunther on their quest for Brünnhilde: 'His rightful bride he'll bring to the Rhine, and he will bring me the ring!'

Brünnhilde refuses Waltraute's request for the return of the ring, Siegfried's token of love, to the Rhinemaidens. We now observe that the ring has little protective power: when Siegfried has forgotten his Brünnhilde and when he wrests the ring from her finger, it fails to protect her. The combined force of Alberich's curse and Siegfried's faithlessness appears to invalidate whatever virtue resides in the ring. It might have saved her from any other intruder, but not from Siegfried. It is impossible to miss the irony of the situation. Wotan had created Siegfried as an independent agent who, unaware of the god's guilty actions, would of his own accord atone for his ancestor's trespasses. But Siegfried's only achievement has been to copy Wotan's moral lapse, when the god wrested the ring from Alberich's hand.

Our earlier assertion that Alberich's curse on the ring does not affect Siegfried, on account of his fearlessness, is substantiated by Alberich himself. In his nocturnal dialogue with his son Hagen, Alberich discloses:

My curse cannot harm this unfearing hero,
for he knows not the ring's repute,
nor makes use of its magical might.

He further directs Hagen's attention to the danger of the ring's return to the Rhinemaidens. Hagen, therefore, will have to use all his ingenuity to retrieve the Nibelung's ring. Hagen, however, promises only to regain the ring. Whether he means to hand it to his father, he does not divulge.

Hagen displays devilish cunning at Gunther and Brünnhilde's wedding reception. Brünnhilde recognizes the ring on Siegfried's finger. But the night before, so she thinks, that ring was forcibly taken from her by Gunther. She now demands to know why Gunther has given it to Siegfried. When both Siegfried and Gunther plead ignorance, she concludes:

He it was
has robbed me of my ring,
Siegfried, the treacherous thief!

Still under the influence of the potion of forgetfulness – that cruel symbol for the fickleness of the human heart – Siegfried protests to Brünnhilde that neither man nor woman had given him the ring. He had it from the dragon's hoard. As for their night together, he declares that his sword separated him from Brünnhilde, whom he had not touched. Brünnhilde, however, well remembers all those nights when she and Siegfried had slept united, with the sword 'snugly asleep in its scabbard'. Clearly, both are referring to different times, and both are right as well as wrong. It is Hagen's craft that has created this deceptive web, and he now does nothing to clear up the confusion in everybody's mind. Siegfried, as perplexed as Gunther, offers a feeble explanation to his bloodbrother:

Greater is my grief than yours,
that our plot went wrong.
The Tarnhelm, I suspect,
was not a good disguise.

The act ends with Hagen, at last, declaring his full allegiance to his father, and anticipating his return to power:

Nibelung lord, Alberich, look upon me!
Bid once again all the Nibelung host
to bow before you, the ring's true lord.

In the final act of *Götterdämmerung*, the Rhinemaidens bewail the loss of their gold. Now that Siegfried has strayed to the banks of the river, they point to the ring on his finger. 'We want it!' they call in unison. Seeing that Siegfried is on his way to join a hunting party, and that he is without booty, they propose to provide him with some game in exchange for the ring. He protests:

Shall paltry paws of humble bears
be bartered for such a ring?

They try a different approach: 'Alas, he is so mean to us!' This hits home. He draws the ring from his finger, ready to surrender it. But now the maidens no longer want it. Their demeanour is changed. Solemnly they declare:

Retain the ring and ward it well,
until you know the ill fate
that lives within your ring.

They proceed to foretell his imminent death, but then they rashly propose another barter:

> Your fate is foretold,
> if you refuse us the ring.

Siegfried is not a man to barter under duress. His reply reveals that he is slowly regaining his former heroic stature, and that the pseudo-Siegfried, Gunther's bloodbrother, husband to the trivial Gutrune, is fading away. It is the real Siegfried who speaks:

> I'd leave it to you, just for love;
> but you threaten my life and my limbs:
> now, were it less than a finger's worth,
> you shall not ransom the ring!

The Rhinemaidens' farewell is sadly astute:

> Oaths he swears and forswears his oaths.
> Runes he knows and rejects the runes.
> The greatest boon was granted him,
> and he disowned it.
> Yet the ring, the accursed ring
> he will not surrender.
> Farewell, Siegfried!
> A noble wife will today inherit your treasure.

Fare well, indeed. Siegfried joins the hunting party and has not long to live. He recounts the story of his life, he tells of the dragon, the ring and the Tarnhelm. Hagen prompts him, adroitly, to come to the point, to the awakening of Brünnhilde, and with it, to his execution. We see the ring again, when Hagen claims it from the dead man's hand as it rises menacingly towards his killer.

During her great funeral oration Brünnhilde draws the ring from Siegfried's finger and promises its swift return to the Rhine:

> From Brünnhild's ashes take it for ever.
> This fire, burning my limbs,
> cleanses the ring of its curse.

As she rides into the flames, to be united in death with Siegfried, Hagen plunges madly into the waters, where the Rhinemaidens grant him what they withheld from his father Alberich – close bodily contact, deadly embrace.

In the course of the tetralogy the ring has passed from its first owner, Alberich, to Wotan, then to the giants collectively. After killing his brother, Fafner became its sole holder. Siegfried obtained it from him, to pass it to Brünnhilde who had it taken away from her by Siegfried. Finally, Brünnhilde gained it once more, only to return it to its rightful owners, the Rhinemaidens.

Two prophecies launched the ring on its travels. The first emanated from Wellgunde who pronounced the possibility of the world and its riches to fall to the man who fashioned a ring from the Rhinegold, a ring that might endow him with measureless power. The other forewarning came from Alberich who, in cursing the ring, also intimidated every subsequent owner by pointing to the ring's power of terrorizing those who covet it and those who wear it. 'Having the ring,' he pronounced, 'means having ill fortune, and not having it means living in hell.'

The Rhinemaidens' use of the subjunctive did not deter Alberich from forging the ring and wielding immense power. True, they held out hopes for 'measureless might', but no court would condemn them for swindling. They could always insist on being quoted verbatim: '... der masslose Macht ihm verlieh' ('... that *might* endow him with measureless might').

When dealing with soothsayers, man is inclined to tailor their sayings to fit his own requirements. Wotan holds the ring because it adds to his prestige, not primarily for such ordinary purposes as ransoming Freia. Fafner slays his brother over the ring and then guards it by sleeping on it, disguised as a dragon. Siegfried regards it as a memento, Brünnhilde as a love token. None of these attitudes contradicts the original terms.

As for Alberich's curse, its potency is unmistakable. Every subsequent owner, except Alberich himself, dies in consequence of having possessed the ring.

The tetralogy ends with the ring's return to the Rhine, and this last journey from Brünnhilde's hand to the Rhinemaidens is its most significant one. It prepares the audience for the final bars of the music, for the assurance of a new beginning, for a world with no need for the ring of power, but with the greater need for the proliferating power of love.

Conclusion

Wagner's tetralogy not only admits but demands examination, argument and re-examination. Its world has become familiar territory today, when we realize that the *Ring* is more than a tale of gods, giants, dwarfs and heroes set to magnificent music. Wotan is not so much a troubled god, but man who has released social, political and physical forces which have a way of sliding beyond his control, and who experiences the dissolution of a world order based on expediency. The *Ring* is, among other things, about man's tragic attempt to reconcile his desire for love and goodness with the necessity of organizing his life. This necessity entails making laws, violating laws, punishing trespasses, succumbing to pragmatism and, inevitably, it seems, to eventual self-annihilation. It is an over-simplification to see in the *Ring* a conflict between power and love: of far greater importance is the fact that Wagner propounds the interdependence of those twin forces. Man seems to need them both to sustain life, yet one destroys the other. This inherent tragedy is at the heart of the *Ring*. Wagner makes his point in *Siegfried*, at the moment of Brünnhilde's awakening. We hear four chords:

To the innocent ear, the short theme symbolizes Brünnhilde and Siegfried's love, and this impression will be reinforced in *Götterdämmerung*, when the same four chords accompany the dying Siegfried's words, 'Brünnhilde, heilige Braut' ('Brünnhilde, my sacred bride'). And yet, the melodic line of B – C – B – D is identical with the theme, first heard in *Rheingold*, of the death-dealing dragon. Towards the end of *Siegfried*, cellos and double basses sound the dragon theme, while clarinets and flutes play what earlier commentators called the motif of Love's Greeting:

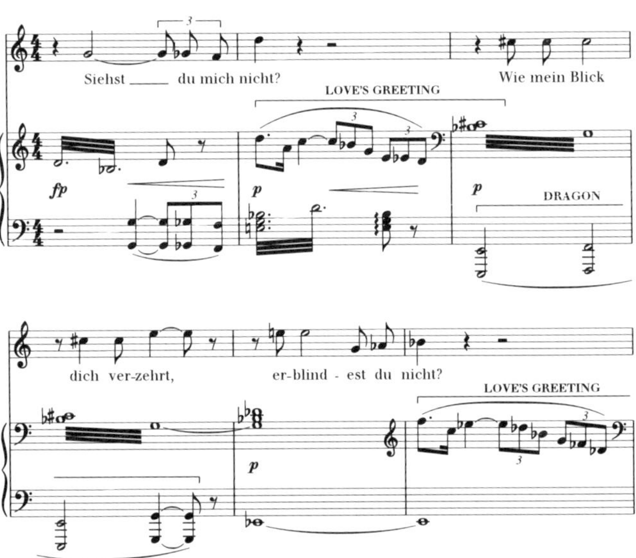

The proximity in the score of the symbols of love and destructive power expresses Wagner's essential philosophy of the *Ring*. He re-creates creation, at the beginning of *Rheingold*, and in the course of the tetralogy he presents us with an exposé of the state of the world and with the condition of man. Wotan, 'enterprising man', and Brünnhilde, 'life-enhancing woman', do not survive the cosmic liquidation, but *Götterdämmerung* ends with the theme which transcends the individual claims of both love and power, by symbolizing the timeless power of love:

Watching the *Ring* is an unsettling business. Yet, its ultimate message admits the feasibility of a future which may yet reveal to man an intrinsic wisdom of the cosmic design, inscrutable though it may be.

A caricature of Wagner conducting (1877)

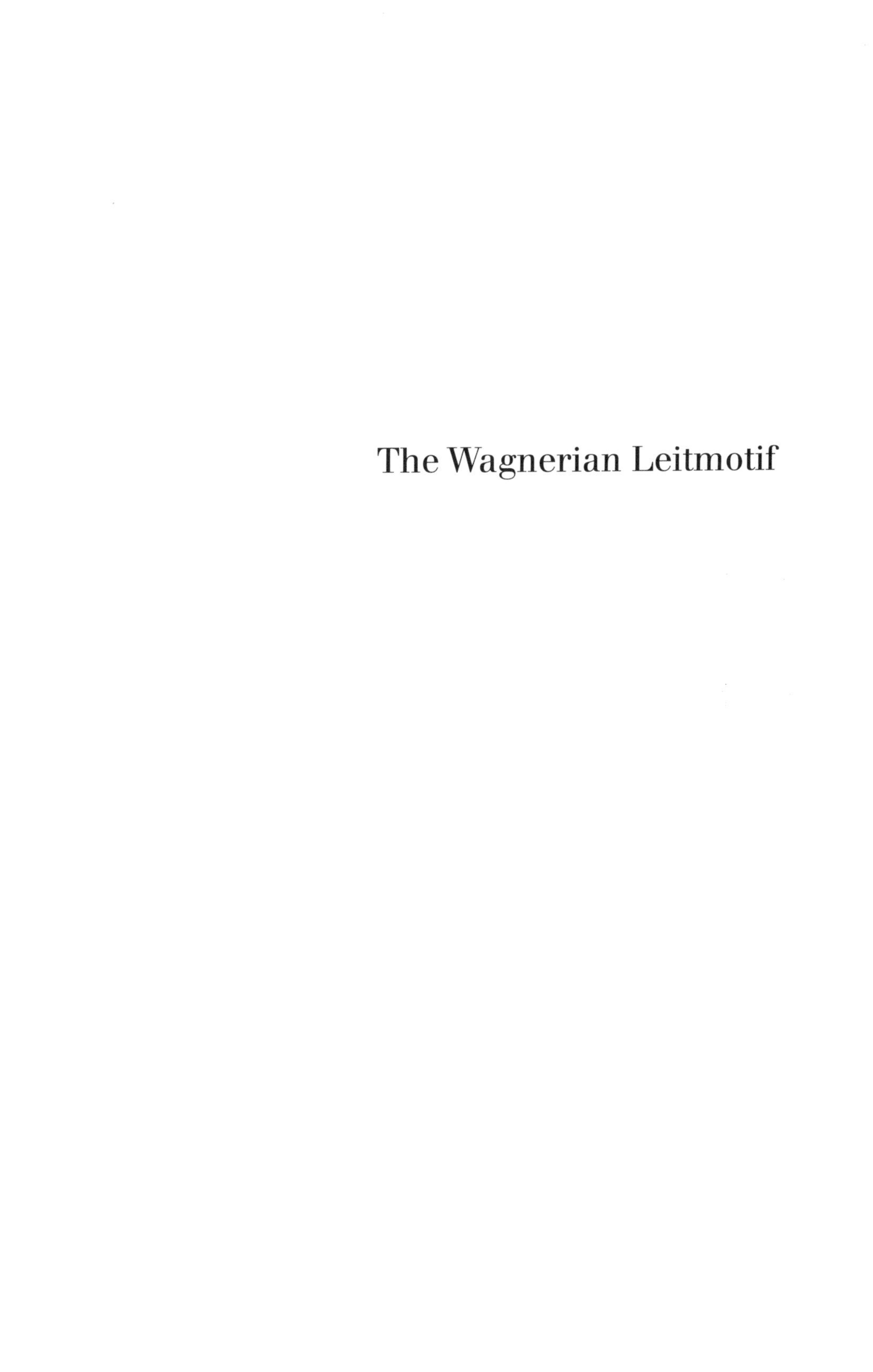

The Wagnerian Leitmotif

The Wagnerian Leitmotif

One of the most fascinating features in the panorama of the *Ring* is Wagner's system of leitmotifs, of which there are over eighty. It has been claimed that listeners or spectators need not know anything about them. If that were true, however, they would be deprived of a vital musical-dramatic dimension: understanding the leitmotifs provides the key to understanding the *Ring*.

The use of the 'leitmotif', a short musical figure associated with a particular character, event or mood, was not unique to Wagner. Earlier composers had employed short musical themes in this way, though none had made such systematic and all-pervasive use of the leitmotif. Beethoven demonstrated the technique to powerful effect in *Fidelio*. Florestan's vision of Leonore, his wife, and of freedom, is conveyed by an arched oboe theme:

Later, when Rocco and Leonore watch the sleeping Florestan, they – and we – hear the same oboe theme, to their spoken dialogue:

> Rocco: Perhaps he is dead?
> Leonore: You think so?
> Rocco: No, he is asleep.

This theme, or leitmotif, fulfils a triple function: it confirms Rocco's impression that the prisoner is not dead; it reveals Florestan's dream of Leonore; and it substantiates this dream in Leonore's actual presence.

Wagner's use of leitmotifs is even subtler and more comprehensive. Beethoven's motif, as it appears in the Rocco–Leonore scene, refers us back to its earlier intimation. It is a motif of remembrance, an *Erinnerungsmotiv*. Wagner's motifs can also foretell (*Zukunftsmotiv*), and they can illustrate a significant present event (*Gegenwartsmotiv*). To alert his audience to the appearance of a new leitmotif, Wagner frequently synchronizes aural and visual aspects. The Alberich motif, for example, sounds when that character is seen for the first time. The

Rhinegold motif sounds as the gold becomes visible. The Giants motif sounds as they enter. The Erda motif sounds as she arises. Each is a motif of the present, or *Gegenwartsmotiv*.

Wagner's use of the leitmotif is consistent with his desire to fuse music, drama, scenery and acting into a *Gesamtkunstwerk*, a totality of the arts. His leitmotifs, too, extend their significance beyond the purely musical. They underpin the action, they comment on it, they help to create receptive moods in the listener, they elucidate, they sometimes tell the audience what the characters on stage do not yet know, they prophesy, and they occasionally contradict the evidence before our eyes. As the dramatic situation changes, so does the instrumentation of the leitmotifs. In short, leitmotifs are our faithful guides through the complexities of the *Ring* tetralogy.

Leitmotif as Dramatic Agent

By looking in detail at Wagner's use of a particular motif throughout the course of the *Ring*, we shall uncover the many different ways in which a leitmotif can involve us in the drama. The Curse motif, first heard after Wotan and Loge deprive Alberich of the ring and Alberich curses the ring and all its future owners, returns as an *Erinnerungsmotiv* throughout the *Ring*. On each encounter the listener will remember its first appearance and its chilling prognosis.

Alberich is obliged, in the fourth scene of *Rheingold*, to ransom his life with his worldly goods, the gold, the Tarnhelm, and the ring. He recalls his earlier curse on love, and proclaims:

As my curse got me the ring,
my curse go with it now!

Accompanied only by a timpani tremolo, the Curse motif is lodged, unusually, not by the orchestra, but by Alberich alone:

Having alerted the listener to the new motif, Wagner repeats it, slightly varied and now accompanied by low woodwind and brass, to Alberich's oracle of doom:

As it gave me
measureless might,
so by its magic
each owner shall die!

The ring passes from Alberich to Wotan, and from Wotan to the giants. Wotan was able to hold the ring for only a brief span: obeying Erda's injunction, he surrendered it and secured his temporary survival. But the accuracy of Alberich's forecast manifests itself as Fafner clubs his brother to death, to become the ring's new owner. A series of vicious death blows (timpani) is heard, followed by the howling of the Curse motif (three trombones). Wotan is uneasy:

Fearful power
I find in the fatal curse.

The Curse motif is then repeated by the trombones.

We next meet the motif in the second act of *Die Walküre*. Wotan bases his hope for the gods survival, and that of the world, on Siegmund, his son. But Siegmund is guilty of adultery and incest, and Fricka, guardian of wedlock, demands his death. Wotan submits, and Brünnhilde is to preside over the sacrifice. Fricka charges her:

Warfather waits for you.
You will discover
how the lot has been cast.

Three trombones endorse the command with their Curse motif, foreshadowing the fatal consequences of Wotan's connivance.

In the following scene, Brünnhilde asks her father: 'What saddens you so?' and the bass trumpet's Curse motif precedes and then envelopes Wotan's non-reply: 'O heilige Schmach!' ('O greatest of shame!')

The god bows to Necessity:

What I love, I now must relinquish,
murder my heart's beloved,
meanly betray
trust and truth.

Three trombones comment with their Curse motif on his decision, in an assertive crescendo, before abating to a contented whisper.

The orchestral prelude to *Siegfried*, Act II, depicts a world of terror, greed, plot and counter-plot. Alberich and Mime have invaded Fafner's territory, forming an unholy trinity. The Curse motif, sounded twice in succession, accurately predicts the ensuing carnage. Alberich awaits Fafner's demise, which the orchestra is emphatic in prophesying. Fafner's own motif is encircled by two Curse motifs, again heralded by three trombones:

In the dispute between Alberich and the Wanderer, the Nibelung rants:

You brag, you boast,
you bluster so boldly,
and yet, how you fear your own fate!

The Curse motif warns both antagonists to keep well away from the blighted ring.

Siegfried kills Fafner, the dragon, but Alberich is not satisfied with a single blood-letting. The gods too must fall:

Laugh on, laugh on,
you light-minded,
luxuriating lot of immortals!
I'll see you all off to your graves!

Four tubas and a timpani tremolo endorse the apocalyptic avowal with their Curse motif.

Fafner, with his dying breath, warns Siegfried to beware of Mime:

He whose words desired the deed,
even now desires your death.
Mark the ending, mark my words!

Here, the Curse motif is as ambiguous as the text. Does the motif validate Fafner's own end? Is it the harbinger of Mime's death? Or even Siegfried's? 'Mark the ending!' said Fafner. The ending of Fafner, Mime or Siegfried? Or the ending of the world, the impending 'Götterdämmerung'?

In the third act, Siegfried wakes Brünnhilde, his destined bride, with a kiss. Their love is momentarily threatened by her realization of the imminent loss of her godhead:

Trapped is in darkness
and troubled my sight.
My eyes are blinded;
the light is lost.

The Curse motif underlines her anxiety and gives warning of Siegfried's imperilled life, but since this is a love scene, Wagner scores the motif for woodwind, *piano*.

In *Götterdämmerung*, the Norns' rope of destiny comes apart. They predict the end of the gods while the Curse motif is played by a bass trumpet, *molto marcato*. Wagner's rare use of that instrument emphasizes the motif's gravity.

Siegfried, who has left his Brünnhilde, makes his way to King Gunther's corrupt court; the bass trumpet cautions him with its Curse motif. If he were to heed it, he might turn back and live. But a Siegfried defies augury.

'Hail, Siegfried! Hero, hail!' Hagen greets Siegfried with the Curse motif, and the trombones curse the hero with their own murderous welcome. The vocal and instrumental motif warns us not to be fooled by Hagen's urbanity, but to recognize the counter-evidence of the leitmotif.

The composer takes us into his confidence:

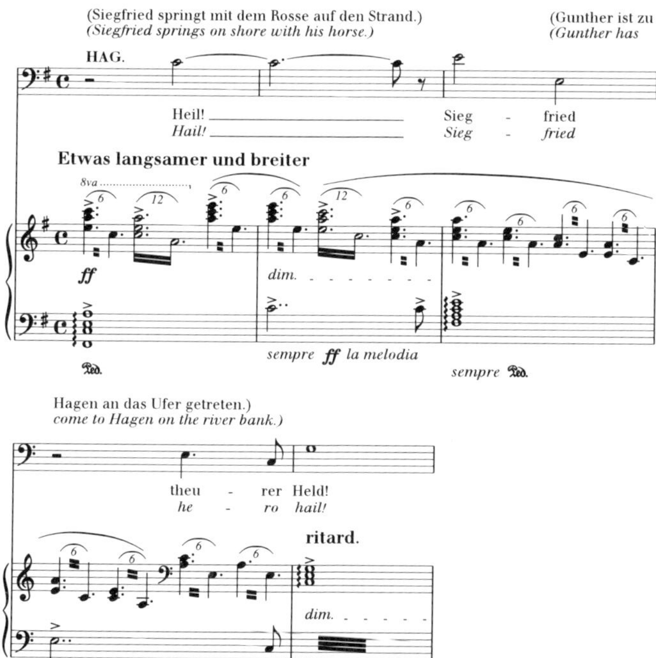

A few moments later Siegfried turns to Hagen:

> You called me Siegfried?
> Strangers are we.

Abetted by a sinister horn, Siegfried sings his own name to the Curse motif. Subconsciously, he accepts the consequences of the curse. His fate is sealed. Siegfried has been trapped into an alliance with the feeble King Gunther and his trivial sister whom he now addresses:

> To your brother offered I support;
> his pride disdained my hand.
> Will you, like him, deny me now,
> or will you be my wife?

We hear Hagen's motif – he is the author of this misalliance – and that of Gutrune, the decoy. Inevitably, the Curse motif follows, sounded by a single horn. Siegfried, fearless but no longer himself, ignores it:

Siegfried and Gunther drink *Blutbrüderschaft* (bloodbrotherhood). They affirm their friendship with an oath, and they share a drinking-horn filled with wine and with their own blood. As they drink, tubas irreverently sneer at the treaty with their Curse motif. Oaths, they say, fidelity, brotherhood? This is what we think of it:

Brünnhilde is alone in her rocky chamber. Siegfried, whose ring is now on her hand, has not yet returned. A bass clarinet moans the Brünnhilde motif but, like a spreading cancer, the Curse motif infests her quietude:

In the second scene of the final act, Hagen calls to Siegfried with his ill-intentioned summons, 'Hoiho!' A trombone, *pianissimo*, precedes him with a gentle Curse motif, Siegfried's angel of death. When Hagen slays Siegfried, he is again accompanied by the motif. Siegfried is out of the way.

Now, in the final scene, Hagen fights with Gunther for possession of the ring:

> The Niblung's dower
> settles on his son!

But his own father's curse, reinforced by the trombones, thwarts the enterprise.

Götterdämmerung is upon us. The world disappears in fire and flood. Brünnhilde has restored the ring to its original element, the waters. Hagen plunges madly into the torrent, to retrieve it from the Rhinemaidens, and the Curse motif sounds for one last time, incomplete.

It lingers on its top note, then ceases to be:

Leitmotif as Confidant

Wagner sometimes uses the leitmotif to address the audience directly. In the third act of *Walküre*, Brünnhilde foretells the birth of Siegfried.

She informs Sieglinde, to the Siegfried motif:

At the end of this act, when Wotan surrounds the slumbering Brünnhilde with an impenetrable wall of flames, he makes the pronouncement:

> No man who fears my sacred spear-point,
> shall fare through this fiery sea!

Wotan sings these lines to the Siegfried motif which, in its few bars, tells the audience that Wotan's spear commands awe; that as long as Wotan wields his spear, nobody will dare cross the wall of flames; that someone fearless enough, however, might try; and that his name is Siegfried.

For our second example we turn to the final act of *Siegfried*. Brünnhilde salutes her awakener and future lover, the fearless young Siegfried. Her ecstatic greeting is accompanied, incredibly, by the Dragon motif, sounded by the cellos and double basses. Why? Because Wagner was familiar with the remotest corners and the deepest abysses of the heart. Brünnhilde is possessed by the desire to possess Siegfried:

> When my eyes feed on yours, then are you not blind?
> When I clasp you close, then do you not burn?

Indeed, Brünnhilde will be instrumental, in *Götterdämmerung*, in Siegfried's death and his eventual incineration.

We have seen that the Wagnerian system of leitmotifs allows direct dialogue between composer and audience, turning the latter into confidants. A similar device can be found in the system of 'kennings' in Old Norse mythology, a device known to Wagner. Kennings form a kind of secret language which, like the leitmotif, is intelligible only to initiates. In this system a poetic description of an object is used, rather than its actual name. Thus gold is 'Rhine fire', sea is 'eel-home', earth is 'evergreen', fire is 'corpse destroyer', night, evocatively, is 'spinner of dreams', clouds are 'windships', a forest 'mountain seaweed', an arm is 'hawk's landing place' and the moon 'tally-of-years'.

At its first appearance, a leitmotif impresses the listener with its brevity, its accentuated orchestral or vocal rendering and, frequently, its visual representation. In the course of the drama the leitmotif is capable of many melodic and rhythmical modifications, of changed harmonization and instrumentation, of diminution (shortening of time values), augmentation (lengthening of time values) and even fragmentation. We shall encounter all of these throughout the *Ring*.

An intriguing situation arises when Wagner synchronizes two or three leitmotifs. In *Rheingold* (Scene 2), Fasolt and Fafner intend to abduct Freia, whose golden apples provide the gods with youth everlasting. Horns sound the Golden Apples motif, while the Giants motif is heard in the low strings:

A triple motif appears in Scene 4, when the aggrieved Alberich is forced to ransom his life with the treasure he has forged:

Origins of the Term

How did the term 'Leitmotiv' arise? According to most commentators the expression was coined by Hans von Wolzogen (1848–1938), pioneer of Wagnerian interpretation, while Wagner did not know the word. Both assumptions are fallacies. Although Wolzogen made ample use of the term, he stated that he had borrowed it from an unidentifiable source. As for Wagner, we read in Cosima's diaries (31 January 1879) that, when playing a fugue by Bach, Wagner drew attention to the reappearance of the fugue theme and remarked, 'People will have to put up with the repetitions of my own leitmotifs.' In his letters and theoretical writings, though, Wagner used different terms, all meaning the same thing: 'themes', 'ground themes', 'ground motifs' or 'musical moments of intuition'. Nietzsche, who had a deeper understanding of Wagner than any of his contemporaries, had another, more accurate word, 'symbols'.

The composer's grandson, Wieland Wagner, revealed similarly inspired insight when he said:

> Leitmotifs are the melodic work material, symbols for metaphysical events. To trace the course of the motifs through the whole Ring amounts to a journey into the realms of depth psychology. (Panofsky, p.53)

A 'journey of discovery'. Wagner knew its purpose and its destination. So did his wife Cosima. In her diaries (2 June 1870) she wrote: 'It must be said that in his rich tapestry of themes which pervade the tetralogy, a language has been created which the world cannot yet conceive.'

The world was indeed slow to conceive, and Wagner did little to contribute to its enlightenment, putting his faith in the self-explanatory power of the score. To his friend August Röckel he wrote, in January 1854: 'There is hardly a single bar in the orchestra which is not based on preceding motifs. But it is futile to talk about this ... '

In bequeathing a work of genius upon the world, Wagner demands our participation, our willingness to appreciate the significance of his system of leitmotifs. In the *Ring* he created the world, and the leitmotifs are the blueprint for that creation.

Characters of the *Ring*

Alberich

Father of Hagen, brother of Mime. Ruler of the Nibelungs, dwarfs living in subterranean Nibelheim. Has renounced love and forged an all-powerful ring from the stolen Rhinegold. Loses his ring to Wotan, then curses it and all future owners. Intends to regain the ring and become ruler of the world. Fails to persuade the dragon (Fafner) to part with it, disputes eventual ownership with Mime, and rejoices over his brother's death. Bribed and cajoled Queen Grimhild to bear him a son, Hagen. Wotan had once engendered Siegfried, in order to restore a status quo. Hagen was sired by Alberich for the same reason. Baritone, in *Rheingold*, *Siegfried* and *Götterdämmerung*.

Brünnhilde

Valkyrie, daughter of Wotan and Erda, and Wotan's shield-maiden. Is punished by Wotan for aiding Siegmund in his battle with Hunding by being cast asleep on a rock, surrounded by a guardian fire. Becomes the bride of Siegfried, who has penetrated the flames and kissed her awake. Receives the cursed ring from him as love token. Is later forced by Siegfried (who has forgotten her) to become King Gunther's bride. Joins in the conspiracy to kill Siegfried. Learns, too late, the truth about Siegfried's Hagen-induced amnesia, makes amends for Wotan's transgressions by restoring the ring to the Rhinemaidens and joins the dead Siegfried in the final conflagration. Soprano, in *Walküre*, *Siegfried* and *Götterdämmerung*.

Donner

Brother of Fricka, Freia and Froh. God of thunder. Baritone, in *Rheingold*.

Erda

Earth-goddess, mother of the three Norns and of Brünnhilde. Represents knowledge of past and future. Warns Wotan to part with the cursed ring, and prophesies the eventual waning of the gods. Deplores Wotan's punishment of Brünnhilde and declines to advise Wotan on restoring the gods' prosperity. Alto, in *Rheingold* and *Siegfried*.

Fafner
Giant, brother of Fasolt, co-builder of Walhall. Kills his brother over possession of the cursed ring. Turns himself into a dragon, with the help of the Tarnhelm (magic cap), and guards the Nibelung hoard. Is killed by Siegfried, but manages to warn him to beware of Mime. Bass, in *Rheingold* and, as Dragon, in *Siegfried.*

Fasolt
Brother of Fafner, co-builder of Walhall, and the milder of the two giants. Is killed by Fafner. Bass, in *Rheingold.*

Freia
Sister of Fricka, Donner and Froh. Also referred to as Holda, she is guardian of the golden apples of youth. Is taken hostage by the giants and held as ransom for Wotan's acquisition of Alberich's treasure. Soprano, in *Rheingold.*

Fricka
Wotan's wife. Sister of Freia, Donner and Froh. Guardian of wedlock. Compels Wotan to connive in the killing of Siegmund. Mezzo-soprano, in *Rheingold* and *Walküre.*

Froh
Brother of Fricka, Freia and Donner. Creates the rainbow bridge on which the gods enter into Walhall. Tenor, in *Rheingold.*

Gunther
King of the Gibichungs, brother of Gutrune, half-brother of Hagen who tricks him into a sham alliance with Siegfried. Receives Brünnhilde from Siegfried's hands, but joins in the plot to kill the hero. Fights with Hagen over possession of the ring and is killed by his deceitful half-brother. Baritone, in *Götterdämmerung.*

Gutrune
Sister of Gunther, half-sister of Hagen. Allows herself to be tricked into alliance with Siegfried. Soprano, in *Götterdämmerung.*

Hagen
Son of Alberich and Queen Grimhild (mother of Gunther and Gutrune). Relentlessly pursues the ring and the Nibelung hoard. Devises Siegfried's temporary amnesia, the hero's alliance with Gutrune, the deception of Brünnhilde and her sham marriage to Gunther. Kills first Siegfried, then Gunther and is drowned by the Rhinemaidens in his final quest for the ring. Bass, in *Götterdämmerung.*

Hunding
Fierce warrior. Marries Sieglinde against her will. Kills Siegmund and is killed by Wotan. Bass, in *Walküre.*

Loge
God of fire. Ambivalent intellectual who is both ally and enemy of the gods. Tenor, in *Rheingold.*

Mime
Nibelung, brother of Alberich, master smith. Rears the young Siegfried, in order to obtain the Nibelung hoard. Makes Siegfried confront and kill the dragon (Fafner). Fails in his attempt to poison Siegfried, who kills him. Tenor, in *Rheingold* and *Siegfried.*

Nibelungs
Subterranean miners in Nibelheim, enslaved by their lord, Alberich. In *Rheingold.*

Three Norns
Weavers of the rope of destiny, seated by the Well of Wisdom, underneath the World Ash Tree. Have knowledge of past, present and future. Alto (First Norn), mezzo-soprano (Second Norn) and soprano (Third Norn), in *Götterdämmerung.*

Three Rhinemaidens
Woglinde, Wellgunde and Flosshilde, guardians of the Rhinegold. Flosshilde is more vigilant than her carefree sisters. In *Götterdämmerung* they are unsuccessful in persuading Siegfried to give them his ring (forged by Alberich from the stolen Rhinegold), and foretell his imminent death. At the end of the tetralogy, they obtain the ring from Brünnhilde's hand. Hagen, who plunges into the river in pursuit of the ring, is drowned by Woglinde and Wellgunde. Soprano (Woglinde), soprano (Wellgunde) and mezzo-soprano (Flosshilde), in *Rheingold* and *Götterdämmerung.*

Siegfried
Son of Siegmund and Sieglinde. Devised by Wotan as fearless hero who is to restore the gods' fortune. Reared by Mime, reforges his father's splintered sword, kills the dragon (Fafner), gains ring and Tarnhelm, kills Mime, vanquishes the guardian of the rock (Wotan as Wanderer), penetrates the circle of flames, kisses Brünnhilde awake and weds her. Falls victim to Hagen's intrigues, which results in his temporary loss of memory, his wooing of Gutrune and his alliance with King Gunther. Disguised by the Tarnhelm, he conquers Brünnhilde on Gunther's behalf, disregards the Rhinemaidens' warning, regains his memory of Brünnhilde and is killed by Hagen. Tenor, in *Siegfried* and *Götterdämmerung.*

Sieglinde

Daughter of Wotan and unnamed mortal woman. Forced into loveless marriage to Hunding. Twin sister and lover of Siegmund, and mother of Siegfried. Dies at Siegfried's birth. Soprano, in *Walküre.*

Siegmund

Son of Wotan and unnamed mortal woman. Twin brother and lover of Sieglinde, and father of Siegfried. Is killed by Hunding. Tenor, in *Walküre.*

Eight Valkyries

Warrior maidens on winged horses, daughters of Wotan (unnamed mother). Restore fallen heroes to life and convey them to Walhall, where they guard the gods against potential enemies. Their names are Wagner's invention: Gerhilde (armed with a spear, soprano) – Waltraute (mighty in battle, alto) – Ortlinde (wields sword with flashing point, soprano) – Helmwige (warrior with helmet, soprano) – Schwertleite (armed with a sword, alto) – Siegrune (bestower of runes of victory, alto) – Rossweisse (rides a shining horse, alto) – Grimgerde (protected by a helmet, alto). All in *Walküre*, Waltraute also in *Götterdämmerung.*

Vassals

Hagen's pliant followers who are meant to witness Siegfried's alleged betrayal of King Gunther and, if need be, exonerate their master for executing the traitor. Tenors and basses, in *Götterdämmerung.*

Walraute

One of the eight Valkyries. Is unsuccessful in persuading Brünnhilde to return the ring to the Rhinemaidens. Forecasts the end of the gods. Mezzo-soprano, in *Walküre* and *Götterdämmerung.*

Wanderer

Wotan, ruler of the gods, roams the world as observer. Challenges Mime to battle of wits, spares the loser's life, prophesies Mime's death at the hands of a fearless hero (Siegfried), opposes Siegfried's quest for Brünnhilde, in order to prove the hero's intrepidity. Has his spear shattered by Siegfried and relinquishes his rule. Bass-baritone, in *Siegfried.*

Women

Ladies from King Gunther's Court and Gutrune's bridesmaids. They briefly comment on Siegfried's alleged treachery, and are present at the final conflagration. Sopranos, in *Götterdämmerung.*

Woodbird
Warns Siegfried to beware of Mime, advises him to obtain Fafner's ring and Tarnhelm, and shows him the way to Brünnhilde's rock. Soprano, in *Siegfried.*

Wotan
Chief of the gods. Husband of Fricka, father of Siegmund, Sieglinde, Brünnhilde and eight Valkyries. Rules the world from his castle, Walhall, built by Fafner and Fasolt. Robs Alberich of gold, ring and Tarnhelm to pay the giants. Embroiled in false treaties and broken promises, he creates the race of the Wälsungs: Siegmund and Sieglinde, and their son Siegfried, who is to rectify Wotan's judicial errors and return the ring to the Rhine. In *Walküre,* Fricka persuades Wotan to sacrifice the adulterous Siegmund. He punishes Brünnhilde's disobedience (she had come to Siegmund's aid) by banishing her, asleep, on a rock. On Brünnhilde's entreaty, he surrounds the rock with impenetrable flames. When Siegfried is killed by Hagen, Wotan commits Walhall and his fellow gods to the flames. Bass-baritone, in *Rheingold, Walküre* and, as Wanderer, in *Siegfried.*

Synopsis of the *Ring*

Das Rheingold

Scene 1: *On the Bed of the Rhine*

Woglinde, Wellgunde and Flosshilde, the Rhinemaidens, are at play, swimming and splashing about. Flosshilde warns her sisters not to neglect their duty, the guarding of the Rhinegold.

The ugly dwarf Alberich appears from below and the beautiful spectacle enchants him. The Rhinemaidens tease him, pretending to find him attractive and then mocking him. Alberich pursues them furiously, when the Rhinegold begins to glow. The Rhinemaidens swim joyously around it, basking in its brilliance. They inform Alberich that a ring could be forged from the gold, and that the wearer of the ring might become all-powerful. They add, however, that this will never be, since the gold can be obtained only by forswearing love, and no living creature would ever do that.

Alberich, maddened by the Rhinemaidens' taunts, renounces love, snatches the gold and disappears with it. The Rhinemaidens bewail their lost gold.

Scene 2: *Open Space on a Mountain Top*

Wotan hails his new fortress, Walhall, which the giants, Fasolt and Fafner, have built for him. His wife Fricka reminds him of the price he has agreed to pay: Freia, her own beautiful young sister. Wotan plays for time, expecting shortly to hear from Loge, his sly adviser, when Freia hastens to the scene, pursued by the giants. Freia's brothers, Donner and Froh, are unable to protect the goddess, while Wotan refuses to accede to the giants' demands. Loge arrives at last. He reports Alberich's theft of the Rhinegold and the dwarf's renunciation of love. He also discloses that Alberich has succeeded in forging a ring from the gold. The giants are now prepared to revoke their original agreement, provided Wotan procures Alberich's gold for them. Wotan, however, wishes to obtain the ring for himself.

The giants carry Freia off, and the gods begin to grow feeble and old, since they are no longer sustained by Freia's golden apples. Wotan resolves to descend to Nibelheim, Alberich's abode. Guided by Loge, he plans to win Alberich's ring and the gold.

Scene 3: *Nibelheim*

Compelled by Alberich, Mime has forged the Tarnhelm, a magic cap with a triple function – it renders its wearer invisible, transports him with lightning speed, and/or transforms him into somebody or something else. Mime's attempt to keep the Tarnhelm for himself is brutally thwarted by Alberich. Wotan and Loge arrive to find Mime lamenting Alberich's cruelty towards himself and his fellow Nibelungs.

Alberich appears, driving his workers before him. He sees himself as the future ruler of the world, and he predicts his eventual ascendancy over Wotan and all his gods. Loge coaxes Alberich into demonstrating the Tarnhelm's magic power. Easily duped, the Nibelung turns himself first into a huge serpent, and then into a tiny toad. Wotan steps on the creature, who is retransformed into Alberich. Loge ties him up and conveys him, with Wotan, to the upper region.

Scene 4: *Open Space on a Mountain Top*

Wotan and Loge have arrived on the mountain height with their prisoner. Wotan demands Alberich's gold for his ransom. With the help of his magic ring, Alberich summons the Nibelungs who appear with the golden treasure. When they depart, Alberich asks for his freedom, but he is forced to surrender the Tarnhelm first. Wotan finally demands the ring and, when Alberich refuses to part with it, he tears it from the dwarf's hand. Alberich then casts a spell on the ring, cursing it and all its future owners.

When Alberich vanishes, the other gods arrive to greet Wotan. The giants return with Freia, whose presence restores the gods' youthful appearance. To ransom Freia, the giants request sufficient gold to cover her up completely, so that she is hidden from their sight. Wotan is forced to surrender the Tarnhelm as well, but when Fasolt examines the piled-up treasure, he can still see Freia's eyes. Fafner points to Wotan's ring, to stop up the chink. Wotan indignantly refuses.

The giants renounce their proposed deal and are about to abduct Freia when Erda appears from below. She warns Wotan to yield the ring and to flee from its curse. She adds that the end of the gods is near, whereupon Wotan throws the ring upon the pile. The giants release Freia, but Alberich's curse is seen to work: Fafner kills his brother for the ring. Donner calls up a storm to clear the air, and Froh directs a path for a rainbow bridge, for the gods to ascend into Walhall.

The Sword motif gives notice of Wotan's bold plan to create a descendant who, armed with Wotan's sword, shall secure the gods' survival. The Rhinemaidens are heard bewailing their lost gold, as the gods enter into Walhall. Loge, however, goes his own way.

Die Walküre

Act 1: *Hunding's House*

Scene 1
A mighty ash tree dominates the room. It is night. Siegmund drags himself inside and collapses by the hearth. Sieglinde, wife of the absent Hunding, revives him, first with water, then with mead. Unaware of their blood relationship, they are drawn to each other. Siegmund is about to leave, but when Sieglinde reveals that 'adversity lives in this house', he decides to await Hunding's return.

Scene 2
Hunding arrives and regards the stranger with suspicion, especially on account of his resemblance to Sieglinde. In recounting his recent armed exploits, Siegmund reveals himself as a champion of the oppressed. He refuses to give his name, and discloses that his family's foes had sacked his home and killed his mother, and that he had lost trace of his father and sister. Hunding recognizes his foe in Siegmund, offers him shelter for the night, but challenges him to a fight in the morning.

Scene 3
Left alone, weaponless, Siegmund recalls that his father had promised him a sword which he would find in the hour of his greatest need. Sieglinde returns, having drugged Hunding's drink. She now urges Siegmund to make good use of the short time left to him. Her account of recent events culminates in the story of a sword which had been lodged in the tree by a stranger and which nobody had ever been able to withdraw. He who could win it would also rescue her from her loveless marriage. The door flies open. The spring air has melted the ice on its hinges, and Siegmund's poetic vision anticipates the discovery of their true relationship:

> To Springtime's passionate splendour
> the stubborn door must surrender.
>
> To seek its sister,
> Spring has flown in.
>
> The sisterly bride
> is set free by her brother.
>
> Now Love is mated with Spring.

The siblings realize who they are and, clinging to each other, they utter their names, Siegmund and Sieglinde. Siegmund pulls the sword from the tree, names it 'Nothung', meaning sword of his 'need', and presents it to his sister as his bridal gift. The orchestra celebrates their ecstatic union.

Act II: *A Wild, Rocky Region*

Scene 1
Wotan commands Brünnhilde, his favourite Valkyrie daughter, to shield Siegmund in his forthcoming fight with Hunding. Fricka, guardian of the sanctity of marriage, reproaches Wotan for his infidelity in begetting the incestuous twins, and demands Siegmund's death. Reluctantly, Wotan agrees to withdraw his protection. Fricka, however, also requests Brünnhilde's non-interference, and Wotan is forced to abandon his son.

Scene 2
In a heart-rending scene between father and daughter, Wotan discloses his thwarted plans for creating a free hero and for the survival of the gods. He is ready to relinquish his guardianship of the world and to hand it over to Alberich. All he can do now is to await his own downfall. In his despair, he revokes his earlier command and orders Brünnhilde to obey Fricka. Brünnhilde protests, but only succeeds in provoking her father's threats of appalling retribution if she were to disobey him.

Scene 3
In their flight from Hunding's house, the twin lovers are resting for a while. Sieglinde's premonition of Siegmund's death in battle has made her collapse.

Scene 4
Brünnhilde appears. True to Wotan's command, she warns Siegmund of his imminent defeat. He defies her, relying on his father's invincible sword. Brünnhilde informs him that Wotan has invalidated the sword's power, but adds that Sieglinde is bearing his child. Siegmund, however, threatens to kill his bride and himself, 'with one stroke'. Overcome with pity for his plight, admiring his heroism, Brünnhilde decides to disregard Wotan's command and promises to protect Siegmund in his battle with Hunding.

Scene 5
The enemies meet. Brünnhilde shields Siegmund, but Wotan himself shatters the sword Nothung with his spear and allows Hunding to kill Siegmund. Brünnhilde gathers the splintered sword and flees with Sieglinde. Wotan's contemptuous gesture

strikes Hunding dead. The god then sets out in furious pursuit of his disobedient daughter.

Act III: *A Mountain Top*

Scene 1
The Valkyries, Wotan's fierce warrior maidens, are on their way from the battlefield to Walhall. Riding through the air, they meet on a summit, fallen heroes slung over their saddles. Brünnhilde is the last to arrive, carrying Sieglinde and the splinters of Siegmund's sword with her. She begs her sisters for help, since Wotan is pursuing her, about to exact punishment for her disobedience. She pleads in vain. None of the Valkyries is prepared to incur Wotan's displeasure. Sieglinde has no will to survive without Siegmund, until Brünnhilde informs her that she is to give birth to Siegfried, Siegmund's son. Brünnhilde hands the splintered sword to the ecstatic Sieglinde and directs her to a forest shelter, where she will be safe from Wotan's wrath and where Siegfried shall be born.

Scene 2
The enraged Wotan arrives. Brünnhilde, who at first hides behind her sisters, steps forward to face her father. Wotan pronounces her punishment. She is to lose her status as a Valkyrie and is to become a mortal woman instead:

> Here on this rock lodged shall you be;
> defenceless, in sleep locked by my spell.
> One man shall conquer the maid,
> when he wakes her and makes her his own.

Her sisters plead with Wotan, but are unable to move him. The god commands them to abandon their disobedient sister.

Scene 3
Wotan and Brünnhilde are alone. Brünnhilde tries to convince her father that, in aiding Siegmund, she had been acting in Wotan's own interest. The god does not agree. Yielding to Fricka's irrefutable arguments, he had commanded Siegmund's death, and Brünnhilde had flouted his injunction. Wotan the law-giver is obliged to abide by the law. In sorrow he sentences Brünnhilde. The former Valkyrie begs her father to modify the punishment by protecting her chaste slumber with an impenetrable wall of fire.

Wotan consents. He takes her godhood away with a kiss, then gently lowers her to a rock beneath a pine tree. He covers her with her shield and summons Loge to ring the rock with a circle of flames. He grips his spear and proclaims:

No man who fears my sacred spear-point
shall fare through this fiery sea!

Sadly the god strides away. His one remaining hope is for a free hero who may eventually shoulder his, Wotan's, burden and make amends for the god's wrongdoings.

Siegfried

Act I: *A Forest Cave*

Scene 1
Mime has set up his forge in the forest where Fafner, in the shape of a dragon, sleeps upon his hoard. Siegfried demands a sword from Mime, but the smith is unable to produce a weapon which the strong young lad cannot break into bits. The impatient Siegfried obtains information from his foster-father about his parents and about the fragments of his father's shattered sword. He orders Mime to reforge the sword and storms away.

Scene 2
Wotan, the Wanderer, enters and invites Mime to stake his head in a trial of knowledge. Each is to ask three questions of the other. Mime is unable to answer the Wanderer's final question, 'Who is to forge the fragments of the shattered sword?' The Wanderer supplies the answer himself: 'He who knows no fear shall forge the sword. As for your head, I leave it to him who has never learnt what fear is.' Left alone, Mime is in a state of terror. He will lose his head to Siegfried, unless he can teach him fear. But if Siegfried learns fear, nobody is to forge the sword which can kill Fafner, thus depriving him, Mime, of the longed-for hoard.

Scene 3
Siegfried returns and asks for his sword, but Mime is anxious to teach him fear. He is unsuccessful, and Siegfried proceeds to melt down the splintered fragments and to reforge his father's sword, while Mime concocts a poisonous brew which he intends to offer Siegfried, as soon as the lad has killed the dragon.

Act II: *The Depth of the Forest*

Scene 1
Alberich is keeping watch near the entrance to Fafner's cave. Wotan arrives, again as the Wanderer, and acquaints Alberich with Mime's designs on the ring. He wakes Fafner so that

Alberich may ask the monster to grant him the ring, in exchange for being warned of Siegfried's approach. Fafner declines and the Wanderer disappears, laughing.

Scene 2
Mime arrives with Siegfried. The dwarf tries, once again, to teach the lad fear, by describing the monster's fearsome aspect and habits. Siegfried, still unafraid, decides to pit his wits and his strength against the dragon, and sends Mime away. He reclines in the shade of a tree and listens to the birds above him. He muses about his dead parents. Trying to imitate the songs of the birds, he fashions a reed pipe. Its sound fails to establish the desired contact, but when he blows his horn the dragon (Fafner) comes out of his lair. Siegfried pierces the heart of the monster who, with his dying breath, warns Siegfried that Mime intends to kill him. Licking the dragon's blood off his fingers causes Siegfried to understand the language of the birds. One of them advises him to take possession of the ring and the Tarnhelm.

Scene 3
While Siegfried is inside the monster's cave, Mime is intercepted by Alberich. Both brothers claim to be legitimate heirs to Fafner's hoard. Siegfried emerges, holding both Tarnhelm and ring, while Alberich and Mime hide and watch. The bird warns Siegfried to beware of Mime, who now comes out of his hiding-place and offers Siegfried a refreshing drink. As a consequence of having tasted the dragon's blood, Siegfried understands not only the birds' language, but also Mime's treacherous thoughts. Mime intends to poison Siegfried in order to gain ring, Tarnhelm and the golden treasure. To prevent this, Siegfried kills Mime. The bird now advises him to make his way through a wall of fire which surrounds the slumbering Brünnhilde, the destined bride of a fearless hero – Siegfried. The bird flutters ahead, and Siegfried follows.

Act III: *The Foot of Brünnhilde's Rock*

Scene 1
The Wanderer calls up Erda to consult her about the future. When she advises him to seek guidance from Brünnhilde instead, he informs her of their daughter's disobedience and punishment. Erda is dismayed and wishes to be released from his spell, but the Wanderer wants to know how the gods' downfall may be averted. Erda is unwilling to prolong the discussion, and the Wanderer announces that he is about to bequeath the world to Siegfried. With that he allows Erda to descend.

Scene 2
Siegfried approaches. The Wanderer's questions about the sword, its origin, its splintering, its reforging, irritate Siegfried, and at last he bids the 'ancient meddler' to take himself off. Wotan bars Siegfried's way with his outstretched spear, which Siegfried shatters, imagining that the Wanderer is in fact the murderer of Siegmund, Siegfried's father. Wotan picks up the splinters of his spear and vanishes.

Scene 3: *Brünnhilde's Rock*
Sounding his horn, Siegfried plunges into the wall of fire. He finds the sleeping Brünnhilde and wakens her with a kiss. She welcomes him rapturously, but soon realizes that her loss of godhood has made her a mortal woman, subject to her new master's impetuosity. Her longing for her deliverer, however, has become so irresistible that she surrenders to her destiny, 'Living in love, triumphant in death!'

Götterdämmerung

Prologue: *Brünnhilde's Rock*

The three Norns, weavers of the rope of destiny, discuss events past, present and to come. Wotan, they relate, had given one of his eyes for drinking from the Well of Wisdom by the World Ash Tree. He then tore a branch from the tree which he shaped into a mighty spear, engraving it with runes of wisdom. This made him lord of the world. But the tree began to wither and the well dried up. A young hero, Siegfried, later shattered Wotan's spear with his sword. The god then ordered the World Ash Tree to be felled. The Norns also retell the story of the building of Walhall by the giants, and they contrast the gods' former stronghold with its present state, as the immortals and their heroes are seated in Walhall, awaiting the end of the world. The logs that once were the World Ash Tree are heaped around Walhall, and soon Wotan will command Loge to set them alight. The Norns find it increasingly difficult to weave their rope, since Alberich's curse adheres to its strands. As the rope breaks, they descend to Erda, their mother.

Day breaks, and Siegfried and Brünnhilde emerge from their cave. She bids him go forth into the world, on fresh adventures. They swear eternal love and fidelity, and exchange tokens of love. Siegfried gives Brünnhilde his ring, and she hands over her horse, Grane, to him. Leaving Brünnhilde in the protection of the wall of flames, he rides away. She watches his descent to the Rhine. The orchestral interlude describes his river journey.

Act I: *The Hall of the Gibichungs*

Scene 1
The feeble King Gunther, lord of the Gibichungs, asks Hagen, his half-brother, to assist him in his quest for prestigious ventures. Hagen, son of Alberich and of Gunther's mother, advises him and his half-sister Gutrune to make advantageous marriages.

Scene 2
When Siegfried arrives at Gunther's court, Hagen makes him fall in love with Gutrune with the help of a potion which causes him to forget Brünnhilde. Prompted by Hagen, Siegfried promises Gunther to obtain Brünnhilde for him. They seal their plot with an oath of bloodbrotherhood and immediately set out on their quest. Hagen remains behind, guarding the hall, confidently awaiting the outcome of the plot – his possession of the ring.

Scene 3: *Brünnhilde's Rock*
Waltraute, Brünnhilde's sister and former fellow-Valkyrie, has secretly left Walhall to visit Brünnhilde. She implores Brünnhilde to return the ring to the Rhine, in order to lift Alberich's curse which is responsible for the present state of the gods, who are passively awaiting their downfall. The logs of the fomer World Ash Tree, she reports, are heaped around Walhall, ready to be ignited by Loge. Brünnhilde refuses to part with Siegfried's token of love, and she sends her sister away. Siegfried, disguised as Gunther (with the help of the Tarnhelm), penetrates the wall of flames and wrests the ring from Brünnhilde. He forces her into her chamber but, true to his oath of bloodbrotherhood, places his sword between himself and Brünnhilde.

Act II *Outside the Hall of the Gibichungs*

Scene 1
Alberich appears to Hagen and urges him to regain the ring.

Scene 2
As Alberich vanishes, Siegfried arrives and informs Hagen of Gunther and Brünnhilde's imminent arrival. Gutrune questions Siegfried about his conquest of Brünnhilde, and wonders whether her new husband has remained faithful to her.

Scene 3
Hagen summons the Gibichung vassals to welcome Gunther and his bride.

Scene 4
When Brünnhilde sees Siegfried at Gutrune's side, she is puzzled and mortified. Noticing the ring on Siegfried's finger, however, she is convinced of Siegfried's treachery and infidelity. Hagen persuades Gunther that Siegfried had broken his oath, when he had conquered and slept with his bloodbrother's new wife. Siegfried is too confused to grasp the meaning of Brünnhilde's wrath. Both he and Brünnhilde swear an oath, protesting their own integrity.

Scene 5
Hagen, Gunther and Brünnhilde plot Siegfried's death. Brünnhilde reveals to Hagen that her magical spells (cast before Siegfried came to the Gibichung court) have made the hero invulnerable. Knowing, however, that he would never flinch from an enemy, she omitted to protect his back.

Act III: *A Wooded Valley on the Rhine*

Scene 1
The Rhinemaidens still hope to regain their stolen gold. They hear Siegfried's hunting horn. The hero has been detached from the hunting party, and the Rhinemaidens promise him rich booty, were he to grant them the ring on his finger. Siegfried refuses to part with Brünnhilde's love token, whereupon the Rhinemaidens prophesy his impending doom unless he gives them the doom-laden ring. Siegfried contemplates parting with the ring, but he will not give it under duress.

Scene 2
Siegfried hears the Gibichung hunting call. Meeting up with the party, he is invited by Hagen to tell them about his ability to understand the language of the birds. This prompts Siegfried to entertain Gunther, Hagen and the assembled huntsmen with the story of his slaying of the dragon and of Mime's death. Skilfully guided by Hagen, Siegfried is set to continue the tale. Aided by Hagen's potion (the antidote to his potion of forgetfulness), Siegfried now remembers and relates his first sight of Brünnhilde and their rapturous union. Hagen murders Siegfried by thrusting his spear into his unprotected back. Siegfried invokes his beloved Brünnhilde, then falls back and dies. His body is borne to the Gibichung hall.

Scene 3
On seeing her dead husband, Gutrune collapses by his bier. Hagen kills Gunther in the struggle over the dead man's ring. Brünnhilde, now grown wise through her suffering, and understanding Siegfried's unwitting treachery, takes the ring from Siegfried's hand. She has the hero's body placed on a

funeral pyre and throws a fiery brand at the logs. She mounts her horse and rides into the flames. The Rhinemaidens retrieve the ring, and while Hagen makes a desperate attempt to gain it for himself, they draw him into the depths of the river. Walhall is destroyed by the flames. The end of the gods has come, and the waters of the Rhine engulf the world, which is purified and redeemed from the curse on love. The Assurance motif suggests the possibility of a new beginning.

The Bayreuth Theatre in 1876;
watercolour by Susanne Schinkel

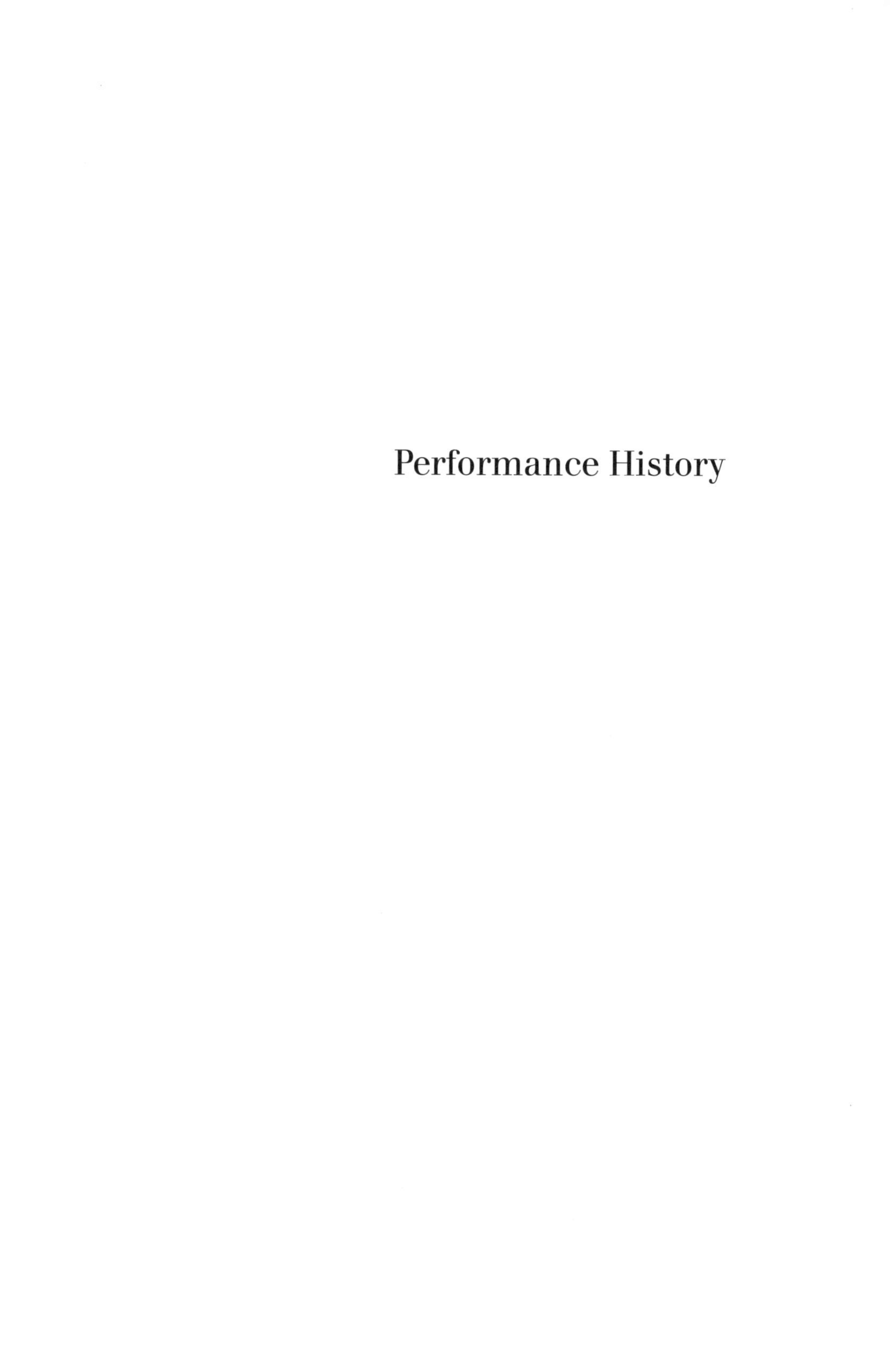

Performance History

Performance History

Overview

If we discount the unauthorized stagings in Munich of *Rheingold* (1869) and *Walküre* (1870), it all began in 1876 with the opening of the Festspielhaus in Bayreuth, when Wagner gave the first performance of the complete *Ring* cycle. Two years later Angelo Neumann presented the *Ring* in Leipzig, and in 1882 gave it in Her Majesty's Theatre in London. Gustav Mahler conducted the cycle at Covent Garden in 1892, and Cosima produced it at Bayreuth in 1896, thirteen years after Wagner's death. All these were, on the whole, homage stagings – they deferred to Wagner's original production of 1876.

Things changed with Siegfried Wagner's reign at Bayreuth, which lasted a quarter of a century, from 1906 to 1930. Wagner's son was a cautious reformer who made good use of electric instead of gas lighting and whose three-dimensional sets superseded the hitherto obligatory painted backdrops.

The first true innovator was Adolphe Appia, whose technique of creating space through lighting led to highly stylized stagings at Basle (1920–25). Twenty years later, in 1940, Sergey Eisenstein produced *Walküre* in Moscow. He pointed the way to realizations of Wagner's works which connected them to the contemporary social scene. With the re-opening, after the war years, of the Festspielhaus in 1951, the ever-changing principles that gave rise to stagings of great originality were symbolism, realism, anti-romanticism and surrealism. Wieland Wagner's stylized representations, buttressed by innovatory lighting, revolutionized the practice of staging his grandfather's works. Significant contrasts to the avant-garde style were provided by Peter Hall (Bayreuth, 1983–6) and Otto Schenk (New York, 1990s). Both producers resurrected Wagner's original stage directions and offered unashamedly romantic interpretations. At the same time, German producers were favouring increasingly provocative stagings, which could be regarded as the operatic equivalent of the theatre of the absurd. Some representatives of this trend are Joachim Herz, Götz Friedrich, Nikolaus Lehnhoff, Richard Jones and the late Ruth Berghaus.

Bayreuth

Richard Wagner, 1876

There were no professional stage producers in Wagner's time. Composers or their assistants did much of the work. They instructed the singers where to enter and where to leave, and they advised on deportment and demeanour. But Wagner needed to make the plots, sub-plots and other complications of the *Ring* tetralogy intelligible to his audiences. To achieve this, he had first to make them intelligible to his singers. He held *Leseproben* (reading rehearsals) for his cast, and even for the chorus, to enable them to understand and grow into their roles. For subsequent *Bühnenproben* (stage rehearsals) he assembled a team of experts who, together with the composer, were the producers of the tetralogy.

Carl Brandt (1828–81), foremost stage technician of his time, was in charge of the lighting and the scenic equipment; he also devised multifarious stage tricks to represent swimming, flying, becoming invisible, changing appearance, a rainbow, fire and other effects. In addition he was responsible for realizing Wagner's principle of synchronization, which required both scenic effects and lighting to be co-ordinated precisely with the music. In the opening scene of *Rheingold*, for example, Wagner requested the gold to be lit with increasing luminosity, where his stage direction reads 'magical golden light streams through the water'. The light reaches its peak of brightness exactly on the last note of a rising horn-call.

Richard Fricke (1818–1903), master of the ballet at Dessau, was the third member of the production team. He helped to turn the singers into respectable actors and matched their deportment to the music. He also encouraged them on their aerial, aquatic and subterranean manoeuvres. Snatches from his Bayreuth diaries reveal the complexity of his task:

> Studied swimming machinery. Anxious and apprehensive … How will the singers find sufficient intrepidity to place themselves into such contraptions? They will be too scared to sing … I said, 'Courage! You will positively enjoy the swim.' The ladder is put in position. Brandt and I help her up. We fasten her to the cradle and begin to drive her gently about. Her face loses its terror. Now Lilli [Lehmann] wants to have her go. Soon all three laugh and frolic. And they do swim. Now Wagner turns up. They do the whole scene for him and they sing beautifully. When they got out of their machines, Wagner thanked them with tears of joy in his eyes, and kissed and cuddled them mightily … Today Wagner put bunches of flowers into the Rhinemaidens' swimming cradles.

Fricke had a harder time with Alberich. Carl Hill was an outstanding singer and a plausible actor, but was prone to dizzy spells. 'Slippery slime,' Alberich cries, 'I stagger and stumble!' Promptly a trap-door opens, and a lift whisks him from the top to the bottom. Hill's protests were countered by the resourceful Fricke. 'In Brandt's machinery, plunging down becomes a positive pleasure!' Hill was terrified, but he let himself be persuaded. 'I would not have done this for anybody in the whole world,' he later declared, 'except for Wagner.' The composer realized the extent of Hill's effort. When the trembling singer arrived at the bottom, he found a bottle of champagne waiting for him. Wagner had labelled it 'Rheingold'.

Joseph Hoffmann (1831–1904), Viennese painter of historical landscapes, was commissioned to design the sets. The style he chose, in consultation with the composer, was late Romantic. Carl Doepler (1824–1905), illustrator and designer, provided costumes which displayed a kind of colour-leitmotif, blue for the gods and red for the Nibelungs. Wagner found the designs too fussy, and Cosima detested them.

The Hall of the Gibichungs; set design by Joseph Hoffmann, Bayreuth 1876

The deliberate absence of a prompt box did not hamper the production team. They placed several prompters in the wings and even behind the scenery, and in case of need the cast would prompt one another.

On the day of the first performance of *Rheingold*, the singers found Wagner's 'Final Request' pinned up on their way to the stage:

> 'Clarity! Never address the audience, but always your fellow performers. During monologues, look either up or down, but never straight ahead. Last wish: Be good to me, my dears! Bayreuth, 13 August 1876, Richard Wagner.'

Carl Doepler's costume design for the character of Mime

Wagner performed his *Ring* cycle three times in the space of two and a half weeks, to tremendous public acclaim. The press was less enthusiastic. Eduard Hanslick disliked the proliferation of technical stage tricks, and he accused the composer of having become the servant of the chief engineer. The dialogues between Wotan and Fricka, and between Wotan and Brünnhilde (*Walküre*, Act II), he found 'abysmally boring', but he was enchanted with the final scene of *Siegfried* and with most of *Götterdämmerung*. Many of his fellow critics admired the multi-coloured vapour effects, such as clouds, invisibility and the transitions from scene to scene. They were not to know that the over-generous use of steam played havoc with the string instruments, which required frequent re-tuning.

Among the cast, filling the minor roles of Rossweisse (*Walküre*) and First Norn (*Götterdämmerung*), was Johanna Jachmann-Wagner, the composer's niece. Wagner was pleased with most, but not all of the singers. His special praise he reserved for Albert Niemann (Siegmund), Carl Schlosser (Mime), Carl Hill (Alberich) and Amalie Materna (Brünnhilde).

The conductor, Hans Richter (1843–1916), displeased Wagner on account of his slow tempos, and in his address to the festival's patrons in 1877 Wagner stated, 'Much was sketchy, much was unsatisfactory; there was neglect, including my own. My ideal was not realized.' He let it be known that there was nobody who could possibly stage an authentic *Ring* after his death.

Wagner had hoped to extend future festival seasons to include all his major works, from *Der fliegende Holländer* to *Parsifal*. After his death, however, Cosima became a virtual hermit who took no further interest in such plans. In 1883 and again in 1884, only *Parsifal* was performed. Wagner's production was initially rehearsed by Emil Scaria (Gurnemanz). By 1886 Cosima had been coaxed back into the Festspielhaus, and under her guardianship, the original *Parsifal* production was accompanied by eight performances of her own new staging of *Tristan und Isolde*. *Parsifal* continued to be presented in 1888

Cosima Wagner; portrait by Hans Thoma

(nine performances), 1889 (nine performances), 1891 (ten performances), 1892 (eight performances) and 1894 (nine performances). Wagner's dream of an extended repertoire was gradually being realized, for Cosima presented her own new *Meistersinger* production in 1888, her new *Tannhäuser* in 1891 and her new *Lohengrin* in 1894.

Cosima Wagner, 1896

While Wagner was alive, Cosima hesitated to contradict him. Thirteen years after his death, she dared to confound his gloomy forecast about the impossibility of anyone else staging an 'authentic' *Ring*. Aided by a new generation of performers and a team of talented scenic artists, she aimed at a revival of the 1876 production which would remedy its faults while preserving its objectives. Electricity had ousted gas, and the consequent possibility of spotlighting, and of using coloured lighting effects, called for imaginative rethinking of the technique of stagecraft.

To acquaint prospective singers with Wagner's intentions, Cosima had in 1892 opened a *Stilbildungsschule* (style training school). Head of this institution was Julius Kniese (1848–1905), Bayreuth's chorus master from 1884 to 1904. For a few years the school flourished, but by 1898 it had only five pupils, and Cosima closed it down. Nonetheless, a handful of promising singers had benefited from Kniese's tuition: Ellen Gulbranson (who sang Brünnhilde in Cosima's 1896 *Ring*), Alois Burgstaller (Siegfried), Hans Breuer (Mime) and Otto Briesemeister (Loge).

Alois Burgstaller as Siegfried in the 1896 production of *Siegfried* at Bayreuth

The scenery of the 1896 revival was created by Max Brückner (1836–1919), who based his sets on the 1876 designs by Joseph Hoffmann. Cosima encouraged him to improve on the older models by filling in more realistic detail.

Hans Thoma (1839–1924) and Arpad Schmidhammer (1857–1921) designed new costumes, which Cosima wanted 'to relate to no particular period'. They responded with far simpler costumes than Doepler had created in 1876, with reduced ornamentation, and a more meaningful colour scheme which provided characteristic colours and symbolic details for each wearer. Freia, for example, was clad in pink (to express youth), Erda in grey (for age) and Froh in green (for cheerfulness). Thoma went further. He tried to relate his colours to the emotional character of each scene. He therefore added a violet veil to Erda's grey robe in her challenging confrontations with Wotan (in *Rheingold* and *Siegfried*). Cosima even tolerated Thoma's more daring interpretations. In *Götterdämmerung* he dressed Siegfried in a suit of armour whose back was decorated with a serpent, the same symbol of guile that adorned Hagen's helmet.

Cosima's initial handicap – being a woman in charge of male singers – soon dissolved as she demonstrated her mental and physical strength. She showed the performers how to leap from rock to rock, how to forge a sword, how to swim, how to shamble like a dwarf and lurch like a giant. This earned the singers' respect, and whenever any of her detailed instructions were queried, she asked Siegfried, 'Was this not how papa did it in 1876?' The dutiful son, who in 1876 had been barely seven, always replied, 'Yes, mama.' This was Cosima's way of legitimizing her directives, and of admitting innovations by the back door.

She required her singers to stand still whenever possible and to present their profiles to the audience. She encouraged expressions of serenity and restrained gestures. She told the singers that their eyes were the mirrors of their souls, and she taught them the 'three-staged glance':

1. Direct your eyes at a point on the floor, some five yards away from you, the lids almost shrouding your gaze; this expresses weariness.
2. Slowly raise your gaze and your lids to eye level; this expresses longing.
3. Draw back your lids to widen the gaze; this expresses recognition.

Set design by Max Brückner for *Das Rheingold*, 1896

During rehearsals Cosima was seated in a curtained area on stage, where she could see, but was not seen. At the end she would distribute copious scribbled memoranda to her cast, to the conductor and even to members of the orchestra, containing words of praise and detailed suggestions for alterations and improvements.

On one matter Cosima remained adamant: the scenic representation must stay realistic, otherwise the audience might not be able to follow the action. When she read Adolphe Appia's revolutionary *Notes sur l'Anneau du Nibelungen* she wrote to Houston Stewart Chamberlain (husband of her daughter Eva), 'Appia seems to be unaware that the *Ring* was performed here in 1876. It follows that the staging is definitive and sacrosanct.'

Outstanding in Cosima's fine cast were Ellen Gulbranson and Lilli Lehmann, who alternated as Brünnhilde, Heinrich Vogl as Loge, Rosa Sucher as Sieglinde and Hans Breuer as Mime. Ellen Gulbranson managed to sing Brünnhilde at Bayreuth until her farewell appearance in 1924. Of the alternating Siegfrieds, the 24-year-old Alois Burgstaller, product of the *Stilbildungsschule*, was generally liked, whereas Wilhelm Grüning was not. George Bernard Shaw wrote that he could not conscientiously advise Englishmen to come to Bayreuth until Grüning came to England.

The old swimming machines had been superseded by colossal, invisible 'fishing rods' at the ends of which Woglinde, Wellgunde and Flosshilde displayed their vocal and physical allure. As one reporter wrote, 'they dived through the waters with the speed of lightning.'

The dragon, though, was almost as great a disaster as its predecessor had been twenty years before. It was said to look like a hippopotamus, and it came tottering sideways out of its cave, presumably for the convenience of the stage hands. A mixed reception was accorded to the Valkyries, small children on wooden horses. Cosima's staging was generally acclaimed, but the press also asked her to remedy scenic infelicities, such as the visible steps in the rocks and the clumsy collapse of Gunther's hall.

Three conductors shared the five cycles of performances. Felix Mottl (1856–1911), who had assisted Wagner in 1876, was now promoted to joint chief conductor, together with the experienced Hans Richter. The third conductor was Siegfried Wagner, who was entrusted with one complete cycle. Richard Strauss was not impressed with Siegfried's stick technique, but Mahler and Shaw found him likeable and full of promise.

Artistically, the 1896 performances eclipsed those of 1876. Both Brückner's naturalistic scenery and Cosima's method of acting persisted, with only gradual reforms, until 1931. During that period there were forty-one performances of the *Ring* cycle at Bayreuth.

Cosima probably felt that Wagner would have revised his pessimistic prophecy had he lived to witness her achievement. She summed up her own and her artists' thoughts in a letter of August 1897 to Prince Hohenlohe:

> Our artists are sad when they part from one another. Many have told me that only here, in Bayreuth, are they truly alive. To witness how the most sublime works of art touch their hearts so directly moves me profoundly.

Cosima and Siegfried Wagner, 1897–1904

The next eight years were a period of consolidation, marked by the grooming of Cosima's son for the triple roles of conductor, producer and future director of the Bayreuth Festivals.

In 1897 Siegfried Wagner shared the rostrum with Hans Richter, but two years later he conducted all *Ring* performances. In 1901 the programme named him, for the first time, as co-producer with his mother, and he also conducted one of the two cycles. The 1904 performances were again shared by two conductors, Hans Richter and Franz Beidler. The latter was Cosima's son-in-law, having married her daughter Isolde. His début was marred by a disagreement, probably engineered by Cosima, between himself and Siegfried, and after conducting *Parsifal* in 1906 he was not invited to Bayreuth again.

Siegfried Wagner, 1906–14

The 1906 programme still listed Cosima Wagner as producer and Siegfried as *Spielleiter*, meaning that he was in charge of Cosima's original staging. Being a devoted son and a diplomat, he conscientiously preserved his mother's concept and instructions, biding his time. Indeed Cosima, having suffered a stroke in December 1906, shortly before her sixty-ninth birthday, handed the direction of the whole Bayreuth undertaking to Siegfried, and never entered the Festspielhaus again. Cosima probably also realized that Bayreuth was in danger of becoming a museum, and that Siegfried must be given an opportunity to re-interpret his father's works. She was a devoted mother.

Siegfried's reign began with his preparations, in 1907, for the following year's festival season. It ended with his death in 1930, just four months after the death of his mother. His talents as a director, producer and conductor were obvious from the beginning, whereas his own operas are now, quite undeservedly, almost forgotten. *Der Bärenhäuter*, *Herzog Wildfang*, *Schwarzschwanenreich* and *Bruder Lustig* are melodious, dramatically compelling and well worth reviving. As a conductor, he earned Hans Richter's accolade, 'I am pleased you have the score in your head, and not your head in the score.'

The year 1907 was marred by a peculiar tragedy. The baritone Theodor Bertram (1869–1907) was a true Bayreuth stalwart, whose Festspielhaus début had been in 1892 as one of the Mastersingers, Konrad Nachtigall. He later sang the Dutchman, Amfortas (*Parsifal*) and, above all, Wotan (in 1901, 1902, 1904 and 1906). One of the oldest surviving recordings from Bayreuth testifies – in spite of the atrocious background noise – to his glorious, noble diction, when Wotan greets Walhall (*Rheingold*, Scene 2). In February 1907 his wife was drowned in a disaster at sea. Bertram took to drink, became insolvent, was plagued by blackmailers and – the final calamity – was not asked to repeat his Wotan at Bayreuth. So he travelled there in 1908, booked into the Station Hotel and hanged himself in his bedroom.

Press and public were wondering whether Siegfried would present a new production of the *Ring* in 1908. His mother had rejected Appia's daring new ideas. Would Siegfried take note of him, or possibly of Gordon Craig (1872–1966)? Craig was Ellen Terry's son, and his innovations in scenic design, costumes and, most notably, in lighting had astonished theatre-goers in London, Berlin and Moscow. Siegfried let it be known that he admired Craig's work, that he was especially interested in refining the lighting apparatus in the Festspielhaus and that he was in close touch with technical advances in that field.

The 1908 *Ring* was still billed as Cosima's production, but Siegfried had developed it quite considerably. He introduced spotlighting, and his acting area featured three-dimensional scenery which superseded the painted backdrop. Albert Schweitzer saw Siegfried at work, and wrote in his *Memories of Cosima and Siegfried Wagner*, 'Siegfried was a marvellous producer ... He told his singers, "Don't imitate me – you are not parrots. Simply intensify your own ideas of your role. Act your part in accordance with your own temperament and character."'

Not everybody liked Siegfried's innovations. He was attacked by some traditionalists for deviating from the Master's ways. In addition, some of his cast let him down. Bernard Shaw said of the first *Rheingold* scene, 'The three Rhinemaidens not being able to sing like salmon, sang like pheasants instead ... Alberich was jolly well out of it.'

A further two *Ring* cycles were given in 1909. Apart from a few cast changes, these repeated and consolidated the previous year's achievements. This time some critics found that Siegfried's reforms had not gone far enough, and they asked for a 'stronger personality' to be in charge of future *Ring* productions. Others wondered whether the festivals were still a meaningful enterprise. Siegfried Wagner answered his critics in his traditional farewell speech to his artists. 'The Festspiele,' he said, 'are going to continue so long as there are people who are willing to dedicate their talents and their strength of purpose to the man who built this house.'

Siegfried's next *Ring* presentation was in 1911. Again he cautiously amended, added and axed. Making better use of the cyclorama, first seen in 1908, he created a new staging of the second scene of *Rheingold*, which was admired by the audience and approved by the press. The Viennese *Neue Freie Presse* wrote, 'Bayreuth has no past. It only has a future.'

Further scenic improvements took place in the two cycles of 1912. Siegfried's admiration for Max Reinhardt's theatrical productions in Berlin inspired him to find new ways of turning his singers into convincing actors. In the 1912 cast-list we find Ottilie Metzger as Flosshilde (*Rheingold*), Grimgerde (*Walküre*), Second Norn, Waltraute and Flosshilde (*Götterdämmerung*). She was to die, thirty-one years later, in Auschwitz.

Audiences at the 1914 *Ring* detected further scenic alterations. New three-dimensional rocks dominated the stage in *Walküre*, *Siegfried* and *Götterdämmerung*. Unobtrusive tracks criss-crossed the rocky expanse, allowing fearless access, lingering and departure.

An appearance record was established by Hans Breuer (1868–1929), who had been singing Mime in *Rheingold* and *Siegfried* ever since 1896, a total of fifty-eight performances. Another Bayreuth veteran was Ernestine Schumann-Heink, who had sung Erda for the first time under Cosima in 1896, and had reappeared in that role in 1897, 1899, 1901, 1902, 1906, 1911 and 1912. In 1914 she took, in addition, the parts of First Norn and Waltraute (*Götterdämmerung*). She had made her professional début at the age of fifteen and ended her career, equally incredibly, at the age of seventy-one, when she sang Erda at the Metropolitan Opera in New York.

A month before the opening of the 1914 festival, the Austrian heir apparent Franz Ferdinand had been assassinated in Sarajevo, and on the day of the performance of *Götterdämmerung* Berlin proclaimed that war was now inevitable. British, French, Austrian and Hungarian visitors made hasty exits from Bayreuth, and the planned twenty performances were curtailed to a mere eight. The large restaurant next to the Festspielhaus was turned into a hospital, and the Festspielhaus was locked up and kept under covers for the duration.

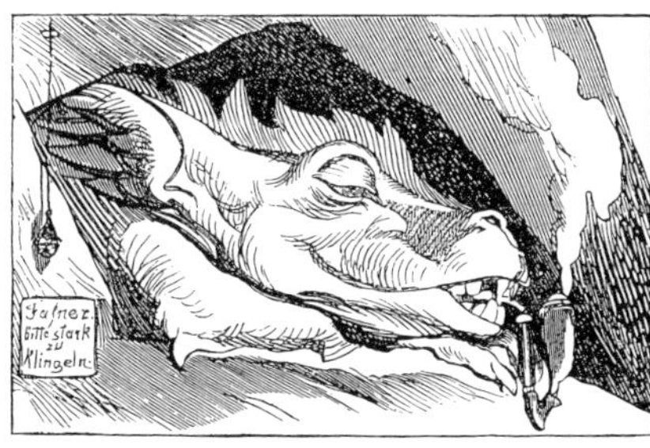

No customers for the next ten years – Bayreuth closes down.

Siegfried Wagner during a rehearsal, c. 1929

Siegfried Wagner, 1924–30

The First World War was over, and it took another five years before Siegfried Wagner was ready to re-open the Festspielhaus. But was Wagner still performable? The catastrophic war and its ruinous financial aftermath had created a climate not altogether conducive to operas with an ethical message. 'Erst kommt das Essen, dann kommt die Moral' (First give us to eat; moral questions can be discussed later) was the moral of Kurt Weill's *Die Dreigroschenoper*: a large part of the population would have agreed with this, but Siegfried Wagner relied on the survival, even in adversity, of the eternal truths in his father's works and on their healing qualities.

With very little capital at his disposal, he persuaded many of his soloists and orchestral players to perform without fees. He also raised funds by conducting numerous concerts. The receipts from these, together with donations from patrons, paid for the installation of improved lighting and for additional three-dimensional scenery, such as the six-columned Hall of the Gibichungs. Siegfried also perfected the moving cyclorama for *Walküre*, which rotated, almost imperceptibly, turning its blue sky at the beginning of the opera into a sombre, black cloudscape by the end of the second act. Reversing the process, the cyclorama turned from the thunderstorm at the beginning of the third act to azure sky for Wotan's farewell to Brünnhilde, before giving way to the sea of fire at the end. The Ride of the Valkyries had at last become a worthy spectacle. Shunning earlier unsuccessful attempts at verisimilitude, the aerial gallop was depicted through the skilful use of blinding lights.

In the cast-list of 1924 was Lauritz Melchior, making his début as Siegmund (*Walküre*). Daniela Thode, Siegfried Wagner's step-sister, was in charge of the costumes. The following year saw the arrival of Friedrich Schorr as Wotan, a part which he made his own until 1931.

The fiftieth anniversary of the festival fell in 1926, but by then Siegfried's funds had dried up, due to extensive building operations. He announced that he and his staff would be toasting the half-century by preparing for next year's festival. 'The best way to celebrate,' he said, 'is to work for the future.'

In 1927 Siegfried was able to fill the main parts with superlative singers, whose achievements can still be appreciated on recordings of the time – Friedrich Schorr's noble Wotan, Lauritz Melchior's ringing, baritonal Siegfried, and the new, stunning Brünnhilde of Nanny Larsén-Todsen, one of the many Scandinavian Brünnhildes to sing at Bayreuth. Frieda Leider, another Brünnhilde, this time from Berlin, shared the role with Larsén-Todsen in 1928, and was to be the darling of Bayreuth for many years.

The year 1930 was an *annus horribilis* for Bayreuth. On 1 April Cosima Wagner died, aged ninety-two, having survived

The Rhinemaidens on wires, Bayreuth 1930

her husband by forty-seven years. Four months later, on 4 August, their son Siegfried died, like his mother, of heart disease. He left his English wife, Winifred, and four children – Wieland (born 1917), Friedelind (1918), Wolfgang (1919) and Verena (1920).

Winifred Wagner, 1931–45

When the widowed Cosima Wagner revived her husband's *Ring* in 1896, she and her advisers resolved not to interfere with the Master's staging. When the widowed Winifred Wagner revived her husband's production in 1931, she and her advisers resolved not to interfere with Siegfried's staging. She instructed her husband's assistant, Alexander Spring, to prepare a replica of the 1930 production. The superlative cast included Friedrich Schorr and Rudolf Bockelmann as Wotan, Nanny Larsén-Todsen as Brünnhilde, Lauritz Melchior as Siegmund, Maria Müller as Sieglinde, Karin Branzell as Fricka and Erna Berger as the most mellifluous Woodbird that has ever been heard.

After a year's pause, in which completely new lighting machinery was installed, Bayreuth staged two *Ring* cycles in 1933, the first year of the Third Reich. Winifred Wagner had appointed Heinz Tietjen to devise a new *Ring*, with scenery by the progressive Emil Preetorious. Hitler, who attended the performances, expected a *Ring* that would pay homage to the National Socialists' concept of monumentalism in art. The old guard of supposed Wagnerians demanded a return to the earlier naturalistic stagings. Winifred Wagner, Tietjen and Preetorious had to steer a course between Scylla and Charybdis.

The Führer's presence coincided with Toscanini's withdrawal from conducting *Meistersinger* and *Parsifal*. Toscanini's telegram to Winifred Wagner displayed an uprightness rare at the time:

> Against all my hopes, the deplorable events which have violated my feelings as an artist and as a human being are still continuing. It is my duty, therefore, to inform you not to count any longer on my coming to Bayreuth, for the sake of your and my own peace of mind.

The cast-list for 1933 contained further illustrious names: Sigrid Onégin as Fricka and First Norn, Franz Völker as Siegmund, Max Lorenz as Siegfried, Emanuel List as Fafner, Hunding and Hagen, and the young Kirsten Flagstad in the beginner's role of Ortlinde, one of the Valkyries. Artistically, this was Bayreuth's golden age. The new scenery by Preetorious revealed a new style which rejected traditional realism in favour of stark, almost bare sets, foreshadowing the radically new stagings of Wieland Wagner in 1951. Preetorius's sets were of no identifiable period, least of all of a Teutonic one. Daniela Thode was dismayed when she saw the new sets. She left Bayreuth, where the new regime was intent on disregarding her stepfather's hallowed instructions.

Heinz Tietjen's innovations included a great increase in the size of the chorus. Wagner employed twenty-six vassals in *Götterdämmerung*, Siegfried increased their number to sixty-four, and Tietjen engaged 101. The stentorian clamour was awesome.

In 1934 Kirsten Flagstad was promoted from Ortlinde to Sieglinde, and the world took note. Tietjen, who was also a most sensitive conductor, shared the rostrum with Karl Elmendorff, but his scenic innovations incurred the displeasure of two of Siegfried's surviving sisters, Isolde and Eva. Even

Set design by Emil Preetorius; Act II, *Die Walküre*, 1938

Richard Strauss joined the malcontents. The less discriminating members of the audience would sing the German national anthem and the Nazi 'Horst Wessel' song at the end of the performances. Winifred ordered printed cards to be handed to the audience which read:

> The Führer requests visitors to refrain from singing the National Anthem or the Horst Wessel Lied, or from similar demonstrations. There is no more suitable manifestation of the glorious German spirit than the immortal works of the Master.

Not only was 1936 the year of the Olympic Games in Berlin, but it was a year of remembrance for Bayreuth. It was the sixtieth year of the festival, and the fiftieth anniversary of the deaths of King Ludwig II and Franz Liszt. The conductors in that momentous year were Heinz Tietjen and Wilhelm Furtwängler.

The following years saw repetitions of Tietjen's and Preetorius's stagings, with a largely unchanged cast. Both press and audiences had by now become accustomed to the new style which, according to Preetorius, was faithful to the spirit of Wagner's intentions, since the works of the *Ring* cycle dealt with allegories and therefore required a modicum of symbolism and the elevation of lighting to a primary carrier of the action.

On 30 July 1939 Hitler bestowed his presence on *Walküre*, and during an interval he awarded the Ehrenkreuz für die deutsche kinderreiche Mutter (Cross of Honour for the German Mother of Numerous Children) to Winifred Wagner.

The season ended on the last day of August. Three days later, the world was at war.

Winifred and Wieland Wagner with Adolf Hitler at the opening of the Festival, 24 July 1938

> Remain calm when you hear the air-raid siren. An interruption of the performance will be announced from the stage. Follow the air-raid wardens and proceed quietly to the shelters. When the alarm is over, the performance will continue exactly where it had come to a halt.

This announcement greeted visitors to the Festspielhaus in 1940.

In attending the final performance of *Götterdämmerung*, Hitler proved a more accurate prophet of the twilight of the Third Reich than the editor of the local paper who proclaimed the 1940 season as 'Festspiele des Sieges' (Victory Festival).

The bulk of the visitors during the war years consisted of German soldiers and munition workers, who were admitted as 'guests of the Führer'. The casts of the years 1940, 1941 and 1942 remained largely unchanged; orchestra members and technical staff were exempt from military service. The audiences, on the other hand, were mostly commandeered. Soldiers on home leave, more and more of them wounded, and male and female workers, all Hitler's guests, ousted the paying civilians.

The war was going badly for Germany, and the *Ring* was no longer performed after 1942. The events of its final tableaux – 'fire seizes the hall of the gods, while men and women watch in great agitation' – had become so commonplace an experience in everybody's lives that there was little point in duplicating it on stage. *Meistersinger* was deemed the appropriate fare for 1943 and 1944. One can only speculate how Sachs's final

War damage to the town of Bayreuth

address, with its renunciation of German arms in favour of German art, affected the audience:

> Not to your forbears, held so dear,
> not to your sword, your shield, your spear,
> no, to your poetry and to a Master's plea
> you owe this day of greatest bliss.
> Be thankful and remember this.

Alas, German art was soon to be in ruins, together with Munich, Nuremberg and Dresden.

It was six years before Wagner could again be heard in the Festspielhaus. Meanwhile, the building underwent a process of alienation which reflected the immediate postwar years. It served successively as a church for American soldiers, as a venue for revues and pop concerts, as a theatre for the Glenn Miller Orchestra and a New York dance troupe called the Rockettes, and later as an opera house for performances of *Madama Butterfly*, *La traviata* and *Fidelio*. It had sustained damage from fire bombs, and its costumes and scenery had been plundered.

Wieland Wagner, 1951–8

The notice that welcomed visitors as they entered the refurbished Festspielhaus in the summer of 1951 was symptomatic of 'new' Bayreuth: 'Our concern is art. Kindly abstain from talking politics.' The new directors, Wieland Wagner (now thirty-four) and his brother Wolfgang (thirty-two), wisely decided on a radical break with the past. Bayreuth had been associated, to many minds, with narrow nationalism, with National Socialism and anti-Semitism, and with the constant recycling of extracts from Wagner's theoretical writings which lent credence to those views. Wieland and Wolfgang drew an unmistakable line between Wagner's political and social theories and his operas. When Wieland produced his 1951 *Ring* cycle, it emerged like a much-loved, faded old painting, restored by modern means to its original glory.

Entrümpelung (eliminating the superfluous) was the new motto. A clear, clean disc-shaped acting area was often dominated by just one item, such as the tree in Hunding's hut, its triangular cordon reflecting the 'triangular' tension between Sieglinde, Hunding and Siegmund.

Wieland's *Entrümpelung* liberated the spectators' imagination (in the way that the Chorus in *Henry V* had asked the audience to 'eke out our performance with your mind'). The immensely effective lighting created coloured spaces unparalleled in the history of operatic production. Sparse scenery and maximum use of lighting effects reduced the running costs of the enterprise – not in itself a consequence of a severely

The tree in Hunding's hut in Act 1 of *Die Walküre* (Wieland Wagner, 1951–8)

restricted budget, but a welcome by-product. The tilted disc-shaped acting area and the cinematic projections on a huge cyclorama produced a forceful effect of dramatic unity, not only from the beginning to the end of a single opera, but also from the beginning to the end of the whole tetralogy. The new *Ring* costumes shed their last resemblances to a 'Germanic' era. They now reflected the influence of ancient Greece, whose dramatists had inspired many themes of Wagner's *Ring*.

As teacher, demonstrator, manager, mentor, interpreter and decoder Wieland was unique. He had inherited the superb acting skills of his father and grandfather, as well as their apostolic convictions. His singers responded in kind. In addition to Ludwig Weber (Fasolt), a survivor of pre-war days, the young cast included Astrid Varnay, another Scandinavian Brünnhilde, Leonie Rysanek (Sieglinde), Sigurd Björling (Wotan), Wolfgang Windgassen, a future Siegfried, as Froh, and Elisabeth Schwarzkopf as Woglinde.

The two conductors were Hans Knappertsbusch and Herbert von Karajan, the one representing noble solemnity and the other buoyant sublimity of sound, the former a Beethoven, the latter a Mozart. Both were equally authoritative. In fact, Wagner's *Ring* not only allows but invites both approaches. The new chorus master was Wilhelm Pitz, who assembled, trained and perfected a chorus whose sonority, power and sheer

The brothers Wieland (left) and Wolfgang Wagner in 1951

beauty of sound may have been approximated after his death, but was never surpassed.

The initial press reactions were generally hostile, but Ernest Newman admired Wieland's production and praised it in the *Sunday Times* as 'timeless and spaceless'. In the course of the next seven years Wieland's *Ring* was given fourteen times, the cast being strengthened as it went along. In 1952 Hans Hotter became Bayreuth's Wotan and was joined by the equally awe-inspiring Gustav Neidlinger as Alberich, with Josef Greindl as Fafner, Hunding and Hagen. Max Lorenz made an ill-advised return, in 1952, as Siegfried, but by the next year Wolfgang Windgassen had grown into the part which he was still singing fifteen years later. In 1953, two unforgettable Wagnerians joined the ensemble: Clemens Krauss as conductor, and Martha Mödl as Brünnhilde. A new name appeared in the cast-list for 1954: Birgit Nilsson, in the tiny part of Ortlinde (*Walküre*). Three years later she sang Sieglinde, and in the 1960s the Swedish soprano was Bayreuth's adored Brünnhilde.

Wotan puts Brünnhilde to sleep at the end of *Die Walküre* (Wieland Wagner, 1951–8)

The final year of Wieland's *Ring* production was 1958. At that time he told the members of the Society of Friends of Bayreuth:

> Wagner's ideas as expressed in his works are valid now as they were then, but his stage instructions are valid only for his own time ... Let us dare to decipher the symbols which Wagner left in his scores for us today to decipher.

Wolfgang Wagner, 1960–64

In the course of altogether eight new *Ring* productions in post-war Bayreuth the press (particularly in Germany) twice arrived at a verdict which utterly contradicted public opinion. Wolfgang Wagner's staging of 1960 was the first occasion, Peter Hall's of 1983 was the second. Using technical wizardry, Wolfgang created a concave disc which consisted of five segments. These he raised, tilted and lowered, individually or in pairs, so that they served for all the settings required in the four operas. The unbroken disc appeared only twice; at the very beginning, when it symbolized an undefiled world, and at the very end, when all five segments sank slowly into their original concave area, the soiled world had disappeared and the promise of a new beginning, suggested by the music, became visible. Where Wieland's disc had been conceived as an acting area, like the Greek *orchestra*, Wolfgang's symbolized the whole world. Concave, it stood for divine space and thought; convex, it represented Nibelheim's nihilism.

Wolfgang Wagner opted for a different cast to that of his brother. Rudolf Kempe had initial difficulties with the peculiar acoustics of the covered orchestra pit, but in the following years he developed into a wise, much-loved interpreter. A serious illness prevented him from conducting in the *Ring*'s final

The concave disc in *Die Walküre*, Act 1 (Wolfgang Wagner, 1960–64)

year (1964), when he was replaced by Berislav Klobucar. Wolfgang Wagner's singers were, overall, not quite as strong as his brother's, but the few exceptions were quite outstanding, such as Birgit Nilsson as Brünnhilde, Gottlob Frick as Hunding and Hagen, Gerhard Stolze as Loge, Thomas Stewart as Gunther and David Ward as Fasolt (1961). Wolfgang's employment of no less than seven different Wotans for his *Ring*'s five-year run suggests either a scarcity of divine power in Walhall, or a modicum of diffidence in Bayreuth's casting office. Hermann Uhde and Hans Hotter were, of course, superb. The others, except for the reliable Theo Adam, are forgotten. In 1963 and 1964 Anita Välkki was the new, powerful Brünnhilde (Scandinavian, what else?).

Two further features must be mentioned. Wolfgang Wagner had his gods clad in most striking costumes, their primary colours practically serving as visual leitmotifs. At the same time his lighting produced thrilling effects, entirely in keeping with the dramatic and musical demands of the moment. The press condemned him for cheap showmanship, and also failed to grasp Wolfgang's concept of the dignity of the gods. Wolfgang would not make Wotan roll on the floor or climb ladders up and down; he saw him as a flawed character, hungry for power, realizing his failings – but a god nevertheless, as noble and sad as the music with which he is endowed. The critics derided this as old-fashioned, and queried Wolfgang Wagner's competence. The audiences were thrilled, and grateful for the uplift and enlightenment provided by this production.

Wieland Wagner, 1965–9

In his second *Ring* production which was, unhappily, disrupted by his untimely death in 1966, Wieland Wagner opted for an interpretation that connected mythological themes with the social conditions of our time. The typical was revealed as the topical. Walhall, for example, was no longer a castle on a mountain top, but a barricaded fortress. 'Walhall is Wall Street,' Wieland explained. Rather than ascending to Walhall, the gods descended.

In this production, the gods were diminished in stature. Still archetypes, they could now be seen as characters with which the modern spectator could identify. Mime became the intellectual manipulator, Wotan the politician *par excellence*, Hagen the single-minded killer, Gutrune the femme fatale, Alberich the anarchist, Brünnhilde the modern woman, Fricka the modern woman's ancestress. Totemist symbols dominated each scene: an ash tree hung with horses' skulls in Hunding's hut, a golden gadget (half key, half pincers) hung over Mime's anvil, while Gunther's hall (*Götterdämmerung*, Act 1) featured an ulcerated, split monolith with more horses' skulls: it was here that Grane's mistress, Brünnhilde, would be trapped.

Wieland Wagner's most striking use of archaic images occurred in the final scene of *Rheingold*. For Freia's ransom,

Siegfried with Mime in *Siegfried* (Wieland Wagner, 1965–9)

Wotan, Fasolt, Loge and Fafner in *Das Rheingold* (Wieland Wagner, 1965–9)

the giants had demanded sufficient gold to cover her up completely. Eight crudely shaped blocks now hid Freia's form, but what we were seeing was a surrogate goddess, a primitive female torso.

Another spectacular achievement was the producer's creation of the dragon. There was no dragon – just a flickering light in the bottom left-hand corner of the stage, and another one in the top right. No manufactured beast could ever rival a monster of such enormity. If the space between its eyes was as vast as the diameter of the Festspielhaus stage, then its tail would be somewhere near Bayreuth's railway station.

Karl Böhm conducted from 1965 to 1967, but after Wieland's death he handed over to Lorin Maazel. Böhm achieved the ideal *Mischklang* (blend of sounds) favoured by the composer and facilitated by the covered orchestra pit, while Maazel went for a more monumental sound. Böhm's approach proved the more convincing. Wieland's cast included some very fine singers whom he had turned into sterling actors. Theo Adam was Bayreuth's Wotan for the whole run of five years, occasionally sharing the role with Thomas Stewart. Wolfgang Windgassen was the ever-present Loge, a memorable portrayal, and an equally superb Siegfried (1965–8). Other outstanding artists were Gustav Neidlinger (Alberich), Martti Talvela (Fasolt), Leonie Rysanek (Sieglinde), James King (Siegmund), Birgit Nilsson (Brünnhilde, 1965–7), Josef Greindl (Fafner, Hunding and Hagen), Berit Lindholm (another Scandinavian Brünnhilde, 1968–9), Karl Ridderbusch (Fasolt, 1967–9) and the young Anja Silja as Freia, Third Norn and once (1967) as the Woodbird.

After Wieland Wagner's death, his assistant Hans-Peter Lehmann was responsible for the staging in 1967, but the absence of the departed genius could be felt. Hans Hotter was entrusted with the following two years' revivals, but even he, the god, could not inspire his singers the way Wieland had done. Wieland Wagner's second *Ring* production set a standard of prodigious virtuosity, one by which all subsequent performances would have to be measured.

Wolfgang Wagner, 1970–75

Wolfgang Wagner built on the scenic elements which had illuminated his earlier staging for his second *Ring* production. He still used the huge segmented disc, but he now furnished it with a central core which focussed the audience's attention on dramatic climaxes. His use of light and colour was even more dazzling than before. He found a shade of blue for the horizon which seemed to most eyes quite a new colour, and quickly became known as 'Bayreuth blue'. The gods were dressed in red, blue and green, and Alberich in violet. The vivid kinetic projections for water, fire and clouds, all perfectly synchronized with the music, revealed the technical state of the art.

Wolfgang Wagner's supreme achievement was the consummate fusion of the abstract and the realistic in his scenic presentation. It must be mentioned, however, that large sections of the press, both in Germany and elsewhere, dismissed this production as retrograde. The American writer Frederick Spotts wrote about the 'reincarnated disc' as a 'scenographic cliché'.

A glance at the cast-list reveals a remarkable measure of consistency. Horst Stein, rock of reliability, conducted all cycles, from 1970 to 1975. Karl Ridderbusch, the discovery of that time,

The construction of the disc at Bayreuth for Wolfgang Wagner's 1970–75 production; *below*, the disk in action during Act II of *Die Walküre*

sang all Fasolts, all Hundings and all Hagens. Theo Adam was every year's Wotan, first sharing with Thomas Stewart, then with Donald McIntyre. Gustav Neidlinger was Alberich in four years out of five. Wolfgang Wagner had a good nose for first-rate new singers. He engaged Gwyneth Jones as Sieglinde for the first three years, then promoted her to Brünnhilde for the next two.

The coming year, 1976, was to mark the centenary of the opening of the Festspielhaus, and Wolfgang Wagner, now the sole administrator of the festival, had a surprise in store, one that was to earn him several written death threats.

Patrice Chéreau, 1976–80

When Wotan planned Siegfried as a free hero, uninvolved in the gods' dealings, he was deluding himself. One's offspring cannot be programmed to be insensitive to kinship and its legacy. When Wolfgang Wagner considered how best to celebrate the centenary of Bayreuth's first *Ring*, he opted for a non-Wagner as producer. No kinship, no legacy. What is more, the chosen man, Patrice Chéreau, had never produced a Wagner opera before. The result was that most of the links to traditional concepts were severed. A radically new approach astonished, insulted and thrilled its audiences. The temple had become a workshop.

Chéreau saw the *Ring* as an allegory of the time of its creation, the nineteenth century. He combined visual aspects from that century and from our own time with an older, 'Germanic' period; in deprecating the heroic aspects of the work, he decided to demythologize it. Understandably, it took the audience some time to accept a spear-carrying Wotan in a frock-coat. Chéreau's detractors would deplore the anachronism; his admirers felt that the fusion of symbols from different times – today's frock-coat and yesterday's spear – only underlined the timeless power of a symbol.

The Rhine became a hydro-electric plant, and the Rhinemaidens were ladies of the *demi-monde*. The gods had become seedy Chekhovian characters and Loge a caricature of Mephistopheles; he danced his ode to beauty with Freia's veil. The giants were carried by unseen porters, who had to lean against pieces of furniture to prevent spillage. The Nibelungs were miners, dainty men and women. Donner released his thunder from a cabin trunk. Freia was buried underneath the gold, which had arrived in plastic bags. Wotan hacked the ring from the hand of Alberich, who for the rest of the proceedings sported four fingers and a red stump. Walhall had become an architect's caprice – an intermarriage of factory complex and bourgeois residence.

In *Walküre*, Hunding arrived in his surrealist villa with twenty henchmen. Wotan, in a quilted house-coat, enacted his

Siegfried and the Rhinemaidens in *Götterdämmerung* (Patrice Chéreau, 1976–80)

great scene with Brünnhilde (Act II) before a vast mirror, to the visual accompaniment of an even vaster pendulum. Its swings mesmerized the audience, and when Brünnhilde contradicted him, Wotan boxed her ears. Siegmund was killed not only by Hunding but also by Wotan, who then immediately clasped his dying son to his heart – a lovely touch. The stormy Ride of the Valkyries was enacted in a churchyard, with three placid horses stepping over the headstones. Brünnhilde was put to sleep halfway up a rocky pyramid, surrounded by minute flames from gas jets.

In *Siegfried*, Mime unwrapped the splintered sword from sheets of newspaper; Siegfried did not forge his own sword, but obtained it from a steam-driven, sword manufacturing machine. The Woodbird had lost its freedom and was now caged, while Erda, instead of rising from below, was rolled onto the stage.

In *Götterdämmerung*, Gunther and Siegfried appeared in evening dress, while Hagen was depicted as a Brechtian commissar. Hagen survived the final catastrophe, since his plunging into the Rhine was deleted; when queried by the press, Chéreau justified the deletion by stating that it was unbelievable that evil could be so easily eliminated.

This anti-mythological staging, with all its intended inconsistencies and mingling of styles, amounted to an utterly riveting interpretation. The production's strongest point was the drama, and the convincing, deeply involved acting by practically every member of the cast. Chéreau proved to be a Svengali in that respect, and his singers were duly grateful. They agreed that the producer had taught them an entirely new craft. On the other hand, the emphasis on the dramatic aspect entailed a certain loss on the musical side. The principle of synchronization, formerly so successful, had been abandoned, and frequently one had the impression that Wagner's music was being used as accompaniment to a thrilling drama.

The music was indeed somewhat devalued by the ascetic conducting of Pierre Boulez, who seemed reluctant to allow the orchestra to express sentiment, excitement or nobility. But the uniformly excellent cast almost atoned for this. Donald McIntyre (Wotan), Yvonne Minton (Fricka), Gwyneth Jones (Brünnhilde), Karl Ridderbusch (Hunding and Hagen) and René Kollo (Siegfried) made this *Ring* an unforgettable feast. In 1977 there was an unusually large number of English-speaking singers in the cast – apart from McIntyre, Minton and Jones there were Norma Sharp as Woglinde and the Woodbird, Patricia Payne as First Norn and Katie Clarke as Helmwige and Third Norn.

Both press and audience were polarized in their reaction. A large number showed unbridled enthusiasm, while many others seemed truly upset and horrified. The author overheard

A scene from *Siegfried* (Patrice Chéreau, 1976–8)

two French visitors after the final performance: 'Zees Frenchman haz killed our Vagnayr!' Both Chéreau and Wolfgang Wagner received letters which announced their impending demise by unspecified means, and outside the box office placards displayed epithets such as 'Opera Buffa', 'Kitsch' and 'Disneyland'. One even quoted Alberich's 'Verflucht sei dieser Ring' ('Cursed be this ring').

Peter Hall, 1983–6

Peter Hall based his production on Wagner's stage directions. In an interview with Bryan Magee (*Musical Times*, February 1983) he declared, 'I don't believe that a producer's function is to indulge his own imagination for the benefit of the work that he is trying to interpret. I think that you ought to make an honest attempt to do what the man asked you to do in the first place.' This frank decision on the producer's part entailed a return to the naturalistic staging of bygone days, aided by the technology of the present.

Peter Hall and William Dudley (in charge of scenery and costumes) designed a slender hydraulic platform, fifteen metres by ten, consisting of eight separable sections that could be lifted, dropped, moved backwards and forwards, as well as rotated through 360 degrees. This platform, either concave or convex, served as an acting area, or as a wall or ceiling for twenty

Wotan and Brünnhilde in *Die Walküre*, Act III (Peter Hall, 1983–6)

different locales. It formed the floor in the Rhine and the Nibelheim scenes. In the same way, the fallen heroes in the third act of *Walküre* and Erda's scene in *Siegfried* used the platform as floor space. Suspended, rising, falling and rotating, it transported Wotan's warrior maidens in *Walküre*, and the slumbering Brünnhilde in *Siegfried* as well as in *Walküre*.

The use of dominant colours was striking for the symbolic value of each colour. Green ruled the Rhine, the costumes of the gods and their habitat in *Rheingold*, the spring night in *Walküre* and the forest in *Siegfried*. Gold was for Alberich's cloak, the ornaments on Hunding's door, the dragon's maw and a strand of the Norns' rope of destiny. Similarly, red, black and grey were tellingly used.

The very beginning was a *coup de théâtre*. Three beautiful, nude maidens were seen darting up and down in real water which seemed to fill the whole extent of the stage. Hall actually used a modern version of the famous Victorian 'Pepper's Ghost', a stage illusion based on reflecting mirrors at an angle of forty-five degrees. The Rhinemaidens swam horizontally, in a shallow basin, but were seen moving vertically when teasing and avoiding Alberich. The giants, in the second scene, were eight feet tall, positioned on cleverly constructed, stable stilts, with huge pickaxes in their hands, giving them three support points and making them fairly manoeuvrable. Their face masks were super-dimensional, allowing them to sing through their chins – not a happy solution.

Wotan and Fricka in *Die Walküre*, Act II (Peter Hall, 1983–6)

In the first act of *Walküre*, just before Siegmund's 'Winterstürme' (storms of winter), the immense door of Hunding's hut, mounted on the concave platform, flew up and revealed the green ash tree in the moonlit night. The Ride of the Valkyries was a space spectacular, the convex platform bearing Brünnhilde's sisters, tethered to the floor, descending from approximately forty-five feet above the stage – a perilous journey, magnificently matching the music. The Three Norns, in the Prologue to *Götterdämmerung*, were seated on the vertical platform, one halfway up on the left, one halfway up on the right, and one high up in the centre, forming a majestic triangle in space. Since much of *Götterdämmerung*, with its Rhenish background and its Gibichung court, is located in a 'Teutonic' space, the producer took care to counterbalance this by introducing extraneous elements, such as Celtic habits and Oriental court obeisances for Hagen's vassals, their heads touching the ground for Gunther's welcome. The first scene of the final act was visually most appealing, Siegfried like another Paris contemplating the three nude Rhinemaidens who stood in a shallow rivulet fed by a waterfall. Later, Siegfried's corpse was carried aloft through the forest, the platform slowly ascending until he disappeared from view. At the end, Loge's fire music accompanied the conflagration of the world, with real flames (inside a huge invisible glass bowl) enveloping the scene. The hammering which Walhall received by bass trumpets and tubas was mirrored in the collapse of walls, roof and foundations, while flutes and violins exulted in the innocent Assurance motif which found its visual counterpoint in the appearance of an empty convex platform as green earth, lit by a rising sun.

A uniformly fine cast, with Siegmund Nimsgern as Wotan, Hildegard Behrens as Brünnhilde, Siegfried Jerusalem as Siegmund and Manfred Jung as Siegfried, was thrillingly conducted in the first year by Georg Solti. The following year Peter Schneider took over from him and proved to be a splendid replacement.

At the end of the first cycle, the audience applauded for seventy-seven minutes, and the artists had to take 128 curtain calls. The press, however, castigated the producer for his *Konzeptlosigkeit* (lack of a concept), the German critics' favoured poison dart. At a press conference Hall tried to answer his detractors:

> I understand many people in this room cannot see the concept. I see the *Ring* as a morality opera about good and evil; it's strongly philosophical, strongly political, but only after it's a myth. And I've tried to put on stage a myth.

There can be little doubt that quite a few of those present would have preferred a statement more in line with that of the former East German producer Harry Kupfer, who in *Neues Deutschland* (June 1980) said of his Bayreuth production of *Der fliegende Holländer*:

> One contributes one's own experiences and one's own realizations, which one gathers practically every day. Only in accordance with such dialectics can the production, based on our Marxist–Leninist view of life, fulfil its ethical and artistic mission.

Peter Hall's *Ring* lasted four years. It was succeeded, in 1988, by a new production by Harry Kupfer.

Harry Kupfer, 1988–92

During the final quarter of the twentieth century, performances of Wagner's operas tended to reflect not only the producer's interpretation of the work in question, but often also his attempt to accommodate the work to his own creative conception. Harry Kupfer's Bayreuth staging of the *Ring* was a case in point. He saw the *Ring* as a parable of man's contamination of his habitat, and arranged for the action to take place in a world devastated either by nuclear war or by catastrophic misuse of advanced technology. In demythologizing the *Ring*, he was able to introduce touches of satire and frivolity, and so establish a sobering contrast to the often harrowing events.

A recurring visual theme of Kupfer's staging was his *Weltstrasse* (road of world history), a cloud-enveloped route stretching into infinity. He also used prolific laser effects for defining a particular space. *Rheingold* began not with the music, but with a dumb show. A man – dead or alive? – lies face down on the ground. Mute spectators are half hidden by smoke. The orchestra begins the prelude, the man rises, laser beams mark the *Weltstrasse*, the Rhinemaidens emerge from a crater, the man is ready to take part in the action; he is Alberich. We are shown that the beginning of *Rheingold* is not a beginning but a replay.

Das Rheingold, Scene 2 (Harry Kupfer, 1988–92)

The Valkyries have landed; *Die Walküre*, Act III (Harry Kupfer, 1988–92)

The second scene of *Rheingold* displayed a skyscraper Walhall in the distance. The gods were a sinister crew, quasi-Mafia types with dark glasses and felt hats, Froh sporting a silk shawl and Donner wearing a shabby T-shirt. The giants were ten feet high, their long mantles hiding their individual mobile conveyances. Their own heads, tiny in comparison with their height, provided an (intended?) comic contrast.

Nibelheim was a subterranean industrial complex. Alberich appeared in a white silk suit, his brother Mime as scientist in white overalls. The Nibelung workers wore radiation-proof suits and goggles. We were persuaded that another cosmic catastrophe was being planned here. At the end of the final scene, the gods ascended to Walhall in a rainbow-coloured lift, after dancing and jumping around for joy over the opera's supposed happy ending.

Walküre began with the obligatory illustrated prelude, during which Siegmund was shown tottering on the *Weltstrasse*, watched over by a smoke-obscured Wotan. The curtain opened on the prelude to the second act with Siegmund and Sieglinde running away on the *Weltstrasse* and Wotan slapping his thighs, for his desired grandson – the free hero – was in the making. The third act provided countless opportunities for Kupfer's favourite mode of acting, low-level horizontality. Wotan and Brünnhilde were directed to roll on the floor, crawl, writhe, lie on their backs, coil and sprawl. The Valkyries, however, had to climb up and down, down and up, on a kind of Jacob's ladder, while singing and carrying heavy armour.

Much of *Siegfried* was a burlesque, with Wotan in jeans and Siegfried in a blue jump-suit. Mime lived in a scrapped nuclear reactor, or possibly a damaged submarine, which locale gave rise to incessant climbing, hiding and horseplay between

Mime and Siegfried, and Mime and the Wanderer (Wotan). There was no forest in the second act, but some dilapidated fortification from a previous war. Wotan could be seen with the Woodbird perching on his spear, while Siegfried sang 'Never before was the forest so fair'. The *Weltstrasse* reappeared at the beginning of *Götterdämmerung*, as the Norns fastened their rope of destiny to a profusion of TV aerials, presumably to obtain news of the world.

Siegfried's Rhine Journey took place on a contaminated, bilious green river, indicating the hero's journey into perdition. The Hall of the Gibichungs was somewhere in a city, with skyscrapers in evidence, Gunther as the boss of a business centre and Hagen as his security officer in black leather, black glasses, black hair. The second act saw Siegfried arrive by sliding down a flight of bannisters, followed by Hagen using the same mode of transportation. Brünnhilde, Gunther's newly won bride, was assigned a different kind of entry. She was carried by four men, folded in a carpet inside a huge fishing net. Gunther then unrolled his booty, Brünnhilde, and presented her to the bystanders.

In the third act, the Rhinemaidens had exchanged their earlier habitation for a disused hydro-electric power station, their hair falling out in fistfuls. The final catastrophe displayed projections of destroyed cities, with Alberich contemplating the conflagration, while a group of merry party-goers, champagne glasses at the ready, watched the proceedings on several giant television screens. Before the final curtain came down, a boy and a girl, with torches in their hands, were trying to find their way. Into a possible future?

Daniel Barenboim was the hypersensitive conductor, and the superb cast included John Tomlinson (Wotan), Graham Clark (Loge), Matthias Hölle (Fasolt and Hunding), Deborah Polaski (Brünnhilde) and Siegfried Jerusalem (Siegmund). Boos and applause were scrupulously divided.

Alfred Kirchner, 1994–

In stark contrast to his predecessor, Harry Kupfer, this producer kept his cast fairly still. He allowed the music to dictate the action, thus establishing a link with the early Wieland Wagner staging of 1951. He also gave unlimited scope to 'Rosalie', his scenery and costume designer, whose creations dominated the proceedings.

A domed platform served as the main scenic element and acting area, on which Kirchner presented the *Ring* as an abstract myth, with hardly a realistic feature. He did not flinch from borrowing previously successful ideas, such as indicating the size of a monster by showing his eyes only (for Alberich's transformation into a serpent), and he relied on Wagner's music when he dropped the curtain at each scene change.

Freia's ransom; *Das Rheingold*, Scene 4 (Alfred Kirchner, 1994–)

Rosalie's costumes, a mixture of the archaic and 'designer' avant-garde, bewildered the audience. Most singers were given unidentifiable objects sprouting from their shoulders, and some wore garments that seemed to inhibit their vocal or physical deportment. Siegfried's romp-suit and pigtail, and Brünnhilde's crinoline trousers were enigmatically inventive. In *Rheingold*, the problem of the giants' height was neatly solved. Uninhibited by stilts or machinery, they simply carried large oval-shaped signs with primitive faces in black and yellow.

The *Rheingold* cast was magnificent. Being allowed to sing standing upright, they could concentrate on delivery and interpretation. John Tomlinson's experienced Wotan again dominated his scenes in Walhall. Siegfried Jerusalem had grown into a masterly Loge, the slick, amoral puppeteer with the spellbinding voice. The fact that on the previous night he was Tristan speaks for his stamina and his vocal husbandry. Bayreuth's recent discovery, René Pape, was a heart-rending Fasolt, the one character in the *Ring* who dies with his integrity unimpaired. Truly amazing is the unbroken line of outstanding Alberichs, from Gustav Neidlinger in 1952, followed by Otakar Kraus (1960), Zoltan Kelemen (1964), Hermann Becht (1979), and now their peer with perhaps the most formidably frightening voice, Ekkehard Wlaschiha. Manfred Jung, a former

Siegfried, returned as a comically creepy Mime, and Hanna Schwarz was mellifluous dignity personified as Fricka.

The Ride of the Valkyries was a scenic masterstroke. Transported in brilliantly lit, slender lifts, the eight warrior maidens descended and rose, singly, in pairs or in groups. The horses were never missed.

The outstanding cast of *Walküre* included Poul Elming's vocally and visually convincing Siegmund, Hans Sotin's mature, demonic Hunding, John Tomlinson's Wotan, this time a little careful with his top notes, and Deborah Polaski's caring, wise and silver-tongued Brünnhilde.

Mime's workshop, in *Siegfried*, was set in a forest of skyscraper sculptures. Siegfried's entrance with his bear provoked loud laughter – the beast was allowed to fool around, making the observer regret that Wagner had not given him a larger part. Kirchner provided further light touches when he made Siegfried loll on a swing, and when the boy's outrageous conduct drove Mime frantic. The forest in the second act was represented by green parasols, hanging upside down from the rafters. This unlikely contrivance became convincing when the magically lit parasols were set into a gently swinging motion at the orchestra's intonation of the Forest Murmurs. The domed platform now resembled the upper part of a globe which had been scored with white lines, representing longitudes and latitudes, with a wide, red-blazing rectangle at the back – globe and fire foreshadowing the end of the cycle.

Another prophecy of the impending end of the gods was provided in the Prologue to *Götterdämmerung*, with its murky red setting for the Norns. Siegfried and Brünnhilde, too, had shed the blue colour in their costumes – the last link with Wotan's world. The trio of second-act conspirators, Hagen, Gunther and Brünnhilde, was visually compelling: the globular platform was topped by a vast rectangular acting area, exquisitely lit, with the rest of the immense stage in total blackness. At the lower left, Gunther was cowering abjectly; to the right, separated by almost the whole width of the stage, smouldered Brünnhilde, gloomy and sick at heart; forming the top of the triangle, Hagen stood leaning on his spear, mentally rehearsing his role as murderer.

Another visual prediction of the final catastrophe occurred at Siegfried's death, when the cross-like pylons that represented the forest collapsed, plunging the scene into darkness. Here the producer dropped the curtain, not just to prepare the stage for the final scene, but to enable the audience to experience the almost unbearably elegiac beauty of the funeral music. Brünnhilde's final monologue was sung to the audience, and when the orchestra sounded the final motif, Assurance, the curtain fell on a world bathed in blue, the colour of the gods, the promise of new earth, new sky.

The Ride of the Valkyries, *Die Walküre*, Act III (Alfred Kirchner, 1994–)

The one constant, ever reliable, ever admirable factor in this and in all preceding *Ring* productions was the orchestra, surely the most devoted, most skilful band of Wagnerians this side of Walhall. Under James Levine they truly served the composer. When the annual longing for Bayreuth takes hold of you – every early spring – it is the sound of the orchestra, emanating from its own mystic abyss, that drives you to Wagner's Festspielhaus on the green hill outside Bayreuth.

Productions outside Bayreuth

Several notable performances from Germany, Switzerland, Britain, France and the USA have been selected from hundreds of *Ring* productions from all over the world. They are all of consequence in interpreting the *Ring* through their influence, positive or negative, on successive producers of the work.

Munich, 1869 and 1870

Seven years before the opening of the Festspielhaus in Bayreuth, King Ludwig gave orders for a performance of *Rheingold* at his own Hoftheater in Munich, in September 1869. The king had spared no expense on the complicated stage machinery and the pleasing scenery, but in Wagner's absence little thought was given to the inner meaning of the *Ring*. The Regisseur (equivalent to today's producer), Reinhard Hallwachs, presented the surface of the story – no mean achievement for a world première – without attempting to search for any intrinsic significance. Over the following 125 years, producers of the *Ring* have been charged with similar offences.

The multi-coloured steam effects were generally admired; Wagner was later to make ample use of this symbolizing and camouflaging agent at Bayreuth. Judith Gautier, Wagner's young French admirer, was however unimpressed. She praised the singers and the orchestra, but held that the decorations and the stage machinery were so ludicrous that they would not pass muster at the Punch and Judy show on the Champs-Élysées. Furthermore, the appearance of King Ludwig caused such a stir in the audience that most of the orchestral prelude remained inaudible. Wagner vented his vexation in a poem:

Spielt nur, ihr Nebelzwerge, mit dem Ringe;
wohl dien' er euch zu eurer Torheit Sold;
doch habet acht: euch wird der Reif zur Schlinge;
ihr kennt den Fluch: seht, ob er Schächern hold.

Do business with my Ring, you little men,
and clutch it with your money-grabbing claws.
Look out, the cursed ring becomes a noose
that hangs you by your mischief-making jaws.

In June 1870 a further command performance, this time of *Walküre*, took place at Munich, again without Wagner's consent or co-operation. The composer, however, swallowed his resentment, for his mind was otherwise engaged – he was about to marry Cosima in Lucerne.

Gutrune gives Siegfried the magic drink in *Götterdämmerung*; set design by Theodor Pixis

Press and public were united in their praise of the new scenery, especially the third-act background for the Ride of the Valkyries by Theodor Pixis. The music, though, did not altogether please. Wotan's great monologue in Act II was found tiring and superfluous, and the *Berliner Musikzeitung* advised its readers to leave before that scene and make their way back to the auditorium before Brünnhilde's scene with Siegmund.

Adolphe Appia, 1924–5

This Swiss master's innovative designs anticipated those of Wieland Wagner by a quarter of a century. Unworried by Cosima's waspish rejection of his scenic suggestions for the Bayreuth stage, he postulated his ideas in two epoch-making works, *La Mise en scène du drame Wagnérien* (The Staging of Wagner's Music Dramas, 1895) and *La Musique et la mise en scène* (Music and Staging, 1897). Appia repudiated the painted backcloth, replacing it with spaces created solely by light. He maintained that light, used inventively, becomes 'living light' that enables the designer-producer to jettison all realistic associations and to parallel the abstraction of the music with the abstraction of the scenic design.

Such an interpretation of Wagner's music by visual means remained largely unacceptable in Appia's own time, yet it led straight to the artistic revolution which Wieland Wagner was to stage in Bayreuth after the Second World War. In their programme for the 1955 Bayreuth Festival, Wagner's grandsons paid tribute to their predecessor:

> Appia's designs from the first quarter of this century – the stylised stage, inspired by the music and by the realization of three-dimensional space – constitute the initial impulses for a reform of operatic stagings which led quite logically to the 'New Bayreuth' style.

Adolphe Appia's stage set for *Die Walküre* in the Basle Opera production, 1925

In 1924 Appia was able to translate his vision into reality. He was asked by Basle Opera to design *Rheingold* for them. This was followed by his *Walküre* in 1925. The 'Old Wagnerians' in the audience were so horrified that they caused a public outcry, and the *Ring* cycle came to a premature end. Appia's ideas, however, were to influence future generations of producers and designers.

Sadler's Wells Opera, 1970–73

Staged at the London Coliseum, sung in Andrew Porter's new English translation, this cycle was produced by Glen Byam Shaw and John Blatchley, but it became instantly known as 'Koltai's *Ring*', much as audiences had spoken of 'Appia's *Ring*'

Siegfried in the forest, *Siegfried*, Act II; set design by Ralph Koltai (Sadler's Wells, 1970s)

or, more recently, of 'Rosalie's *Ring*'. Wieland and Wolfgang Wagner were never upstaged by their scenic artists, since they themselves were producers and designers in one.

Ralph Koltai, for Sadler's Wells, opted for visually arresting stage settings that combined abstract symbolism with touches of realism. The stage was not bare, as Appia had demanded, but rocks and forest were embodied by metallic shafts, bars and spheres. Koltai had created a *Ring* not of the past or the present, but of a coming age, a space age.

Rita Hunter (Brünnhilde), Alberto Remedios (Siegfried) and Norman Bailey (Wotan) were the pillars of this English cycle, with the conductor Reginald Goodall, *echt* Wagnerian in the Knappertsbusch mould.

London, Royal Opera, 1974–82
Producer: Götz Friedrich

Götz Friedrich and his designer Josef Svoboda used a rectangular, moving platform as their multi-purpose acting area. The drama was allowed to unfold on, under and above it. Making ample use of his favoured device, Brecht's 'alienation' effect, the producer frequently removed a character from the action and placed him or her in a position where they could communicate with the audience directly. To that effect he saw Wagner's characters as archetypes: Wotan – according to his programme notes – as a head of government, Fasolt and Fafner as union leaders, the Nibelungs as proletarians and Alberich as the founder of a revolutionary movement. The producer further enlightened his audience by telling them of 'Wotan's attempt to secure his threatened rule over the world ... by means of biological, anachronistic, counter-revolutionary, anarchistic ideas and deeds.'

Berlin, Deutsche Oper, 1987
Producer: Götz Friedrich

Thirteen years after his Covent Garden production, Götz Friedrich had revised and refined his ideas about the *Ring* for his acclaimed Berlin production. 'Our stage is to be understood as a Time Tunnel,' he wrote in the programme. 'Every character, every situation is both present and past. What is above is turned upside down and becomes the below ... The beginning is the end and the end is a new beginning.' Friedrich's Time Tunnel, inspired by Henry Moore's drawing *The Tube*, served as permanent set for the whole cycle, emphasizing its timelessness and constituting a unifying medium.

Peter Sykora, surrealist scenic artist, created decor and costumes, and conductor Jesus Lopez Cobos, the third member of the production team, led his orchestra in such a way that Wagner's text could be clearly understood. *Rheingold* was seen as a 'divine comedy', *Walküre* as 'Wotan's downfall', *Siegfried* as a 'dark fairy-tale intermezzo', and *Götterdämmerung* as an 'end before a possible new beginning'.

Rheingold opened with the whole cast huddled in the Time Tunnel, heavily wrapped up, refugees from some disaster. After almost a minute, the orchestral prelude began, the Rhinemaidens shed their vestments, and gods, giants and dwarfs left the tunnel, allowing the play to begin. Again.

In the course of the opera, Alberich advances from workman (Scene 1) to factory boss (Scene 3), controlling his miners on six video screens. The gods wear white masks, symbolizing youth; when the giants abduct Freia, the gods lose their masks. Wotan acquires the ring by hacking off Alberich's hand. Freia is forced to help the giants with the transport of the gold, and the rainbow problem is solved by the glow of its spectrum within the Time Tunnel. The Woodbird (*Siegfried*, Act II) is a Papagena-like apparition that descends and ascends in an air-ship. King Gunther's hall in the first act of *Götterdämmerung* features an expansion of the magnifying panes which the producer first used in his Covent Garden staging. They enlarge and distort, and they serve one character to spy on another. Gunther and Gutrune are presented as a pair of incestuous lovers. The Rhinemaidens (Act III) have grown old and spend

The Time Tunnel in the set by Götz Friedrich (Deutsche Oper, 1987)

most of their time rolling on the floor, while Siegfried is portrayed as an anti-hero. His death, shortly after his 'mich dürstet' ('I am thirsty') is made to resemble that of Christ, and Gunther is shown as another Pontius Pilate.

Clearly, this production team had inventive concepts of the characters in their *Ring*. A fly-on-the-wall report of several rehearsal sessions with cast and production team (in the programme notes, September 1985) illustrates this:

> *Götterdämmerung*, Hagen – Alberich. Alberich comes creeping in, like an ancestor or a descendent of Trotsky in exile. Hagen, eyes closed, is fast asleep, a wild synthesis of elephant, black panther and rhino. His father had never cared for him ... Hagen thinks it time for the old man to drop down dead. When Alberich sees that he has lost his power over Hagen, he becomes more and more hysterical (as in his quarrel with Mime). Panting, with a cracking voice, he becomes unintelligible. Maybe Alberich has escaped from a lunatic asylum? There he had proclaimed, in his delusion of grandeur, that he was the lord of the world, the emperor with the golden ring.

When the cycle was performed in 1987 to enthusiastic audiences in Japan, the chief of the fire brigade agreed to break, just for once, the strict law against fire on the stage. The performances ended in a gigantic, controlled conflagration, so that – in the fire chief's own words – 'the audience should not think that our fire brigade did not appreciate Wagner's music.'

Munich, Bayerische Staatsoper, 1987
Producer: Nikolaus Lehnhoff

A small step from Götz Friedrich's Berlin Time Tunnel to Nikolaus Lehnhoff's Munich Space Station (a smaller one for mankind). Designer Erich Wonder's science fiction sets, utopian and indeterminate, dominated this staging which was not afraid to contradict, occasionally, the aural with the visual aspects. Conductor Wolfgang Sawallisch supported this anti-romantic view by emphasizing the score's severity rather than its sublimity. His tempos, therefore, were uniformly rapid.

The curtain rose before the orchestral prelude to *Rheingold*, with Loge (Robert Tear) scribbling the words 'Once upon a time' on a wall. The Rhinemaidens' habitat was a salon, and Alberich materialized from behind the sofa. The second scene (Wotan and Fricka on a mountain top) took place on the wing of an aircraft. At the end (the gods' entry into Walhall), Loge played the Rhinemaidens' lament on a gramophone, then he threw away his white gloves and left with the *Financial Times* under his arm.

Hunding's hut (*Walküre*, Act I) was a classy residence with an armour-plated entrance door. The second act represented

Siegfried and the Wanderer, *Siegfried*; stage set by Nikolaus Lehnhoff (Bayerische Staatsoper, 1987)

Wotan's command centre on board a space vehicle, while the Valkyries (Act III) assembled on a mid-air station, where they made merry with the dead heroes. In *Siegfried* (Act III) the Wanderer (Wotan) met his grandson on a gigantic sculptured face, its eyes closed but nostrils wide open.

The ending of *Siegfried* took place, again, on the space station, where Brünnhilde, according to the English programme notes, 'tries to explain the concepts of immaculate love to Siegfried, who has helplessly turned away. But Siegfried defends his passion for Brünnhilde without reservation. In her desperation, Brünnhilde lifts the spear that protected her as a Valkyrie. Siegfried seizes it from her and urges her to join him in matrimony. Sensuality overpowers her and escalates to a frenzied pitch and ends in her surrender to Siegfried.' René Kollo (Siegfried) and Hildegard Behrens (Brünnhilde), having presumably not read these notes, sang and acted most beautifully.

In his Berlin production, Götz Friedrich's Gunther and Gutrune were portrayed as incestuous lovers. In Munich, Nikolaus Lehnhoff shed further light on the siblings' moral habits: Gutrune was not only in love with her own brother, but also with her half-brother Hagen. For a description of the final scene of the cycle, we return once more to the English programme notes. We are in 'a dilapidated bunker. Gutrune has lost her mind and haunts this morgue, dancing ... Siegfried's dead body is thrown on the funeral pyre.'

Paris, Théâtre du Châtelet, 1994
Producer: Pierre Strosser

Anxious to avoid their predecessors' miscalculations, *Ring* producers in the 1990s were searching for new solutions to an uncomfortable riddle – how to present Wagner's work to modern audiences without either making it look dated (winged

Poster for the production at the Théâtre du Châtelet (Pierre Strosser, 1994)

helmets, beards etc.), or supplying a visual sub-text of their own. They also had to consider whether a new staging should be the result of a team effort, or whether producer, scenic artist or costume designer should be the prime mover.

Pierre Strosser, in the first complete *Ring* in Paris for four decades, decided to eschew concept and interpretation for most, but not all of the time. He therefore reduced the scenery to a bare minimum, allowing the action to take place on a slanted platform with a panorama at the rear, on which he projected an indefinable landscape. He further decided to demythologize, desymbolize and 'de-Germanize' the text. The result was an unpretentious, tractable staging which often let the music make its own points. Strosser was assisted in this by Jeffrey Tate, whose very slow tempos, allied to a transparent orchestral sound, allowed most of the words to be clearly understood. Not that Strosser let Wagner have his way throughout. There were lapses. Where the composer enjoined his singers in 1876, 'Never address the audience, but always your fellow performers', Strosser asked his singers not to address their fellow performers, but the audience. A performance that rejected archetypes and symbols, that minimalized props and scenery, became an unspectacular spectacle. The predominant colours were grey and black, the forest (in *Siegfried*) was reduced to a single tree, no moral problems were posed, and corruption had not visibly tainted mankind. The receptive audience showed enthusiastic appreciation, and were unconcerned about several lengthy stretches in the course of the tetralogy which came near to a staged concert performance.

Where Strosser attempted dramatic effects, he succeeded or failed – according to the spectator's response – to illuminate the text. In *Rheingold* Fafner did not club his brother to death (as the music demands) but strangled him. The Rhinegold itself was a glowing, frosted glass globe, about one foot across, which grew to twice its size when it became part of the treasure. The Rhinemaidens were not frolicsome but becalmed, the Valkyries were static; the gods were not godlike, the giants were not gigantic. To compensate for their ordinary size, Fafner and Fasolt were attended by a further sixteen 'mini-giants', whereas Alberich was allotted only four Nibelung slaves. The finale was a *coup de théâtre*: accompanied by the deafening sound of splintering timber, a black wall pierced the floor and rose to occupy the whole of the background. It was Walhall, Wotan's wish-fulfilment. The gods entered their fortress through a small door in the centre which closed just in time to exclude Loge.

The rear wall served as the back of Hunding's house (*Walküre*, Act I). Sieglinde was seated in an armchair, reading a book, before Siegmund's arrival. To revive the exhausted man, she offered him a glass of sherry. In the third act, the dead heroes, two dozen or more, were left lying on the stage during Wotan's farewell to Brünnhilde, forming a counterpoint to the slumbering Valkyrie. Instead of a circle of flames, a billowing red cloth was dropped, to shield Wotan's sleeping child.

No dragon in *Siegfried*, no Rhine Journey in *Götterdämmerung*. Fafner himself confronted Siegfried in the one-tree forest, and Siegfried simulated his boat trip – novel and convincing – by emerging from the door which had already served as the entrance to Walhall (*Rheingold*, Scene 4) and strolling diagonally down the stage, while a group of people slowly ascended towards and past him, suggesting Siegfried's rapid forward motion.

Seattle, 1986–95
Producer: François Rochaix

1995 was the last year of a presentation that had been running for ten years. The producer's concept had remained the same. Seattle Opera's house magazine informs us:

> Wotan is the director of a world theatre. In *Rheingold* Wotan plans his performances and controls his actors; in *Walküre* his lead actress points out his faulty reasoning, and his favourite actress rebels against him; in *Siegfried* another favourite actor tries to destroy the theatre and causes him to give up; in *Götterdämmerung* Wotan gives his theatre over to his enemy, who destroys the theatre completely.

Within this self-imposed structure, producer François Rochaix and Robert Israel (scenic designs and costumes) created a fast-moving, colourful and occasionally amusing *Ring* which tried hard to synchronize action and music. The audience was particularly appreciative of the Valkyries' flying horses. The dragon, too, caused a considerable stir – a Heath Robinsonish beast which belched smoke, fire and vomit (at a reported construction price of $100,000).

In 1986 the producer was asked about his concept. He replied, 'The *Ring* is full of contradictions, conflicts and ambiguities that Wagner created. To try to resolve those ambiguities ... involves compromises that we are unwilling to make. Instead, we've left the contradictions there for the audience to deal with.' If the resultant production lacked grandeur and did not always inspire the audience with a sense of awe, it was busy, genial and irreverent, fit for attracting a generation of newcomers to the *Ring*. Rochaix's idea of having Wotan present the performance – the play within a play – may well inspire future producers to explore this avenue.

An almost entirely American cast included Monte Pederson (Wotan), Nadine Secunde (Sieglinde, and Brünnhilde in *Sieg-*

The Valkyries preparing to land; *Die Walküre*, Act III (Seattle, François Rochaix, 1986–95)

fried) and Marilyn Zschau (Brünnhilde in *Walküre* and *Götterdämmerung*). The singer-friendly conductor was Hermann Michael. It should be noted that the 1986 performance was conducted by an octogenarian. French maestro Manuel Rosenthal was heard lamenting, 'My dream is to conduct the *Ring*, but no one will ever ask me to do it.' Seattle did – as good a reason for starting a ten-year cycle of the *Ring* as any.

London, Royal Opera, 1994–6
Producer: Richard Jones

This *Ring* made a lukewarm reception impossible. Audiences and press were either apoplectically against it or euphorically in favour. 'This *Ring* is a real event, theatrical as well as musical, full of fresh insights,' wrote Anthony Arblaster in *Wagner News*. But Geoffrey Norris pondered in the *Daily Telegraph*, 'The dustbin which Hagen carries in Act I is a symbol of what could usefully be done with the production.'

The reason for such polarization lay in Richard Jones's constant searching for the meaning of Wagner's symbols, and in his presentation of his findings in as striking a manner as possible. For example, the giants in *Rheingold* were Siamese twins who broke apart when fighting over the golden treasure. Wotan was made to carry a traffic sign for a spear.

In the first act of *Walküre* the twin lovers Siegmund and Sieglinde were kept far apart, never touching until the very end of the act. In the second act Fricka arrived, not in a chariot drawn by rams, but in an armour-plated limousine. Being the guardian of holy wedlock, she wore a satin wedding dress. The second act ended, compellingly, with Hunding, Wotan, Brünnhilde and Sieglinde witnessing Siegmund's betrayal and death, with blood on their hands. Jones further illuminated Wotan's agony when, in his farewell to Brünnhilde, he was not the dominant figure, but the sad god who had to be comforted by his rejected daughter.

Götterdämmerung began with the house lights on, until the First Norn asked 'What glow glimmers there?' Clad in frumpish cardigans, the Norns were depicted as news-gathering snoops, clearly echoing Thomas Mann's description of their activities as 'cosmic tittle-tattle'. Siegfried and Gunther's oath, their bloodbrotherhood, was translated into its modern equivalent – they shared a syringe. Hagen's watch took place on a dustbin, with the watchman wearing Gunther's crown. In the second act, during the Brünnhilde–Waltraute scene, Brünnhilde disappeared at Waltraute's narration, allowing the audience to see Waltraute's head and shoulders only, one of the frequent instances when cinematographic technique was exploited. Hagen's vassals, in the second act, wore pyjamas and tin hats, and to show Brünnhilde's humiliation, she was dragged on with a paper bag over her head. The breakup of the Gibichung hall is precisely indicated in the score, but the producer anticipated it by several bars – a pile of cardboard boxes, denoting the palace walls, was made to collapse spectacularly. At the very end, a dark figure (Wotan, Siegfried, Death, or

Brünnhilde in *Götterdämmerung*, Act II (Royal Opera House, Richard Jones, 1994–6)

Wagner?) led Brünnhilde towards a red chimney pot, the remains of Walhall.

Like the Seattle *Ring* this production offered a painless introduction for the newcomer to Wagner. Jones's interpretations of Wagner's symbols kept the spectators' eyes riveted on the stage, but probably diverted their attention from the music.

Appraisal

Wagner's *Ring* is permanently provocative. Its metaphorical idiom, its veiled message, its sublimity and its terror continue to tease spectators and presenters. If it is true that a work of genius can, by definition, never be fully grasped by either beholder or interpreter, then it should not surprise us that the staged *Ring* will always divide its audience into assenters and dissenters.

What is it, in every new performance of the *Ring*, that delights one section of the audience and distresses another? Producers who observe all or most of Wagner's stage directions may succeed in acquainting modern audiences with the composer's intentions. They risk, however, irritating those who fail to establish a connection between Wagner's tetralogy and the problems of our own time. They are apt to turn to avant-garde stagings which try to decode Wagner's symbols and spell out their relevance. Such productions, too, are apt to perplex the spectator whenever the producer lacks discernment and introduces stage directions which contradict the music. When Fafner kills his brother (*Rheingold*, Scene 4), Wagner *composes* the clubbing to death – ruthless timpani beats. If Fasolt is throttled (as in Strosser's 1994 Paris production), the producer strangles the composer. Likewise, scenic riddles – Hagen's dustbin, Brünnhilde's paper bag, Gunther and Gutrune as lovers, Valkyries playing with corpses, sword splinters wrapped in newspaper, a gramophone record playing the Rhinemaidens' lament, orchestral preludes with mimed action – are likely to engage the audience's attention to such an extent that the music loses its hold.

What, then, is the producer to do?

> Let Wagner's intentions be recognizably translated, by modern means for modern audiences.
>
> There is great terror in Wagner's drama; let there be not great ugliness on the stage.
>
> Singers are at their best when they are comfortable; let them not roll or climb when singing.

Refrain from undervaluing the spectator's intelligence.

Eschew trivialization, marginalization, distortion, political subtexts and effects without cause.

Do not irritate the audience; breastplates and grandiose gestures can cause as much offence as a caged woodbird or a hacked off hand.

Let there be no illustrated orchestral preludes; the music is able to make Wagner's points.

Let producer, scenic artist, costume designer, conductor and cast agree to serve Wagner.

History of Composition

Das Rheingold

1848 Wagner writes *Die Nibelungensage (Mythus)*, his first prose sketch for the poems of the future *Ring* cycle
1851 Prose sketch of *Rheingold* written
1852 Prose draft of *Rheingold* written; verse draft completed
1853 Private publication of completed *Ring* Poem; composition of *Rheingold* begun
1854 Composition of *Rheingold* completed on 26 September

First performance:
22 September 1869, at the Royal Court Theatre, Munich

First performance (as part of the *Ring* cycle):
13 August 1876, at the Festspielhaus, Bayreuth

First UK performance:
5 May 1882, at Her Majesty's Theatre, London

Die Walküre

1848 Wagner writes *Die Nibelungensage (Mythus)*, his first prose sketch for the poems of the future *Ring* cycle
1851 Prose sketch of *Die Walküre* written
1852 Prose and verse drafts of *Walküre* written
1853 Private publication of complete *Ring* Poem
1854 Composition of *Walküre* begun
1856 Composition of *Walküre* completed on 23 March

First performance:
26 June 1870, at the Royal Court Theatre, Munich

First performance (as part of the *Ring* cycle):
14 August 1876, at the Festspielhaus, Bayreuth

First UK performance:
6 May 1882, at Her Majesty's Theatre, London

Siegfried

1848 Wagner writes *Die Nibelungensage (Mythus)*, his first prose sketch for the poems of the future *Ring* cycle
1851 Prose sketch, prose and verse draft of *Der junge Siegfried* written
1853 Private publication of completed *Ring* Poem
1856 *Der junge Siegfried* renamed *Siegfried*; composition of *Siegfried* begun
1857 Composition of *Siegfried* interrupted
1869 Composition of *Siegfried* continued, after an interval of twelve years
1871 Composition of *Siegfried* completed on 5 February

First performance (as part of the *Ring* cycle):
16 August 1876, at the Festspielhaus, Bayreuth

First UK performance:
8 May 1882, at Her Majesty's Theatre, London

Götterdämmerung

1848 Wagner writes *Die Nibelungensage (Mythus)*, his first prose sketch for the poems of the future *Ring* cycle
1848 Prose and verse draft of *Siegfrieds Tod* written
1850 Musical sketches for *Siegfrieds Tod*
1853 Private publication of completed *Ring* Poem
1856 *Siegfrieds Tod* renamed *Götterdämmerung*
1869 Composition of *Götterdämmerung* begun
1874 Composition of *Götterdämmerung* completed on 21 November

First performance (as part of the *Ring* cycle):
17 August 1876, at the Festspielhaus, Bayreuth

First UK performance:
9 May 1882, at Her Majesty's Theatre, London

Commentaries Then and Now

'The cathedral chapter of Seville once instructed their architect: "Build us a temple of which future generations will say, it was sheer madness to undertake such an extraordinary work." Yet there the cathedral stands.'

Franz Liszt to Richard Wagner, 1851

'How strange! Only when I compose do I fully understand the essential meaning of my works. Everywhere I discover secrets which hitherto had remained hidden to my eyes.'

Wagner to Liszt, 1856

'Wagner is so unashamedly arrogant, that his heart is not touched by criticism; that is, if he has a heart, which I doubt.'

Georges Bizet, 1871

'La musique de Wagner réveille le cochon plutôt que l'ange.' (Wagner's music arouses the swine rather than the angel.)

Le Figaro, Paris, 1876

'With the last chords of the *Twilight of the Gods*, I had the feeling of liberation from captivity.'

Pyotr Ilyich Tchaikovsky, 1878

'The story [of *Siegfried*] is a chaotic mass of triviality and filth. Where it is not silly, it is dirty.'

The Sunday Herald, London, 1882

'Herr Scaria, as the hateful Wotan, got through his dismal recitatives with astonishing determination ... That the *Nibelungen Ring*, in spite of its occasional power and beauty, can ever be popular, is more than we expect.'

The Era, London, 1882

‘When I left the Festival Theatre, unable to utter a word, I realized that I had experienced the summit of greatness and pain, and that I was going to carry it with me, unblemished, for the rest of my life.’

Gustav Mahler (on *Parsifal*), 1883

‘It was I who first recognized the artist for whom the whole world now mourns. It was I who saved him for the whole world.’

King Ludwig II, 1883

‘Triste – triste – triste. Wagner é morto.’

Giuseppe Verdi, 1883

‘Wagner is the antidote *par excellence* to all that is German.’

Friedrich Nietzsche, 1888

‘The scenery must be reduced to a minimum, so as not to obstruct the imagination.’

Adolphe Appia, 1895

‘What a curious mixture of sublimity and absolute puerile drivel are all these Wagner operas.’

Arthur Sullivan, 1897

‘This helmet is a very common article in our streets, where it generally takes the form of a tall hat. It makes a man invisible as a shareholder ... when he is really a pitiful parasite on the commonwealth, consuming a great deal, and producing nothing, feeling nothing, knowing nothing, believing nothing, and doing nothing except what all the rest do.’

George Bernard Shaw, 1898

‘Wagner, the discoverer of the myth as a basis for his music dramas, the saviour of opera through the myth ... makes us believe that music's *raison d'être* is to be mythology's handmaiden.’

Thomas Mann, 1935

‘Wagner’s heritage must not be mummified and reduced to an exhibit in a museum, through misconceived loyalty. His timeless vitality must be realized afresh at every new staging.’

Wieland Wagner, 1952

‘Like Faust, Wagner was driven on to experience the best and the worst in himself, until he really knew what it is like to be a human being, with a thoroughness few mortals either need or could achieve.’

Robert Donington, 1963

‘Wagner is so great that he is still growing. And that means that nobody has seen him yet.’

Salvador Dalí, 1974

‘The prodigality of Wagner’s orchestration, the size of his orchestra, his inclusion of unusual instruments in order to extend the possibilities of novel sound experiences – all these would clearly be characteristics of a capitalist bourgeoisie which thirsts for affluence and power.’

Pierre Boulez, 1976

‘Wagner was probably the greatest mind of the nineteenth century.’

Reginald Goodall, 1980

‘Wagner has used music as a drug, as an intoxicant, as a philosophy of life. This is a phenomenon unknown before his time in the history of music and of culture. Its consequences were fatal.’

Hartmut Zelinsky, 1982

‘The *Ring* is inexhaustible ... precisely because it deals with eternal things and the way mortals face or fail to face their meetings with eternity.’

Bernard Levin, 1991

The *Ring* Orchestra

For his early operas Wagner used instrumental forces similar to those of his predecessors. Weber and Donizetti influenced the orchestral structure of *Die Feen* and *Das Liebesverbot*, while the *Rienzi* and *Holländer* orchestras were modelled on Meyerbeer's. The *Ring*, however, required something quite different. To satisfy the demands of the prolific multiformity of his poem, Wagner increased his woodwind instruments from three to four in each section. He doubled the number of horn players from four to eight and, similar to his woodwind practice, he used four trumpets and four trombones. He then decided that for certain passages he required a sound with the characteristics of both the horn and the trombone. Such an instrument, however, did not exist.

To the composer's own specifications, the Berlin firm of Moritz built a quartet of 'Wagner tubas', two tenor and two bass instruments – tenor tubas in B flat whose pitch corresponds to that of the euphonium, and bass tubas in F whose pitch corresponds to that of the tuba in F. These newly constructed Wagner tubas are elliptical in shape and have horn mouthpieces. In the *Ring* orchestra they are played by the fifth, sixth, seventh and eighth players of the French horn section. They provide the sombre, solemn, weighty yet gentle sound which Wagner needed, for example, in the second scene of *Rheingold* when Wotan greets Walhall, his newly built mountain home.

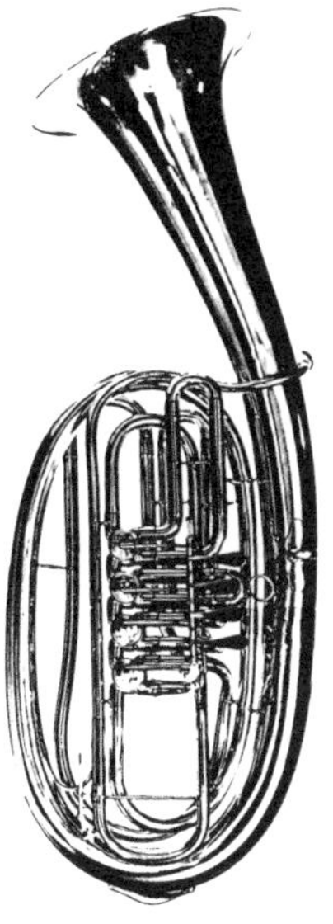

The Wagner tuba, built to the composer's own specifications

These were not the only innovations in Wagner's *Ring* orchestra. He also had a bass trumpet built, in order to obtain a less bright but rather eerie, penetrating sound which combines some of the characteristics of the trumpet with those of the trombone. In the first act of *Walküre*, for instance, to Wagner's stage direction, 'Sieglinde indicates a spot on the tree trunk', the bass trumpet announces the Sword motif. The perilous situation demands the warning tone of the bass trumpet, in preference to its more fiercely metallic forbear. Wagner further buttressed his brass section by introducing the contrabass tuba. Its ominous, menacing growl can be heard at the beginning of the first act of *Siegfried*, as it sounds the Treasure motif, representing Fafner asleep on his golden hoard. Similarly, the introduction of the contrabass trombone resulted in a further reinforcement of the brass department. Its carrying power and sepulchral authority marks the passage towards the end of the prelude to the third act of *Siegfried*, where the Wanderer (Wotan) 'strides to a cavernous opening in the rock', escorted by the Treaty motif.

While woodwind, brass and percussion sections show some slight variation in the course of the tetralogy, Wagner's strings remain constant. He always employs the same sixteen first violins, sixteen second violins, twelve violas, twelve cellos and eight double basses. This formation enabled him to divide his forces into subsections, as he did in *Rheingold*, Scene 1. To portray the elation of the Rhinemaidens at the dazzling sight of the shining Rhinegold, he first uses twelve violins in three parts, then sixteen violins in four parts, followed by twenty-four violins in six parts and, finally, thirty-two violins in eight parts. Thus constituted, the composer's orchestra was equipped to cope with the demands of the poet.

Wagner augmented his orchestral forces by adding a vast array of off-stage sound effects:

Das Rheingold
18 anvils (transition between Scenes 2 and 3; transition between Scenes 3 and 4)
Harp (Scene 4, to accompany the Rhinemaidens' lament)

Die Walküre
Stierhorn (alphorn) (Act II, when Hunding challenges Siegfried)
Thunder machine (end Act II, Wotan pursuing Brünnhilde)

Siegfried
Hammer (Act I, used first by Mime, later by Siegfried)
Cor anglais (Act II, Siegfried cutting reed pipe)
Horn (Act II, Siegfried attracting the dragon with its sound)
Thunder machine (Act I, Wanderer in Mime's cave; Act II, Wanderer enters and leaves forest; Act III, end of prelude; Act III, Siegfried shatters Wanderer's spear)

Götterdämmerung
Horn (orchestral transition from end of Prologue to beginning of Act I; Act I, before Siegfried's arrival at Gunther's court; Act I, before Siegfried's appearance on Brünnhilde's rock; prelude to Act III; Act III, scene 1, Rhinemaidens; Act III, beginning of scene 2)
Several horns (orchestral postlude to Act II; prelude to Act III, Act III, end of scene 1)
3 stierhorns (Act II, Hagen summoning the vassals; prelude to Act III)
4 harps (Act III, scene 1, Rhinemaidens)

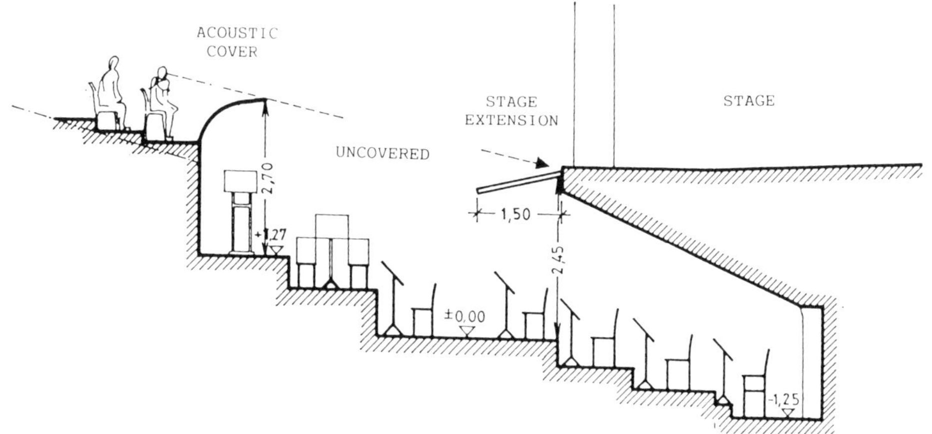

The auditorium of the Festspielhaus

The structure of the orchestra pit in the Bayreuth Festival Theatre forced Wagner to consider the placing of his instrumentalists according to principles never before considered by any other conductor or director. The orchestra pit offered three different positions for his players: they could be placed below the acoustic cover, in the uncovered section, or below the stage extension.

In order to obtain an optimum balance of orchestral sound, Wagner placed violins, violas and double basses below the acoustic cover. Cellos, flutes, oboes, cor anglais and harps were seated in the uncovered section, while clarinets, bassoons, French horns, trumpets, trombones, tubas and percussion were located in the section closest to the stage. To achieve his desired *Mischklang* (sound blend), Wagner further experimented by splitting up instrumental species into sub-sections, arriving at a most unusual, but entirely successful orchestral layout:

Stage Extension

percussion	timpani	trombones	tuba
bass clarinet	double bassoon	trumpets	horns
	bassoons		

Uncovered

harps	cellos	oboes	cor anglais	cellos	harps
	flutes	piccolo			

Acoustic Cover

basses	2nd violins	violas	violas	1st violins	basses
	2nd violins			1st violins	

CONDUCTOR

List of Orchestral Forces

Das Rheingold

Strings: 16 first violins
16 second violins
12 violas
12 cellos
8 double basses

Woodwind: 1 piccolo
3 flutes
3 oboes
1 cor anglais
3 clarinets
1 bass clarinet
3 bassoons

Brass: 8 French horns
3 trumpets
1 bass trumpet
3 tenor trombones
1 bass trombone
1 contrabass trombone
4 Wagner tubas (2 tenor and 2 bass)
1 contrabass tuba

Percussion: timpani
cymbals
triangle
bass drum
gong
6 harps

Offstage: 18 anvils
1 harp

Die Walküre

Strings: as before

Woodwind: 2 piccolos
3 flutes
3 oboes
1 cor anglais
3 clarinets
1 bass clarinet
3 bassoons

Brass:	8 French horns
	3 trumpets
	1 bass trumpet
	3 tenor trombones
	1 bass trombone
	1 contrabass trombone
	4 Wagner tubas (2 tenor and 2 bass)
	1 contrabass tuba
Percussion:	timpani
	cymbals
	triangle
	tenor drum
	glockenspiel
	gong
	6 harps
Offstage:	Stierhorn

Siegfried

Strings:	as before
Woodwind:	2 piccolos
	3 flutes
	4 oboes
	1 cor anglais
	3 clarinets
	1 bass clarinet
	3 bassoons
Brass:	8 French horns
	3 trumpets
	1 bass trumpet
	3 tenor trombones
	1 bass trombone
	1 contrabass trombone
	4 Wagner tubas (2 tenor and 2 bass)
	1 contrabass tuba
Percussion:	timpani
	cymbals
	triangle
	tenor drum
	glockenspiel
	gong
	6 harps
Offstage:	cor anglais
	horn

Götterdämmerung

Strings: as before

Woodwind: 2 piccolos
3 flutes
4 oboes
1 cor anglais
3 clarinets
1 bass clarinet
3 bassoons

Brass: 8 French horns
3 trumpets
1 bass trumpet
3 trombones
1 bass trombone
1 contrabass trombone
4 Wagner tubas (2 tenor and 2 bass)

Percussion: timpani
tenor drum
cymbals
triangle
glockenspiel
6 harps

Offstage: 4 horns
3 Stierhorns
4 harps

Bibliography

In listing over 120 titles, this bibliography covers less than one per cent of all publications on Wagner and his works. This selection does however offer much valuable information for the present-day reader. For those looking for 'required reading', Cosima's diaries are a must, as is the Spencer and Millington translation of Wagner's letters. Recommended studies and biographies include Cooke's *I Saw the World End*, Mann's *Pro and Contra Wagner*, *The Wagner Compendium* (edited by Millington), Müller and Wapnewski's *Wagner Handbook*, Newman's *The Life of Richard Wagner*, Wapnewski's *Der traurige Gott* and Weston's *The Legends of the Wagner Drama*.

Editions/Literary Works

Ellis, W. A. ed. and trans. *Richard Wagner's Prose Works* (London, 1972)

Kaiser, J. ed. *Die Musikdramen* (Munich, 1978)

Wolzogen, H. von and Sternfeld, R. eds. *Sämtliche Schriften und Dichtungen* (Leipzig, 1911–16)

Diaries/Letters

Bergfeld, J. ed. *Richard Wagner: Tagebuchaufzeichnungen 1865–1882: 'Das braune Buch'* (Zurich, 1975; Eng. trans. 1980 as *The Brown Book*)

Burk, J. N. ed. *Letters of Richard Wagner: the Burrell Collection* (London, 1951)

Glasenapp, C. F. ed. *Familienbriefe von Richard Wagner (1832–1874)* (Berlin, 1907; Eng trans. 1911/repr. 1972)

Golther, W. ed. *Richard Wagner an Mathilde Wesendonk: Tagebuchblätter und Briefe 1853–1871* (Leipzig, 1904, 30/1906; Eng. trans. 1911)

Gregor-Dellin, M. and Mack, D. eds. *Cosima Wagner: Die Tagebücher* (Munich and Zurich, 1976–7; Eng. trans. 1978–9)

Gregor-Dellin, M. ed. *Mein Leben* (Munich, 1963; Eng. trans. 1983)

Hausegger, S. von, ed. *Richard Wagners Briefe an Frau Julie Ritter* (Munich, 1920)

Heckel, K. ed. *Briefe Richard Wagners an Emil Heckel: zur Entstehungsgeschichte der Bühnenfestspiele in Bayreuth* (Berlin, 1899, 3/1911; Eng. trans. 1899)

Hueffer, F. ed. *Briefwechsel zwischen Wagner und Liszt* (Leipzig, 1887, rev. 3/1910 by Kloss, E.; Eng. trans. 1888/repr. 1973)

Karpath, L. ed. *Richard Wagner: Briefe an Hans Richter* (Berlin, 1924)

Kerr, C. V. trans. *The Bayreuth Letters of Richard Wagner* (London, undated)

Kietz, G. A. *Richard Wagner in den Jahren 1842–1849 und 1873–1875: Errinerungen von Gustav Adolph Kietz* (Dresden, 1905)

Kloss, E. ed. *Richard Wagner an Freunde und Zeitgenossen* (Berlin, 1909)

Kloss, E. ed. *Richard Wagner an seine Künstler* (Berlin, 1908)

La Mara [pseud. of Lipsius, M.], ed. *Richard Wagners Briefe an August Röckel* (Leipzig, 1894, 2/1912; Eng. trans. 1897)

Lenrow, E. ed. and trans. *The Letters of Richard Wagner to Anton Pusinelli* (New York, 1932/repr. 1972)

Scholz, H. ed. *Richard Wagner an Mathilde Maier (1862–1878)* (Leipzig, 1930)

Schuh, W. ed. and trans. *Die Briefe Richard Wagners an Judith Gautier* (Zurich, 1936)

Spencer, S. and Millington, B. eds. and trans. *Selected Letters of Richard Wagner* (London, 1987)

Strobel, G., Wolf, W. *et al* eds. *Richard Wagner; Sämtliche Briefe* (Leipzig, 1967–)

Strobel, O. ed. *König Ludwig II. und Richard Wagner: Briefwechsel, mit vielen anderen Urkunden* (Karlsruhe, 1936–9)

Wolzogen, H. von, ed. *Richard Wagner an Minna Wagner* (Berlin, 1908; Eng. trans. 1909/repr. 1972)
Wolzogen, H. von, ed. *Richard Wagner's Briefe an Theodor Uhlig, Wilhelm Fischer, Ferdinand Heine* (Leipzig, 1888; Eng. trans. 1890)

Wagner's Sources for the *Ring*

Auden, W. H. and Taylor, P. B. trans. *Poetic Edda* (London, 1981)
Byock, J. L. trans. *Volsunga Saga* (Berkeley, 1990)
Grimm, J. *Deutsche Mythologie* (Gütersloh, 1875–8; Eng. trans. 1883–8)
King, K. C. ed. *Das Lied vom Hürnen Seyfrid* (Manchester, 1958)
Panzer, F. *Das Nibelungenlied* (Stuttgart, 1955)
Sturluson, S. *Edda* (Eng. trans. 1987, by Faulkes, A.)

Books

Appia, A. *La Mise en scène du drame Wagnérien* (Paris, 1895)
Appia, A. *Die Musik und die Inszenierung* (Munich, 1899; Eng. trans. 1962)
Barth, H. ed. *Bayreuther Dramaturgie* (Stuttgart, 1980)
Barth, H., Mack, D., Voss, E. eds. *Wagner: a Documentary Study* (London, 1975)
Bauer, H.-J. *Richard Wagner Lexikon* (Vienna, 1975/repr. 1988; Eng. trans. 1975)
Bauer, H.-J. *Richard Wagner* (Berlin, 1995)
Bauer, O. G. *Richard Wagner: Die Bühnenwerke* (Berlin, 1982)
Benvenga, N. *Kingdom on the Rhine* (Harwich, 1983)
Bermbach, U. *In den Trümmern der eigenen Welt* (Berlin, 1989)
Bertram, J. *Mythos, Symbol, Idee in Richard Wagners Musik-Dramen* (Hamburg, 1957)
Blunt, W. *The Dream King: Ludwig II of Bavaria* (London, 1970)
Blyth, A. *Wagner's 'Ring'* (London, 1980)
Borchmeyer, D. *Das Theater Richard Wagners* (Stuttgart, 1982)
Bory, R. *Richard Wagner: Sein Leben und sein Werk in Bildern* (Frauenfeld, 1938)
Bronnenmeyer, W. *Vom Tempel zur Werkstatt* (Bayreuth, 1970)
Bülow, M. *Hans von Bülow* (Stuttgart, 1925)
Burbidge, P. and Sutton, R. eds. *The Wagner Companion* (London, 1979)
Chamberlain, H. S. *Richard Wagner* (Munich, 1896, 3/1911; Eng. trans. 1897/repr. 1974)
Chancellor, J. *Wagner* (London, 1978)
Cook, P. *A Memoir of Bayreuth 1876* (London, 1979)
Cooke, D. *I Saw the World End* (London, 1979)
Culshaw, J. *Reflections on Wagner's 'Ring'* (London, 1976)
Dahlhaus, C. *Die Musikdramen Richard Wagners* (Velber, 1971; Eng. trans. 1979)
Deathridge, J. and Dahlhaus, C. *The New Grove 'Wagner'* (London, 1984)
Di Gaetani, J. L. ed. *Penetrating Wagner's 'Ring'* (Cranbury, 1978)
Donington, R. *Wagner's 'Ring' and its Symbols* (London, 1963)
Eger, M. *Wenn ich mit Wagnern den Krieg mache* (Vienna, 1988)
Ellis, W. A. *Life of Richard Wagner* (London, 1900–08)
Ewans, M. *Wagner and Aeschylus* (London, 1982)
Fay, S. and Wood, R. *The Ring: Anatomy of an Opera* (London, 1984)
Fehr, M. *Richard Wagners Schweizer Zeit* (Aarau, 1934/repr. 1953)
Fischer-Dieskau, D. *Wagner und Nietzsche* (Eng. trans. 1976)
Fricke, R. *Bayreuth vor dreissig Jahren* (Dresden, 1906)
Garten, H. F. *Wagner the Dramatist* (London, 1977)
Gay, P. *Jews and Other Germans* (London, 1977)
Golther, W. *Die sagengeschichtlichen Grundlagen der Ring-Dichtungen Richard Wagners* (Berlin, 1902)

Gregor-Dellin, M. *Richard Wagner* (Munich, 1980)
Gutman, R. *Richard Wagner* (London, 1968)
Hanslick, E. ed. Pleasants, H. *Vienna's Golden Years of Music 1850–1900* (New York, 1950/repr. 1969)
Herzfeld, F. *Minna Planer* (Leipzig, 1938)
Hollingdale, R. J. *Nietzsche, Wagner and the Philosophy of Pessimism* (London, 1982)
Holman, J. K. *Wagner's Ring* (Portland, Oregon, 1996)
Kaiser, J. *Leben mit Wagner* (Munich, 1990)
Karbaum, M. *Studien zur Geschichte der Bayreuther Festspiele (1876–1976)* (Regensburg, 1976)
Kühnel, J. *Richard Wagners 'Ring des Nibelungen'* (Siegen, 1991)
Lee, M. O. *Wagner's 'Ring'* (New York, 1990)
Lehmann, L. *Mein Weg* (Leipzig, 1913, 2/1920; Eng. trans. 1914/repr. 1977)
Lippert, W. *Wagner in Exile* (London, 1930)
Lorenz, A. *Das Geheimnis der Form bei Richard Wagner, i: Der Ring des Nibelungen* (Berlin, 1924/repr. 1966)
Mack, D. *Der Bayreuther Inszenierungsstil 1876–1976* (Munich, 1976)
Mack, D. ed. *Theaterarbeit an Wagners Ring* (Munich, 1978)
Mack. D. ed. *Cosima Wagner: Das Zweite Leben* (Munich, 1980)
Magee, B. *Aspects of Wagner* (London, 1988)
Magee, B. *The Philosophy of Schopenhauer* (Oxford, 1983)
Magee, E. *Richard Wagner and the Nibelungs* (Oxford, 1990)
Mann, T. *Leiden und Grösse Richard Wagners* (Berlin and Frankfurt, 1960; Eng. trans. 1985, as *Pro and Contra Wagner*)
Marek, G. R. *Cosima Wagner* (New York, 1981)
Millington, B. *Wagner* (London, 1992)
Millington, B. ed. *The Wagner Compendium* (London, 1992)
Millington, B. and Spencer, S. eds. *Wagner in Performance* (New Haven and London, 1992)
Müller, U. and Müller, U. eds. *Richard Wagner und sein Mittelalter* (Salzburg, 1989)
Müller, U. and Wapnewski, P. eds. *Wagner Handbook* (London, 1992)
Nattiez, J.-J. *Wagner Androgyne* (Princeton, 1993)
Neumann, A. *Errinerungen an Richard Wagner* (Leipzig, 1907; Eng. trans. 1908/repr. 1976)
Newman, E. *The Life of Richard Wagner* (London, 1933–47)
Newman, E. *Wagner as Man and Artist* (London, 1914/repr. 1963)
Newman, E. *Wagner Nights* (London, 1949)
Nietzsche, F. *Der Fall Wagner* (Leipzig, 1988; Eng. trans. 1967)
Osborne, C. *The Complete Operas of Richard Wagner* (London, 1990)
Panofsky, W. *Wagner, eine Bildbiographie* (Munich, 1963)
Petzet, D. and Petzet, M. *Die Richard-Wagner-Bühne Ludwigs II* (Munich, 1970)
Porges, H. *Die Bühnenproben zu den Bayreuther Festspielen des Jahres 1876* (Eng. trans. Cambridge, 1983) [Eyewitness account of Wagner's rehearsing of the *Ring*]
Porter, A. trans. *Richard Wagner: The Ring* (London, 1976)
Prawy, M. *Richard Wagner, Leben und Werk* (Munich, 1982)
Rappl, E. *Wagner Opernführer* (Regensburg, 1967)
Richardson, J. *Judith Gautier* (London, 1986)
Robb, S. trans. *Richard Wagner: The Ring of the Nibelung* (New York, 1960)
Sabor, R. *The Real Wagner* (London, 1987)
Shaw, G. B. *The Perfect Wagnerite: a Commentary of the Nibelung's Ring* (London, 1898, 4/1923/repr. 1972)
Skelton, G. *Wieland Wagner* (London, 1971)
Skelton, G. *Wagner at Bayreuth* (London, 1976)
Skelton, G. *Richard and Cosima Wagner* (London, 1982)
Spencer, S. ed. *Wagner 1976: a Celebration of the Bayreuth Festival* (London, 1976)

Spencer, S. trans. *Wagner's Ring of the Nibelung* (London, 1993) [with commentaries by Millington, B. and others]
Spotts, F. *Bayreuth: a History of the Wagner Festival* (New Haven, 1994)
Stein, J. *Richard Wagner and the Synthesis of the Arts* (Detroit, 1960)
Strobel, O. *Richard Wagner: Skizzen und Entwürfe zur Ring-Dichtung* (Munich, 1930)
Taylor, R. *Richard Wagner* (London, 1979)
Turing, P. *New Bayreuth* (London, 1969)
Umbach, K. *Richard Wagner: ein deutsches Ärgernis* (Hamburg, 1982)
Voss, E. *Studien zur Instrumentation Richard Wagners* (Regensburg, 1970)
Wagner, W[olfgang]. *Lebens-Akte* (Munich, 1994)
Wapnewski, P. *Die Szene und ihr Meister* (Munich, 1978)
Wapnewski, P. *Der traurige Gott: Richard Wagner in seinen Helden* (Munich, 1978)
Wapnewski, P. *Weisst du wie das wird ...?* (Munich, 1995)
Watson, D. *Richard Wagner* (London, 1979)
Westernhagen, C. *Wagner* (Zurich, 1968; Eng. trans. 1979)
Weston, J. L. *The Legends of the Wagner Drama* (London, 1896/repr. 1977)
Wolzogen, H. *Thematischer Leitfaden durch die Musik zu Richard Wagners Festspiel 'Der Ring des Nibelungen'* (Leipzig, 1876)
Würzbach, F. *Nietzsche* (Munich, 1966)
Zelinsky, H. *Richard Wagner: ein deutsches Thema* (Frankfurt, 1976)

Discography

This list includes all recordings which the author has been able to comment on. It does not prefer studio recordings to live performances, modern to historical, stereo to mono, or vice versa. The author's comments reflect his verdict on what constitutes a valid Wagnerian performance, and he pleads sincerity but not infallibility.

Complete Performances of the *Ring*

1950
Wilhelm Furtwängler
La Scala Orchestra and Chorus

Das Rheingold
Wotan: F. Frantz
Alberich: A. Pernerstorfer
Loge: J. Sattler
Fricka: E. Höngen
Mime: P. Markworth
Erda: M. Weyth-Falke
Fafner: A. Emmerich
Fasolt: L. Weber

The glories of this recording are Furtwängler's authoritative conducting, and, from an otherwise undistinguished cast, the magnificent, most affecting Fasolt of veteran Ludwig Weber.

Cetra CDC26 (Mono)

Die Walküre
Siegmund: G.Treptow
Sieglinde: H. Konetzni
Hunding: L. Weber
Wotan: F. Frantz
Brünnhilde: K. Flagstad
Fricka: E. Höngen

Furtwängler's noble, idiosyncratic but inspired conducting and Kirsten Flagstad's profound, generous-toned Brünnhilde make this set a collector's windfall, in spite of the two cuts and the audience participation.

Cetra CDC15 (Mono)

Siegfried
Siegfried: S. Svanholm
Mime: P. Markwort
Wanderer: J. Herrmann
Alberich: A. Pernerstorfer
Fricka: L. Weber
Erda: E. Höngen
Brünnhilde: K. Flagstad

The La Scala orchestra is not known for its Wagnerian achievements, but here they give an inspired account under the magic Furtwängler baton. Svanholm's Siegfried is accurate, no more, but his Brünnhilde is Kirsten Flagstad, and that is the reason why this set is essential to have or to borrow.

Cetra CDC27 (Mono)

Götterdämmerung
Siegfried: M. Lorenz
Brünnhilde: K. Flagstad
Gunther: J. Hermann
Hagen: L. Weber
Gutrune: H. Konetzni
Waltraute: E. Höngen
Alberich: A. Pernerstorfer

A historic document of great importance! Furtwängler makes his orchestra respond to the sublety of his rubato. Max Lorenz and Kirsten Flagstad are simply overwhelming, notwithstanding the tenor's cavalier treatment of rhythmical niceties. Weber's Hagen is awe-inspiring; there is not a single weak link in this impressive cast. The sound is very acceptable for its age. Let us give thanks for Wilhelm Furtwängler.

Cetra CDC28 (Mono)

1952
Joseph Keilberth
Bayreuth Festival Orchestra and Chorus

Das Rheingold
Wotan: H. Uhde
Alberich: G. Neidlinger
Loge: E. Witte
Fricka: I. Malaniuk
Mime: P. Kuen
Erda: M. Bugarinovic
Fafner: K. Böhme
Fasolt: L. Weber

This is the first live recording at postwar Bayreuth. Orchestra and cast are in superb form, with Uhde, Neidlinger and Weber quite outstanding. The sound is remarkably good for its age.

Paragon PCD 84015-17 (Mono)

Die Walküre
Siegmund: G. Treptow
Sieglinde: I. Borkh
Hunding: J. Greindl
Wotan: H. Hotter
Brünnhilde: A. Varnay
Fricka: I. Malaniuk

This is of particular historical interest for connoisseurs of the postwar 'New Bayreuth' style: slenderized, meticulous orchestral sound (what an underrated conductor Keilberth was), jettisoning *bel canto* for psychological role identification (listen particularly to Hotter's Wotan, Greindl's Hunding and Varnay's Brünnhilde). The new idiom was to be perfected and sustained over the following decades.

Paragon PCD84017-84020 (Mono)

Siegfried
Siegfried: B. Aldenhoff
Mime: P. Kuen
Wanderer: H. Hotter
Alberich: G. Neidlinger
Fricka: K. Böhme
Erda: M. Bugarinovic
Brünnhilde: A. Varnay

The glories of this set are manifold – Hotter's majestic, yet vulnerable Wotan, Kuen's definitive Mime, Neidlinger's Alberich (Bayreuth's finest and long-serving demon) and Astrid Varnay's fiery Brünnhilde. Siegfried and Erda are adequate, but the postwar Bayreuth orchestra is a revelation.

PARAGON PCD84021-84024 (Mono)

Götterdämmerung
Siegfried: M. Lorenz
Brünnhilde: A. Varnay
Fricka: H. Uhde
Hagen: J. Greindl
Gutrune: M. Mödl
Waltraute: R. Siewert
Alberich: G. Neidlinger

The listener can relish the presence of Bayreuth's superb dramatic sopranos, Varnay (as Brünnhilde), and Mödl as Gutrune and Third Norn. Both ladies give object lessons to future generations on phrasing, breath control and role identification. The postwar chorus, hand-picked and trained by Wilhelm Pitz, is a thundering revelation as Hagen's Vassals.

PARAGON 84025-84028 (Mono)

1953
Clemens Krauss
Bayreuth Festival Orchestra and Chorus

Das Rheingold
Wotan: H. Hotter
Alberich: G. Neidlinger
Loge: E. Witte
Fricka: I. Malaniuk
Mime: P. Kuen
Erda: M. von Ilosvay
Fafner: J. Greindl
Fasolt: L. Weber

An altogther magnificent issue and a benchmark for the rest of the century. The playing is superb, and Hans Hotter's Wotan and Gustav Neidlinger's Alberich are still unsurpassed.

FOYER 15CF2011 (Mono)

Die Walküre
Siegmund: R. Vinay
Sieglinde: R. Resnik
Hunding: J. Greindl
Wotan: H. Hotter
Brünnhilde: A. Varnay
Fricka: I. Malaniuk

The cast is almost identical to Keilberth's 1952 recording, but at the helm is Clemens Krauss, one of the three towering Wagner conductors of that time (the others being, of course, Furtwängler and Knappertsbusch). The sound is excellent for its time, and the singers especially come over fresh and tangible. They are, without exception, at the top of their considerable prime. Ramon Vinay and Regina Resnik as the twin lovers are even better than their 1952 predecessors, while the orchestra glows with the fire of a band that revels in responding to a master.

LAUDIS LCD44003 (Mono)

Siegfried
Siegfried: W. Windgassen
Mime: P. Kuen
Wanderer: H. Hotter
Alberich: G. Neidlinger
Fricka: J. Greindl
Erda: M. von Ilosvay
Brünnhilde: A.Varnay

Clemens Krauss remains unsurpassed. The superb cast is again almost identical to Keilberth's, but the presence of the young Wolfgang Windgassen adds lustre to this set. The refurbished sound is fine almost throughout, and the voices are well forward.

FOYER 4-CF22009 (Mono)

Götterdämmerung
Siegfried: W. Windgassen
Brünnhilde: A. Varnay
Gunther: H. Uhde
Hagen: J. Greindl
Gutrune: N. Hinsch-Gröndahl
Waltraute: I. Malaniuk
Alberich: G. Neidlinger

With the possible exception of the Gutrune, this set features an all-star cast, Windgassen solving the world-wide Heldentenor scarcity single-voiced. The Bayreuth master musicians under Krauss (one year before his untimely death) have no peers this side of Valhalla.

FOYER 15-CF2011 (Mono)

1953
Wilhelm Furtwängler
Rome Radio Symphony Orchestra and Chorus

Das Rheingold
Wotan: F. Frantz
Alberich: G. Neidlinger
Loge: W. Windgassen
Fricka: I. Malaniuk
Mime: J. Patzak
Erda: R. Siewert
Fafner: G. Frick
Fasolt: J. Greindl

Furtwängler does his very best with a second-rate orchestra, but what wonderful soloists! Wolfgang Windgassen as Loge, Gustav Neidlinger as Alberich, Julius Patzak as Mime, Gottlob Frick as Fafner, Sena Jurinac as one of the Rhinemaidens and Elisabeth Grümmer as Freia – a million-dollar cast.

EMI CZS7671242 (Mono)

Die Walküre
Siegmund: W. Windgassen
Sieglinde: H. Konetzni
Hunding: G. Frick
Wotan: F. Frantz
Brünnhilde: M. Mödl
Fricka: E. Cavelti
A triumph of mind over matter. The innocent orchestral players, quite unused to Wagner, were converted by the conductor into willing and able Wagnerians, dray horses into derby winners. The set is a must for the sake of worshipping the combination of Furtwängler, Windgassen, Mödl and Frick.
EMI CDZC67127 (Mono)

Siegfried
Siegfried: L. Suthaus
Mime: J. Patzak
Wanderer: F. Frantz
Alberich: A. Pernerstorfer
Fricka: J. Greindl
Erda: M. Klose
Brünnhilde: M. Mödl
Furtwängler, Mödl (Brünnhilde), and Suthaus (Siegfried) make this a memorable set. The present reviewer is probably alone in thinking that Julius Patzak's Mime was better than his Schubert (he was a celebrated Lieder singer). Rita Streich's Woodbird remains the sweetest on record.
EMI CZS767123-2 (Mono)

Götterdämmerung
Siegfried: L. Suthaus
Brünnhilde: M. Mödl
Gunther: A. Poell
Hagen: J. Greindl
Gutrune: S. Jurinac
Waltraute: M. Klose
Alberich: A. Pernerstorfer
Furtwängler again achieves good results from the orchestra. The wonders of this performance, however, are the singers. Which other set can boast the glorious Sena Jurinac in such minor parts as Gutrune, Third Norn and Woglinde? Ludwig Suthaus is a silver-tongued, *bel canto* Siegfried, a foil to the intensely dramatic Brünnhilde of Martha Mödl. Add Josef Greindl's rumbustious Hagen and Margarete Klose's warmly solicitous Waltraute, and you will want to listen to this set many times.
EMI CDZD67136 (Mono)

1956–8
Hans Knappertsbusch
Bayreuth Festival Orchestra and Chorus

Das Rheingold
Wotan: H. Hotter
Alberich: G. Neidlinger (1956–7), F. Andersson (1958)
Loge: L. Suthaus (1956–7), F. Uhl (1958)
Fricka: G. von Milinkovic (1956–7), R. Gorr (1958)
Mime: P. Kuen (1956–7), G. Stolze (1958)
Erda: J. Madeira (1956), M. von Ilosvay (1957–8)
Fafner: A. van Mill (1956), J. Greindl (1957–8)
Fasolt: J. Greindl (1956), A. van Mill (1957), T. Adam (1958)
Knappertsbusch (slow, solemn, noble) is in the class of Furtwängler and Krauss. The Bayreuth orchestra play like angels possessed, and Hotter (Wotan) and Neidlinger (Alberich) are worthy contestants for the world. There are some intriguing cast changes for the 1958 recording, with minus points for the new Alberich and Loge, but hosannas for Rita Gorr's Fricka and Gerhard Stolze's Mime.
Laudis LCD15-4021 (Mono)

Die Walküre
Siegmund: W. Windgassen (1956), R. Vinay (1957), J. Vickers (1958)
Sieglinde: G. Brouwenstijn (1956), B. Nilsson (1957), L. Rysanek (1958)
Hunding: J. Greindl (1956–8)
Wotan: H. Hotter (1956–8)
Brünnhilde: A. Varnay (1956–8)
Fricka: G. von Milinkovic (1956–7), R. Gorr (1958)
The 1956 version is expensive and hard to come by. In 1957 the newly arrived Birgit Nilsson stormed her way through the part of Sieglinde, before she became Bayreuth's matchless Brünnhilde. In 1958 Rita Gorr did for Fricka what Hans Hotter had been doing for Wotan all those years: two monumental interpretations, alas on different recordings. Hans Knappertsbusch, one of the three immortals, gives us a more dramatic (and faster) reading in 1958 than in the more lyrical earlier versions. The Bayreuth sound is gorgeous. I would plump, after some introspection, for the 1958 version, on account of Jon Vickers (what *mezza voce*!) and Rita Gorr (imperious, burnished, intense). Her Fricka remains peerless.
1956: King Records KICC2274/88
1957: Laudis 4011
1958: Arkadia HP48013
(All Mono)

Siegfried
Siegfried: W. Windgassen (1956 and 1958), B. Aldenhoff (1957)
Mime: P. Kuen (1956–7), G. Stolze (1958)
Wanderer: H. Hotter
Alberich: G. Neidlinger (1956–7), F. Andersson (1958)
Fafner: A. van Mill (1956), J. Greindl (1957–8)

Erda: J. Madeira (1956), M. von Ilosvay (1957–8)
Brünnhilde: A. Varnay
These performances made the Bayreuth of the mid century a Mecca for connoisseurs and newcomers alike. Knappertsbusch's deep Wagnerian insight and Wieland Wagner's stunning production remain beacons undimmed. Windgassen's Siegfried, Hotter's Wotan, Neidlinger's Alberich and Varnay's Brünnhilde may have been equalled but never surpassed. My own preference is the 1958 version. Valhalla on earth.
1956: King Records KICC2274/88
1957: Laudis LCD15–4021
1958: Arcadia HP48013 (All Mono)

Götterdämmerung
Siegfried: W. Windgassen
Brünnhilde: A. Varnay
Gunther: H. Uhde (1956–7), O. Wiener (1958)
Hagen: J. Greindl
Gutrune: G. Brouwenstijn (1956), E. Grümmer (1957–8)
Waltraute: J. Madeira
Alberich: G. Neidlinger (1956–7), F. Andersson (1958)
This is probably Knappertsbusch's greatest achievement at Bayreuth. His searing intensity illuminates every scene and propels the singers to heights hitherto only dreamt of. An almost unbelievable feature of the 1956 version is the doubling of the parts of Brünnhilde and Third Norn by Astrid Varnay (a tour de force on the stage, with hardly any time to change from Norn to goddess). 1958 is again my preference, with Windgassen at his height, Elisabeth Grümmer as the sweetest of Gutrunes (a shady character needing some vocal redemption), and the most impressive trio of Norns in Jean Madeira, Ursula Boese and Rita Gorr.
1956: Seven Seas KICC2274/88
1957: Laudis LCD 15–4021
1958: Hunt LSMM34041–4

1958, 1965, 1962, 1964
Georg Solti
Vienna Philharmonic Orchestra and State Opera Chorus

Das Rheingold
Wotan: G. London
Alberich: G. Neidlinger
Loge: S. Svanholm
Fricka: K. Flagstad
Mime: P. Kuen
Erda: J. Madeira
Fafner: K. Böhme
Fasolt: W. Kreppel
Lush strings, gorgeous brass, passionate conducting and Kirsten Flagstad's golden-toned Fricka, who makes this a First Lady's set.
Decca 4141012 DH3

Die Walküre
Siegmund: J. King
Sieglinde: R. Crespin
Hunding: G. Frick
Wotan: H. Hotter
Brünnhilde: B. Nilsson
Fricka: C. Ludwig
This marks the stereo watershed. Georg Solti and John Culshaw, his sonic wizard, perform marvels in hi-fi. This set introduced a whole new generation to the *Ring* and had them hooked until – well, ten years later along came or strolled Reginald Goodall, and thirteen years after him Haitink and Levine set new standards. Solti's cast consisted of high flyers only, probably the best of their time. If you want to be taken on a breathless musical journey, from climax to climax, then this your set.
Decca 4141052DH4

Siegfried
Siegfried: W. Windgassen
Mime: G. Stolze
Wanderer: H. Hotter
Alberich: G. Neidlinger
Fafner: K. Böhme
Erda: M. Höffgen
Brünnhilde: B. Nilsson
In spite of its age, this studio-produced stereo set, digitally remastered, remains an exciting journey, with Solti revelling in the silken string tone, the ravishing woodwind and the climactic brass sonorities of the Vienna Philharmonic. Windgassen and Nilsson set the third act alight, and Joan Sutherland's Woodbird is an added, if unintelligible, bonus.
Decca 414100-2DM15

Götterdämmerung
Siegfried: W. Windgassen
Brünnhilde: B. Nilsson
Gunther: D. Fischer-Dieskau
Hagen: G. Frick
Gutrune: C. Watson
Waltraute: C. Ludwig
Alberich: G. Neidlinger
An unsurpassable cast without exception offers superb interpretations and vocal brilliance. Windgassen and Nilsson are totally committed – listen to the end of Act 1, with Siegfried turning into a most unwilling anti-hero, and Brünnhilde plumbing the depths of divine despair. Fischer-Dieskau and Claire Watson raise the doubtful prestige of the feeble Gibichung siblings with their mellifluous portrayals, while Christa Ludwig's Waltraute has never been bettered. Which other set can boast such Rhinemaidens as Lucia Popp and Gwyneth Jones?
Decca 414115-2DH4

1967
Karl Böhm
Bayreuth Festival Orchestra and Chorus

Das Rheingold
Wotan: T. Adam
Alberich: G. Neidlinger
Loge: W. Windgassen
Fricka: A. Burmeister
Mime: E. Wohlfahrt
Erda: V. Soukupova
Fafner: K. Böhme
Fasolt: M. Talvela

This is an inspired performance only slightly marred by stage noise. Böhm's reading is dynamic, shapely and wise. If Theo Adam is not quite as insightful as Hotter, we still have Windgassen's brilliant, worldly-wise Loge and, as a bonus, Anja Silja as the youngest and most emotive Freia ever.

PHILIPS 412475-2PH2

Die Walküre
Siegmund: J. King
Sieglinde: L. Rysanek
Hunding: G. Nienstedt
Wotan: T. Adam
Brünnhilde: B. Nilsson
Fricka: A. Burmeister

Neither Fricka nor Hunding are quite in the class of their predecessors in Karajan's 1967 recording, but Böhm establishes here the antithesis to Karajan's approach: he takes risks, dramatizes, reduces the orchestral bulk to chamber music proportions, as in the Winter Storms of Act I and in Brünnhilde's pleading with Siegmund in Act II; he also impels his forces to eruptions of mayhem (the opening to Act III), and drowns us in almost unbearable waves of searing emotion (Wotan's account of the state of the world in Act II).

PHILIPS 4124782PH4

Siegfried
Siegfried: W. Windgassen
Mime: E. Wohlfahrt
Wanderer: T. Adam
Alberich: G. Neidlinger
Fricka: K. Böhme
Erda: V. Soukupová
Brünnhilde: B. Nilsson

Windgassen and Nilsson are without equal as the lovers. Böhm transforms the Bayreuth players into a chamber music ensemble of virtuosos, capable of gossamer filigree (Forest Murmurs) and brazen bravado alike (end of Act III).

PHILIPS 412483-2PH4

Götterdämmerung
Siegfried: W. Windgassen
Brünnhilde: B. Nilsson
Gunther: T. Stewart
Hagen: J. Greindl
Gutrune: L. Dvoráková
Waltraute: M. Mödl
Alberich: G. Neidlinger

Outstanding in this superb cast are, of course, Nilsson and Windgassen, but what a finely honed, burnished baritone this set can boast in Thomas Stewart's Gunther. Anja Silja's Third Norn marked, alas, her last appearance at Bayreuth and, until recently, in the Wagner repertoire. Böhm's Straussian inclinations make such passages as Siegfried's Rhine Journey a jaunty voyage rather than a trip into disaster. This set, remarkably, features three renowned Brünnhildes in minor parts: Martha Mödl (Waltraute), Ludmilla Dvoráková (Gutrune) and Helga Dernesch (Wellgunde).

PHILIPS 412488-2PH4

1967, 1966, 1968–9, 1970
Herbert von Karajan
Berlin Philharmonic Orchestra

Das Rheingold
Wotan: D. Fischer-Dieskau
Alberich: Zoltan Kelemen
Loge: G. Stolze
Fricka: J. Veasey
Mime: E. Wohlfahrt
Erda: O. Dominguez
Fafner: K. Ridderbusch
Fasolt: M. Talvela

Not every Wagnerian will take easily to Karajan's unruffled view of the score, but what singing by a star-studded cast! Fischer-Dieskau is an ideal, young Wotan, passionate, divinely musical. The giants are the finest pair ever, Martti Talvela gaining every listener's heartfelt sympathy, and Karl Ridderbusch endowing the uncouth Fafner with such warmth and beauty that one wishes he would not kill his brother. Happily, both will survive on future discs – Talvela as Hunding, and Ridderbusch as Hagen.

HUNT 12CDKAR223

Die Walküre
Siegmund: J. Vickers
Sieglinde: G. Janowitz
Hunding: M. Talvela
Wotan: T. Stewart
Brünnhilde: R. Crespin
Fricka: J. Veasey

The superlative cast must have appreciated the glorious sound-cushion which the Berlin Philharmonic presented to them. Wise old Herbert von Karajan knew and loved this score (in performance he conducted with his eyes closed) and he guides his singers as he guides us, his listeners, safely through every dramatic maze. Some of the *Ring*'s terror is smoothed over, but the gain in sheer beauty of sound is enormous. Gundula Janowitz

(Sieglinde) is more nightingale than woman, while Josephine Veasey's Fricka throbs with vibrancy and zest. Thomas Stewart's Wotan is the marvel of this recording: his soft-grained baritone has a most appealing bronze edge to it which enables him to ride the mighty storms and to find deeper and deeper profundities in Wotan's confrontation with Fricka and in his farewell to his favourite child, Régine Crespin's impassioned Brünnhilde.

DG 415145-2

Siegfried
Siegfried: J. Thomas
Mime: G. Stolze
Wanderer: T. Stewart
Alberich: Z. Kélémen
Fafner: K. Ridderbusch
Erda: O. Dominguez
Brünnhilde: H. Dernesch

Karajan, as always, goes for perfection in sound, and his singers are decidedly non-heavyweights. Jess Thomas and Helga Dernesch turn the final scene into an unteutonic *bel canto* feast, while the vastly underrated Thomas Stewart gives a touching portrayal of the god on the brink of abdication and despair. Karajan celebrates beauty in every scene, even in Mime's smithy and in the dragon's lair. The recording is studio-produced and digitally remastered.

DG 415150-2GH4

Götterdämmerung
Siegfried: H. Brillioth
Brünnhilde: H. Dernesch
Gunther: T. Stewart
Hagen: K. Ridderbusch
Gutrune: G. Janowitz
Waltraute: C. Ludwig
Alberich: Z. Kelemen

Karajan + Berlin Philharmonic Orchestra = Perfection. It is a matter of personal taste whether Wagner can bear perfection. Technically, the set is a miracle, though the two main protagonists are overshadowed by the exquisite Gutrune of the young Gundula Janowitz, the mighty Hagen of Karl Ridderbusch and, again, by Thomas Stewart's angst-ridden Gunther.

HUNT 12CDKAR223

1973–7
Reginald Goodall
English National Opera Orchestra and Chorus

Das Rheingold (sung in English)
Wotan: N. Bailey
Alberich: D. Hammond-Stroud
Loge: E. Belcourt
Fricka: A. Howard
Mime: G. Dempsey
Erda: A. Collins
Fafner: C. Grant
Fasolt: R. Lloyd

The orchestra under Goodall rises to Wagnerian heights not attained before or since. Norman Bailey (Wotan) and Derek Hammond-Stroud (Alberich) are utterly convincing, vocally and histrionically. Wagner in English can work. Under Goodall it does.

EMI CMS7641102 (recorded 1975)

Die Walküre (sung in English)
Siegmund: A. Remedios
Sieglinde: M. Curphy
Hunding: C. Grant
Wotan: N. Bailey
Brünnhilde: R. Hunter
Fricka: A. Howard

This is a monument to a greatly loved and greatly neglected Wagnerian. Reginald Goodall's meticulous, time-consuming but so rewarding preparatory work with his singers pays top dividends. The orchestra glows with controlled passion, and the leisurely pace allows them and the cast to score point after point. The glories of this set are Norman Bailey's Wotan and Rita Hunter's Brünnhilde.

EMI CMS7639182 (recorded 1975)

Siegfried (sung in English)
Siegfried: A. Remedios
Mime: G. Dempsey
Wanderer: N. Bailey
Alberich: D. Hammond-Stroud
Fricka: C. Grant
Erda: A. Collins
Brünnhilde: R. Hunter

Goodall's spacious tempos again reveal hidden treasures in Wagner's score. They also allow his singers time to prepare their phrases with leisurely breath control. Rita Hunter's Brünnhilde, Alberto Remedios's Siegfried and Norman Bailey's Wanderer/Wotan are the inspired stars of this set, which may well become a collector's prize.

EMI CMS763595-2 (recorded 1973)

Götterdämmerung (sung in English)
Siegfried: A. Remedios
Brünnhilde: R. Hunter
Gunther: N. Welsby
Hagen: A. Haugland
Gutrune: M. Curphey
Waltraute: K. Pring
Alberich: D. Hammond-Stroud

Goodall takes his singers, his orchestra and his listeners on a reposeful, but always arresting global journey; the meticulously rehearsed orchestra surpasses its normal standards. Rita Hunter's Brünnhilde is thrilling, and Alberto Remedios' Siegfried truly heroic.

EMI CMS764-2442 (recorded 1977)

1980
Pierre Boulez
Bayreuth Festival Orchestra and Chorus

Das Rheingold
Wotan: D. McIntyre
Alberich: H. Becht
Loge: H. Zednik
Fricka: H. Schwarz
Mime: H. Pampuch
Erda: O. Wenkel
Fafner: F. Hübner
Fasolt: M. Salminen

Pierre Boulez is a most sensitive conductor, but the true Wagnerian sound eludes him. Even the Bayreuth orchestra sounds a trifle uninvolved. McIntyre's Wotan is majestic, tortured and volatile; his German is impeccable. Hanna Schwarz (Fricka), Heinz Zednik (Loge) and Matti Salminen (Fasolt) head an otherwise fair-to-middling cast.

PHILIPS 4344212 PH2

Die Walküre
Siegmund: P. Hofmann
Sieglinde: J. Altmeyer
Hunding: M. Salminen
Wotan: D. McIntyre
Brünnhilde: G. Jones
Fricka: H. Schwarz

Fast tempos, less than ideal casting, but a terrific Hunding (Matti Salminen) and a great Fricka (Hanna Schwarz). Wagner wins.

PHILIPS 4344222PH3

Siegfried
Siegfried: M. Jung
Mime: H. Zednik
Wanderer: D. McIntyre
Alberich: H. Becht
Fricka: F. Hübner
Erda: O. Wenkel
Brünnhilde: G. Jones

The finest singing comes in the Wanderer–Mime scene in Act I, and the most idiomatic orchestral playing can be heard in the Forest scene in Act II. The rest is worthy to fair, speedy, and with all the notes in place.

PHILIPS 434423-2PH3

Götterdämmerung
Siegfried: M. Jung
Brünnhilde: G. Jones
Gunther: F. Mazura
Hagen: F. Hübner
Gutrune: J. Altmeyer
Waltraute: G. Killebrew
Alberich: H. Becht

After those outstanding casts of previous *Götterdämmerung* recordings, the present one is found wanting. The orchestral playing is fine, of course, but often hurried and matter-of-fact.

PHILIPS 4344242-PH4

1980–84
Marek Janowski
Dresden Staatskapelle, Rundsunkchor Leipzig, Chor des Deutschen Staatsoper Dresden and Rundsunkchor Berlin

Das Rheingold
Wotan: T. Adam
Alberich: S. Nimsgern
Loge: P. Schreier
Fricka: Y. Minton
Mime: C. Vogel
Erda: O. Wenkel
Fafner: M. Salminen
Fasolt: R. Bracht

Wonderful, inspired playing by the Dresden virtuosos. Peter Schreier presents a definitive Loge, while Yvonne Minton, as Fricka, is a worthy successor to Kirsten Flagstad. The underrated Siegmund Nimsgern is a towering, awesome Alberich. This fine recording has one drawback: it is unbanded, and you will have to do a lot of searching if you wish to hear a particular passage.

EURODISC 610055-7
(recorded 1980)

Die Walküre
Siegmund: S. Jerusalem
Sieglinde: J. Norman
Hunding: K. Moll
Wotan: T. Adam
Brünnhilde: J. Altmeyer
Fricka: Y. Minton

Wonderful orchestral sound, intelligent direction, a truly great pair of lovers in Siegfried Jerusalem at his youthful best, and Jessye Norman (exciting casting) in her prime. Theo Adam's Wotan is reliable rather than inspired, but Kurt Moll and Yvonne Minton are at hand to delight us with an awesome Hunding and a regal Fricka. The unexpected bonus is the finest octet of Valkyries ever, with such stars as Cheryl Studer, Eva-Marie Bundschuh, Anne Gjevang, Uta Priew and Ortrun Wenkel – unbeatable.

EURODISC GD69005
(recorded 1981)

Siegfried
Siegfried: R. Kollo
Mime: P. Schreier
Wanderer: T. Adam
Alberich: S. Nimsgern
Fricka: M. Salminen
Erda: O. Wenkel
Brünnhilde: J. Altmeyer

As with Janowski's previous sets, the casting is inspired, and the orchestral sound ravishes the ear. Both Siegfried and the Wanderer (Kollo and Adam) are at the top of their career, and to have such superb artists as Matti Salminen (Fafner), Siegmund Nimsgern (Alberich) and Peter Schreier (Mime) is a generous and much appreciated bonus. The digital recording is excellent.

EURODISC GD69006
(recorded 1984)

Götterdämmerung
Siegfried: R. Kollo
Brünnhilde: J. Altmeyer
Gunther: H. G. Nöcker
Hagen: M. Salminen
Gutrune: N. Sharp
Waltraute: O. Wenkel
Alberich: S. Nimsgern

Kollo in his vocal prime as Siegfried, the terrific Matti Salminen as Hagen, and the Dresden State Orchestra – these are the triple glories of this set. The recording is superb, with a most appealing balance of voices and instruments.

EURODISC GD69003 (recorded 1983)

1988–91
Bernard Haitink
Bavarian Radio Symphony Orchestra and Chorus

Das Rheingold
Wotan: J. Morris
Alberich: T. Adam
Loge: H. Zednik
Fricka: M. Lipovsek
Mime: P. Haage
Erda: J. Rappé
Fafner: K. Rydl
Fasolt: H. Tschammer

This is a singer-friendly version. Haitink's evident affinity with Wagner's grandeur and brooding mystery results in a reading that moves and soothes in turn. His singers respond by giving deeply considered performances. Our critics take pleasure in belittling James Morris's Wotan; he is, in fact, superb, and has more Wagnerian insight in his little finger than – ah well. Mariana Lipovsek's honey-voiced Fricka and Heinz Zednik's knowing, thoroughly musical Loge are the other glories of this set.

EMI CDS7498532 (recorded 1988)

Die Walküre
Siegmund: R. Goldberg
Sieglinde: C. Studer
Hunding: M. Salminen
Wotan: J. Morris
Brünnhilde: E. Marton
Fricka: W. Meier

This set, and those following, take us into a new area of technical near-perfection. The orchestral sound is spacious, and integrates most effectively with the singers. Haitink, of course, excels as ever with this very fine orchestra. His cast serves him well – even the much-maligned Rainer Goldberg gives a sterling performance as Siegmund. Most of the others maintain an impressive level of excellence, but we do have a Brünnhilde whose decibels are an acquired taste.

EMI CDS7495342 (recorded 1988)

Siegfried
Siegfried: S. Jerusalem
Mime: P. Haage
Wanderer: J. Morris
Alberich: T. Adam
Fricka: K. Rydl
Erda: J. Rappé
Brünnhilde: E. Marton

A veritable 'curate's Siegfried', with a marvellous Siegfried (Siegfried Jerusalem) and the great James Morris again as the Wanderer, but with more pedestrian offerings elsewhere. The orchestra under Haitink is very fine indeed, but Christianity forbids an appraisal of the oscillating Brünnhilde. Siegfried deserves a steadier bride.

EMI CDS754290-2 (recorded 1990)

Götterdämmerung
Siegfried: S. Jerusalem
Brünnhilde: E. Marton
Gunther: T. Hampson
Hagen: J. Tomlinson
Gutrune: E. M. Bundschuh
Waltraute: M. Lipovsek
Alberich: T. Adam

As in this conductor's *Siegfried*, both the recording and the orchestral sound are quite exceptional. Again, his cast serve him devotedly and successfully, especially Siegfried Jerusalem as a mature but most appealing Siegfried, John Tomlinson as a Hagen whose beauty of voice makes him the more dangerous, and a tremendous Gunther whom Thomas Hampson endows with a Lieder singer's lyrical warmth. What a great pity about Brünnhilde, whose over-generous vibrato mars her scenes. In spite of this, Haitink provides plenty of insights and long stretches of Wagnerian discovery.

EMI CDS754485-2 (recorded 1991)

1988–9
James Levine
Metropolitan Opera Orchestra and Chorus

Das Rheingold
Wotan: J. Morris
Alberich: E. Wlaschiha
Loge: S. Jerusalem
Fricka: C. Ludwig
Mime: H. Zednik
Erda: B. Svendén
Fafner: K. Moll
Fasolt: J.-H. Rootering

Levine obtains refined, beautiful, dramatic and imaginative playing from his superb orchestra. His tempos are leisurely, but always convincing. James Morris is outstanding as Wotan, with veteran Christa Ludwig (Fricka) sounding as fresh as she did twenty-five years earlier. Siegfried Jerusalem's Loge is in Windgassen's class, and Ekkehard Wlaschiha (Alberich) in Neidlinger's. The giants are breathtaking.

DGG 4452952 GH2 (recorded 1988)

Die Walküre
Siegmund: G. Lakes
Sieglinde: J. Norman
Hunding: K. Moll
Wotan: J. Morris
Brünnhilde: H. Behrens
Fricka: C. Ludwig
Ravishing playing and variable singing. Levine takes his time, as he should (Wagner took twenty-five years), and his players respond with brilliantly expressive sounds, particularly the brass section. Sieglinde (the glorious Jessye Norman) outclasses her sibling, and Hildegard Behrens must be seen as well as heard, for her voice really serves her marvellous acting. Wotan and Hunding are supreme, and it is lovely to hear Christa Ludwig once again as Fricka, just as magisterial and mellifluous and ageless as twenty-three years earlier, in the Solti recording.
DG 4233892GH4 (recorded 1988)

Siegfried
Siegfried: R. Goldberg
Mime: H. Zednik
Wotan: J. Morris
Alberich: E. Wlaschiha
Fricka: K. Moll
Erda: B. Svendén
Brünnhilde: H. Behrens
State-of-the-art recording, gorgeous brass sound and utter refinement in woodwind and strings, with even the smallest parts in the cast taken by the world's best (Kurt Moll's Fafner and Kathleen Battle's Woodbird) – such are the credentials of this *Siegfried* from New York. James Morris wears Hotter's mantle with authority and ease, as the Wotan of the eighties and nineties.
DG 429407-2GH4 (recorded 1988)

Götterdämmerung
Siegfried: R. Goldberg
Brünnhilde: H. Behrens
Gunther: B. Weikl
Hagen: M. Salminen
Gutrune: C. Studer
Waltraute: H. Schwarz
Alberich: E. Wlaschiha
This is a set overflowing with felicities. The New York orchestra is brilliant, and James Levine's many years in Bayreuth have made him an outstanding Wagnerian. His cast is uniformly superb. Reiner Goldberg, disliked by many critics is, to my ears, a strong, mellifluous Siegfried. His Brünnhilde, Hildegard Behrens, gives unsparingly of her ample resources, dramatically awesome, and heart-rending in her distress. In Matti Salminen's Hagen, Cheryl Studer's Gutrune, Ekkehard Wlaschiha's Alberich and Hanna Schwarz's Waltraute we have the world's top performers in their respective roles. A great set.
DG 445354-2GX14 (recorded 1989)

1991–2
Daniel Barenboim
Bayreuth Festival Orchestra and Chorus

Das Rheingold
Wotan: J. Tomlinson
Alberich: G. von Kannen
Loge: G. Clark
Fricka: L. Finnie
Mime: H. Pampuch
Erda: B. Svendén
Fafner: P. Kang
Fasolt: M. Hölle
At his best, Barenboim's interpretation does full justice to Wagner's design, but he is also given to quite a few less persuasive changes of speed. Outstanding in a not always convincing cast are Graham Clark's athletic Loge, Brigitta Svendén's vibrant Erda and Matthias Hölle's quite superb Fasolt.
TELDEC WEA 4509911852 (recorded 1991)

Die Walküre
Siegmund: P. Elming
Sieglinde: N. Secunde
Hunding: M. Hölle
Wotan: J. Tomlinson
Brünnhilde: A. Evans
Fricka: L. Finnie
Richard Strauss is supposed to have said, 'Maybe I'm not the world's finest composer, but I'm certainly the very best of all the second-best ones.' Daniel Barenboim almost convinces us that he is Furtwängler's successor, but not quite. The Bayreuth orchestra is superb, of course, but have we not heard it in even better form? John Tomlinson is an outstanding Wotan, but there is Robert Hale and there is James Morris. Anne Evans is capable of insightful and highly intelligent delivery, but there are Brünnhildes who move you more. The twin lovers are very nearly excellent, and so is Linda Finnie's Fricka. The only one who has no peers is Matthias Hölle as Hunding: stentorian, awesome, gripping. The *Ring* recording of the decade? Almost.
TELDEC WEA4509911862 (recorded 1992)

Siegfried
Siegfried: S. Jerusalem
Mime: G. Clark
Wanderer: J. Tomlinson
Alberich: G. von Kannen
Fricka: P. Kang
Erda: B. Svendén
Brünnhilde: A. Evans
As in Barenboim's *Rheingold* and *Walküre*, the cast has great strengths in Tomlinson's Wotan/Wanderer and in Clark's Mime. Siegfried Jerusalem, in

1992, was probably the finest of Siegfrieds. The rest of the cast does not quite live up to those Valhallian heights. The orchestral sound, strangely, is not what one remembers from the live performance at Bayreuth. Perhaps the critic was right who said of the resultant sound, 'it comes re-synthesized in Teldec's electro-acoustic mincing machine' (*Wagner News*, February 1996). Nevertheless, a recording that can boast such a marvellous Wotan/Wanderer, Siegfried and Mime as this must be taken seriously.

TELDEC 4509-94193-2
(recorded 1992)

Götterdämmerung
Siegfried: S. Jerusalem
Brünnhilde: A. Evans
Gunther: B. Brinkmann
Hagen: P. Kang
Gutrune: E. M. Bundschuh
Waltraute: W. Meier
Alberich: G. von Kannen

Barenboim's most convincing performance of the present cycle has the orchestra more realistically recorded than in *Siegfried*. Siegfried Jerusalem, as always, is a pillar of strength, while the rest of the cast is fine to competent. Head and shoulders above everybody else, though, is Waltraud Meier's Waltraute: she must be heard in her scene with Brünnhilde in Act I, a blazing tour de force.

TELDEC 450994194-2
(recorded 1991)

Performances of Individual Music Dramas

[Keilberth's *Walküre* is part of a complete *Ring* recording]

Das Rheingold

1993
Christoph von Dohnányi
Cleveland Orchestra
Wotan: R. Hale
Alberich: F.-J. Kapellmann
Loge: K. Begley
Fricka: H. Schwarz
Mime: P. Schreier
Erda: E. Zaremba
Fafner: W. Fink
Fasolt: J.-H. Rootering

Dohnányi proves himself, at this first attempt, an inspired, energetic, seasoned Wagnerian. He obtains absolutely magnificent playing from the Cleveland magicians, and his cast does him proud. Apart from a slightly underpowered Fafner, we get top performances from gods, dwarfs and giant. The new Alberich is Franz-Josef Kapellmann. Make a note of this name – he will go very, very far. To cast Kim Begley as Loge was a stroke of genius: he is sensational. Nearing the end of his distinguished career, Peter Schreier presents a Mime that will be almost impossible to follow. Robert Hale's Wotan is equal to that of James Morris, both in beauty of tone and in investing the god with that elusive mixture of grandeur and melancholy. Technically this recording represents state-of-the-art.

DECCA 443690-2DH02

Die Walküre

1938
Carl Leonhardt
Radio Stuttgart Orchestra
Siegmund: F. Krauss
Sieglinde: M. Reining
Hunding: J. von Manowarda
Wotan: R. Bockelmann
Brünnhilde: E. Schlüter
Fricka: H. Jung

Both orchestra and conductor belong to the second division, so does half the cast. The recording is past its shelf-life, but just listen to Wotan and Brünnhilde. Manowarda and Schlüter produce the authentic Wagner sound, majestic, warm, vocally assured and making time stand still. Skip Act I and wallow in the rest.

PREISER 90151 & 90207
(Mono)

1941
Erich Leinsdorf
Metropolitan Opera Orchestra
Siegmund: L. Melchior
Sieglinde: A. Varnay
Hunding: A. Kipnis
Wotan: F. Schorr
Brünnhilde: H. Traubel
Fricka: K. Thorborg

Technically, this is quite a trial. Once you are attuned to the frying-pan background, you realize that age has dealt more kindly with the voices than with the orchestra, and you can experience just about the finest Wotan (Friedrich Schorr), Siegmund (Lauritz Melchior), Hunding (Alexander Kipnis) and Fricka (Kerstin Thorborg) of their (and our) time.

MYTO MCD913.41 (Mono)

1951
Ferenc Fricsay
Städtische Oper, Berlin
Siegmund: L. Suthaus
Sieglinde: M. Müller
Hunding: J. Greindl
Wotan: J. Herrmann
Brünnhilde: P. Büchner
Fricka: M. Klose
In spite of its age, the sound is quite acceptable. Ferenc Fricsay inspires the Berlin players and his cast. We get terrific performances from the twin lovers, Siegmund and Sieglinde (Ludwig Suthaus, liquid honey, and Maria Müller, burnished, intense), and from Josef Herrmann's great-hearted Wotan.
Myto 3MCD933.81 (Mono)

1954
Joseph Keilberth
Bayreuth Festival Orchestra
Siegmund: M. Lorenz
Sieglinde: M. Mödl
Hunding: J. Greindl
Wotan: H. Hotter
Brünnhilde: A. Varnay
Fricka: G. von Milinkovic
1954 was the year when Bayreuth was able to luxuriate in two world-beating Brünnhildes, Astrid Varnay and Martha Mödl. So they cast them alternately as Brünnhilde and Sieglinde. On this set Varnay is Wotan's daughter, and Mödl his grandchild. Both being marvellous actresses, they had to be heard and seen, but their vocal rendering gives us a glimpse of their star quality. Max Lorenz was the Siegmund and Siegfried of his time – alas, that was quite some time ago. But we still have Hotter's immortal Wotan and Greindl's grisly Hunding.
Melodram CD36102 (Mono)

1954
Wilhelm Furtwängler
Vienna Philharmonic Orchestra
Siegmund: L. Suthaus
Sieglinde: L. Rysanek
Hunding: G. Frick
Wotan: F. Frantz
Brünnhilde: M. Klose
Fricka: R. Siewert
The conductor's death in the same year, alas, cut short the projected complete *Ring* with the irresistible combination of nonpareil orchestra and conductor. Ludwig Suthaus was a most mellifluous Siegmund, whose heartache becomes ours, while Leonie Rysanek – another star actor-singer – is a silver-tongued, vulnerable, yet also indomitable Sieglinde. The Wotan of Ferdinand Frantz is firm, authoritative and utterly reliable. But can one find greater depth in the role of Wotan? Hotter can.
EMI CHS7630452 (Mono)

1961
Erich Leinsdorf
London Symphony Orchestra
Siegmund: J. Vickers
Sieglinde: G. Brouwenstijn
Hunding: D. Ward
Wotan: G. London
Brünnhilde: B. Nilsson
Fricka: R. Gorr
Twenty years after his first *Walküre* (with the New York Metropolitan Orchestra) Erich Leinsdorf conducts a searing, utterly convincing performance with the LSO. With Gorr once again as Fricka, with Vickers and Brouwenstijn as the fated twins and with Nilsson this time the ecstatically glowing Brünnhilde, this is a heart-warming set.
Decca 4303912DM3 (Mono)

Götterdämmerung

1942
Karl Elmendorff
Bayreuth Festival Orchestra and Chorus
Siegfried: S. Svanholm
Brünnhilde: M. Fuchs
Gunther: E. Koch
Hagen: F. Dalberg
Gutrune: E. Fischer
Waltraute: C. Kalab
Alberich: R. Burg
This wartime performance features the great Marta Fuchs (who started her career as an alto), as a supercharged, golden-toned Brünnhilde who casts her formidable shadow over the rest of the performers. Strangely, the recording features many singers of the alternative Festival cast, rather than the top drawer. Thus the recording gives us Set Svanholm's dry Siegfried instead of Max Lorenz's, Friedrich Dalberg's unmagnetic Hagen instead of Josef von Manowarda's and, unhappily, a nondescript Waltraute in place of Margarete Klose. A set of missed opportunities.
Preiser 90164 (Mono)

Videography

Details are given below of four performances of the *Ring* on video and laserdisc. For comments on visual presentation see the Performance History essay in this volume. For comments on aural aspects see the discography.

Place	Bayreuth	Munich	New York	Bayreuth
Orchestra	Festival	Bavarian. State	Met. Opera	Festival
Conductor	P. Boulez	W. Sawallisch	J. Levine	D. Barenboim
Producer	P. Chéreau	N. Lehnhoff	O. Schenk	H. Kupfer
Year	1980	1989	1990	1992
Video	Philips 070401/2/3/4 3PHE2	EMI MVX9 91275-3	DG 072 418/19/20/21 3GH2	Teldec 4509 91123-3
Laserdisc	070 401-4 1PHE2/3	LDX9 91275-1	072 418-21 1GH2/3/3/3	4509 91122/3-6 and 94193/4-6

Rheingold				
WOTAN	D. McIntyre	R. Hale	J. Morris	J. Tomlinson
FRICKA	H. Schwarz	M. Lipovsek	C. Ludwig	L. Finnie
LOGE	H. Zednik	R. Tear	S. Jerusalem	G. Clark
MIME	H. Pampuch	H. Pampuch	H. Zednik	H. Pampuch
ALBERICH	H. Becht	E. Wlaschiha	E. Wlaschiha	G. von Kannen
FREIA	C. Reppel	N. Gustavson	M. Häggander	E. Johansson
FROH	S. Jerusalem	J. Hopferwieser	M. Baker	K. Schreibmayer
DONNER	M. Egel	F. Cerny	A. Held	B. Brinkmann
ERDA	O. Wenkel	H. Schwarz	B. Svendén	B. Svendén
FASOLT	M. Salminen	J. Rootering	J. Rootering	M. Hölle
FAFNER	F. Hübner	K. Moll	M. Salminen	P. Kang
WOGLINDE	N. Sharp	J. Kaufmann	K. Erickson	H. Leidland
WELLGUNDE	I. Gramatzki	A. M. Blasi	D. Kesling	A. Küttenbaum
FLOSSHILDE	M. Schiml	B. Calm	M. Parsons	J. Turner

	Bayreuth, 1980	Munich, 1989	New York, 1990	Bayreuth, 1992
Die Walküre				
SIEGMUND	P. Hofmann	R. Schunk	G. Lakes	P. Elming
SIEGLINDE	J. Altmeyer	J. Varady	J. Norman	N. Secunde
HUNDING	M. Salminen	K. Moll	K. Moll	M. Hölle
WOTAN	D. McIntyre	R. Hale	J. Morris	J. Tomlinson
BRÜNNHILDE	G. Jones	H. Behrens	H. Behrens	A. Evans
FRICKA	H. Schwarz	M. Lipovsek	C. Ludwig	L. Finnie
Siegfried				
SIEGFRIED	M. Jung	R. Kollo	S. Jerusalem	S. Jerusalem
MIME	H. Zednik	H. Pampuch	H. Zednik	G. Clark
WANDERER	D. McIntyre	R. Hale	J. Morris	J. Tomlinso
ALBERICH	G. von Kannen	H. Becht	E. Wlaschiha	E. Wlaschiha
FAFNER	M. Salminen	P. Kang	F. Hübner	K. Moll
WALDVOGEL	N. Sharp	J. Kaufmann	D. Upshaw	H. Leidland
ERDA	O. Wenkel	H. Schwarz	B. Svendén	B. Svendén
BRÜNNHILDE	G. Jones	H. Behrens	H. Behrens	A. Evans
Götterdämmerung				
SIEGFRIED	M. Jung	R. Kollo	S. Jerusalem	S. Jerusalem
BRÜNNHILDE	G. Jones	H. Behrens	H. Behrens	A. Evans
GUNTHER	F. Mazura	H. G. Nöcker	A. Raffell	B. Brinkmann
HAGEN	F. Hübner	M. Salminen	M. Salminen	P. Kang
GUTRUNE	J. Altmeyer	L. Balslev	H. Lisowska	E. Bundschuh
WALTRAUTE	G. Killebrew	W. Meier	C. Ludwig	W. Meier
ALBERICH	H. Becht	E. Wlaschiha	M. Salminen	G. von Kannen

Leitmotifs of the *Ring*

In this alphabetical list of all leitmotifs in *the Ring*, letters 'R', 'W', 'S' and 'G' are added to indicate in which opera the leitmotif appears.

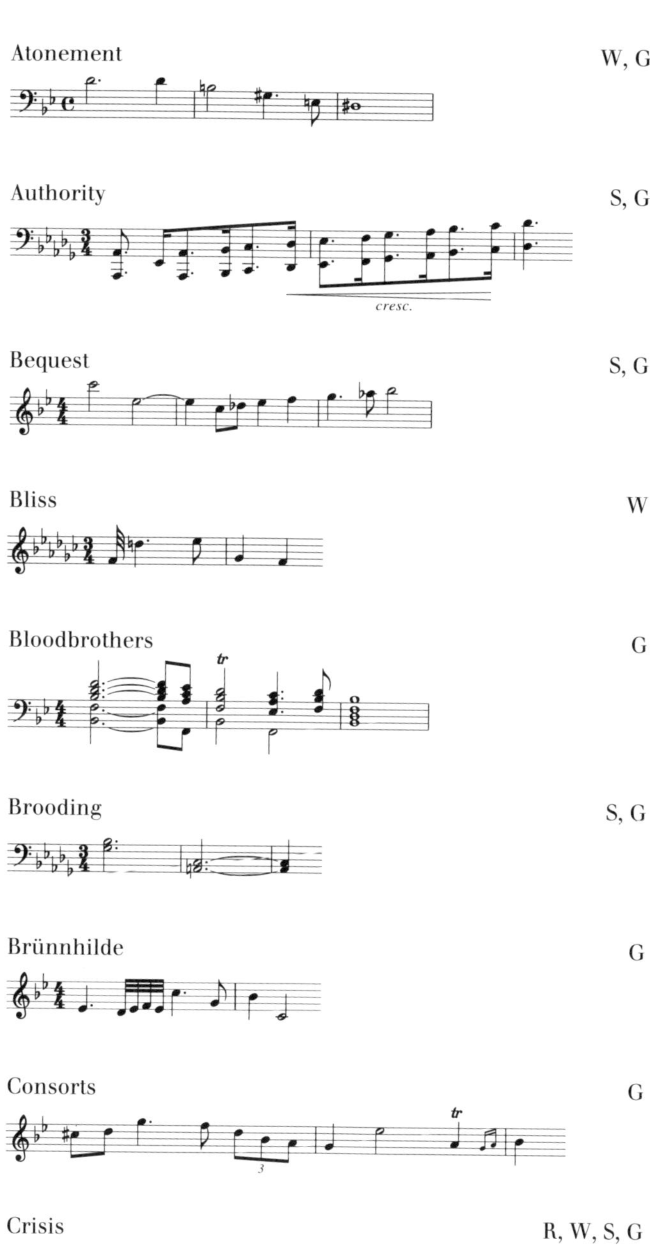
Atonement
W, G
Authority
S, G
cresc.
Bequest
S, G
Bliss
W
Bloodbrothers
G
tr
Brooding
S, G
Brünnhilde
G
Consorts
G
tr
3
Crisis
R, W, S, G

Crocodile
S
MIME
Als zul - len - des Kind zog ich dich auf,
Curse
R, W, S, G
Death
W, S, G
pp
pp
Dragon
R, W, S, G
Enchantment
R, S
Erda
R, W, S, G
Fafner
S, G
pp
Fate
W, S, G
Forge
R, S, G

Freedom
S, G
SIEGFRIED
Aus dem Wald fort in die Welt ziehn: nim-mer kehr ich zu-ruck'
Freia
R, W, S, G
Genesis
R, S, G
Giants
R, W, S
Gibichungen
G
Golden Apples
R, G
Gold's Dominion
R, G
Götterdämmerung
R, S, G
Grief
R, W, S, G
Gutrune
G

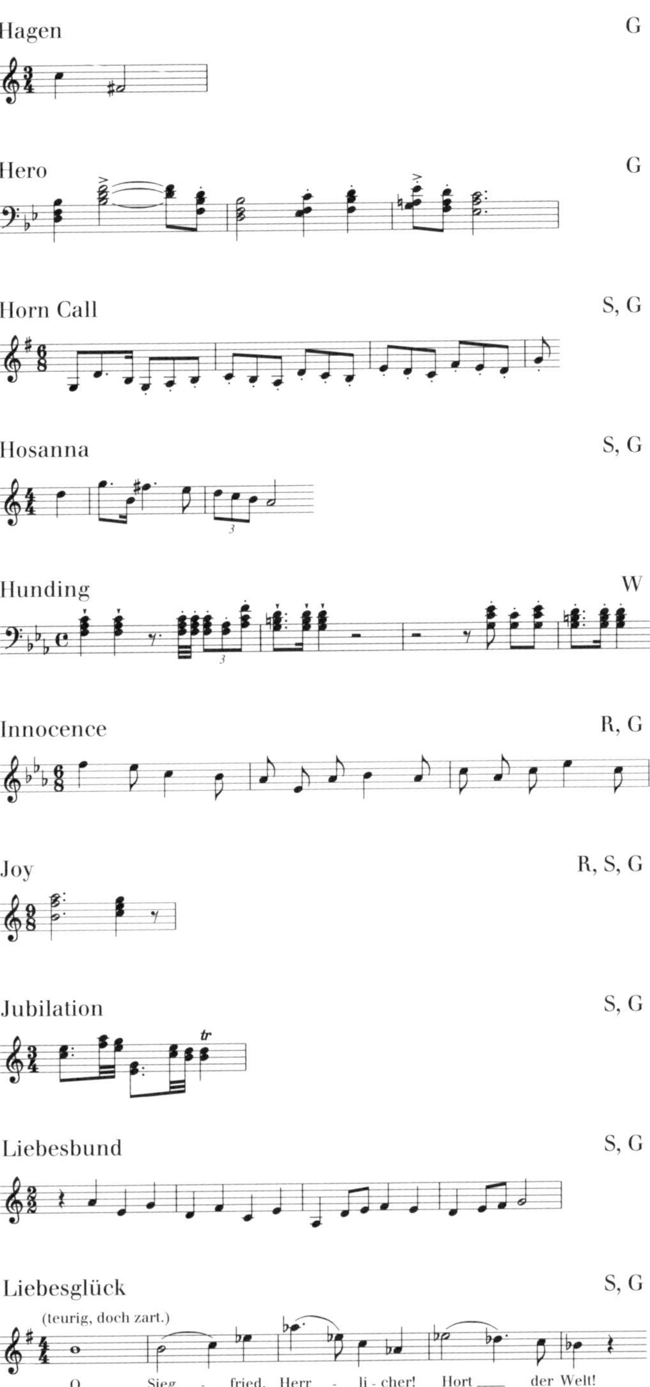
Hagen
G
Hero
G
Horn Call
S, G
Hosanna
S, G
Hunding
W
Innocence
R, G
Joy
R, S, G
Jubilation
S, G
Liebesbund
S, G
Liebesglück
S, G
(teurig, doch zart.)
O Sieg - fried, Herr - li - cher! Hort ___ der Welt!

Liebesnot
R, S, G
Liebe-Tragik
R, W, S, G
Loge
R, W, S, G
Longing
S
Magio Fire
W, S, G
Murder
G
Vln.
Ww.
Vlc.
Nibelungen Hate
R, W, S, G
Nothung
W, S, G
No - thung!
Oblivion
W, S, G

Rainbow
R
Revenge
G
Revival
S, G
Rhinegold
R, W, S, G
Ride
W, S, G
ff
Ring
R, W, S, G
Sanctuary
W, S, G
Shuffle
S
Siegfried
W, S, G
Sieglinde
W, S, G

Siegmund
W
Storm
W
Sword
R, W, S, G
Tarnhelm
R, S, G
Thunder
R, W
Treasure
R, S, G
Treaty
R, W, S, G
Troth
R, W, S
Valkyrie Cry
W, S, G
Walhall
R, W, S, G

Wälsungen
W, S, G
Wälsung Ordeal
W, S, G
Wanderer
S
Woodbird
S, G
Wotan's Child
W, S, G
Wotan's Farewell
W, S
Wotan's Frustration
W, S, G

Photographic Acknowledgements

AKG London: frontispiece, 18, 47, 59, 66, 69, 164, 168, 179r, 200
AKG/Private Collection, Munich: 53
Archiv Bernd Mayer, Bayreuth: 180
Bayreuther Festspiele GmbH: 182
Bayreuther Festspiele GmbH/Jean-Marie Bottequin: 190
Bayreuther Festspiele GmbH/Heinz Eysell: 182, 184, 187r
Bayreuther Festspiele GmbH/Anne Kirchbach: 197
Bayreuther Festspiele GmbH/Siegfried Lauterwasser: 183, 186, 189, 191
Bayreuther Festspiele GmbH/Wilhelm Rauh: 185, 187l, 192, 194, 195, 199
Deutsches Theatermuseum, Munich: 201r
The Hulton Getty Picture Collection Ltd, London: 99
Kranichphoto Berlin: 203
Anne Kirchbach/Bayerische Staatsoper: 205
Mary Evans Picture Library, London: 64, 82, 85, 89l, 105, 179l
Myths of the Norsemen from the Eddas & Sagas, H. A. Guerber (Harrap & Co., 1914): 76, 81, 89r, 92, 94
Nationalarchiv der Richard-Wagner-Stiftung Bayreuth: 20, 21, 24, 29, 35, 39, 42, 134, 169, 170, 171
Performing Arts Library, London/Clive Barda: 209
Seattle Opera/Matthew McVay: 208
Süddeutscher Verlag Bilderdienst, Munich: 55
Asgard and the Gods: Tales and Traditions of our Northern Ancestors, W. Wagner (W. Swan Sonnenschein & Allen, 1880): 91, 96
Théâtre du Châtelet, Paris: 206
Ullstein, Berlin: 176
Victoria & Albert Museum Picture Library, London/Anthony Crickmay: 201

Index

Page numbers in italics refer to picture captions.